# STEALTH
# PATROL

# STEALTH
# PATROL

## THE MAKING OF
## A VIETNAM RANGER

BILL SHANAHAN

AND

JOHN P. BRACKIN

DA CAPO PRESS
A Member of the Perseus Books Group

Copyright © 2003 by Bill Shanahan and John P. Brackin

Designed by Brent Wilcox
Set in 11-point Sabon by the Perseus Books Group

Cataloging-in-Publication data for this book is available from the Library of Congress.

First Da Capo Press edition 2003
ISBN 0-306-81273-8

Published by Da Capo Press
A Member of the Perseus Books Group
http://www.dacapopress.com

Da Capo Press books are available at special discounts for bulk purchases in the U.S. by corporations, institutions, and other organizations. For more information, please contact the Special Markets Department at the Perseus Books Group, 11 Cambridge Center, Cambridge, MA 02142, or call (800) 255-1514 or (617) 252-5298, or e-mail j.mccrary@perseusbooks.com.

1 2 3 4 5 6 7 8 9—07 06 05 04 03

# ACKNOWLEDGMENTS

Several former Lurps and Rangers deserve special mention for their cooperation and assistance in helping us put this material together. Among those deserving special thanks are Pete Campbell, Dave Brueggemann, and Patrick Tadina. They contributed their time, their thoughts, and their memories; their influence is evident throughout the text. Thanks also to William Palmer, Dick Davis, Dick James, Leroy Pipkin, and Kenneth Murray; they all graciously shared their thoughts and memories, and in Kenneth Murray's case, several of his pictures from LZ English. And thanks finally to Reed Cundiff, who generously provided us with a list of names to appear on the company roster. Without his help, it would've been a much shorter list.

In addition to those former Rangers who helped us out, we'd also like to thank a number of others who helped us at various points along the way. Thanks especially to those who helped with John's trip to Vietnam: Brice Brackin, Rhett Thompson, Forrest Briggs, Nguyen Do Huynh, and Nguyen Van Bong. Thanks also to those who helped with the submission process: Jenny Shields, Perry Balian, Susan Bluestein Davis, Sheldon Webster, Phillip Thompson, and Amy L. Abrames. And to those whose help can best be described as miscellaneous (though valuable nonetheless): Vickie Shanahan, Catherine Lewis, Meg Balian, Dorsey McDaniel, Rick Perdue, Jamie Cordes, Bob Forhan, and Lois Brackin.

And last but not least, we'd like to thank Robert Pigeon, for believing in the project when it was still just a proposal; and our families, for supporting us throughout. To all, thank you very much.

# CONTENTS

# A Glimmer of Hope

I was sitting there in my hooch, finishing off the last little bit of my canned lunch, when I first heard his voice, coming from just outside the tent. I didn't know who it was—I didn't recognize his voice—but I could hear him loud and clear, and there was no mistaking what he was saying:

"Looking for a Private Shanahan. Anybody here go by that name?"

I craned my neck around to see this big, blond, imposing-looking figure, leaning through the door, sort of hunched over and coming in at me—on top of me practically, with his right hand extended and a broad smile that just about covered his whole face.

I set my rations down on the ground and flipped over to shake his hand—and when I did I noticed my friend and squad leader Bill Pfister standing over behind him.

Pfister called in from over his shoulder. "Hey, Shan, wake up, man. I got somebody I want you to meet."

Of course, before he'd even finished his sentence, the new guy, a sergeant, was shaking my hand and telling me his name: "Leroy Pipkin. Damn glad to meet you."

He was tall and broad-shouldered, but I could tell pretty much right off that his most prominent feature was his personality. His blond hair was slightly longer than normal—not long or unkempt, but just slightly longer than what most of the guys in the line company had—and his shirttail hung freely around his waist. He also wore a strange-looking necklace, homemade probably, that draped loosely across his chest, and he carried a camouflaged flop hat and a lit cigarette in his left hand. In general, I got the impression that he was something of a maverick, and right off I had to wonder why he was looking for me.

"Bill Shanahan," I said. "How you doing?"

I stood up to greet him.

"I'd offer you a chair, but there don't seem to be too many around this place."

In truth, there wasn't a whole lot of anything around that place. We were set up at some nondescript airstrip—we'd been there for about a week—and it was about as barren as any I'd seen. As bleak and empty as a dried-out lakebed.

"Ah, that's all right," he said. "I prefer to stand anyways—but what I'm here for, Bill, is to talk to you a little bit about the Lurps."

*No sense in beating around the bush,* I thought. I was beginning to wonder about that myself.

"I talked to your CO, and he gave me your name, said you might make a good candidate for the team—actually I asked him to give me his three best men, and he gave me your name, so I guess that means you're coming pretty highly recommended—"

He glanced over at Pfister. "And plus, your buddy here vouched for you."

He spoke in a clipped cadence, his words tumbling out quickly, one on top of the other, and his voice was deep and throaty, the way a bear might sound, if he could talk, after a night of drinking.

"Now, I've already been talking to Pfister here a little bit, but I'll just tell you what I told him. Basically I'm here recruiting guys for the Lurps. Now, I know you might not know who we are—or at least not too much about us—but basically what we do is, we're a special recon detachment. The word 'Lurp' actually stands for 'long-range patrol,' and that's exactly what we do—long-range patrols. We operate in teams of five—maybe six—members apiece, and we don't fool around with all this ninety-man line company stuff. In the Lurps, every man counts—and that's why we only take the best—"

He paused and took a drag from his cigarette. He put a friendly hand on Pfister's shoulder—gotta make sure we're getting this—then began again. "Now, our job is basically information gathering. We get an assignment to recon an area, and we'll go in there, for usually three or four days at a time, and look for VC and NVA—and let me just tell you: you *will* be seeing VC out there—and I mean I'm talking about at a distance of from me to that rock over there—and they won't even know you're there—"

He continued on like that for a while, describing the various aspects of the company and the way they operated, but one thing in particular caught my attention. Amid the promises of ground support and tiger fatigues, I locked on to the idea that running missions with these guys would mean a whole lot less people.

"—three-day missions, choppers drop us in, three days later they come and pick us up—"

In the line company, because of our numbers, we were constantly being harassed by all of these smaller enemy forces—I mean, we made so much noise clomping through the jungle that everybody within a five-mile radius knew we were coming—and from what I could tell, this guy seemed to be offering a real alternative.

"—in the Lurps, *we're* the ones pulling the ambushes—"

Of course, I didn't really know anything about the Lurps, outside of what all he'd just said—which actually just sounded like a lot of rah-rah army talk—but I dern well knew about the line company, and the prospect of running with a smaller team seemed to make a lot of sense. If it meant cutting out the noise, then I was pretty much game for anything.

I looked over at Pfister, who was leaning against the tent with his arms crossed and his head cocked; he appeared to be listening carefully, as he didn't speak and just tipped his head in agreement with Pipkin's words. I looked back to Pipkin.

"—hey, I know what it's like, all that shit on your back—ammo, mortar, M-60 rounds, damn steel pot rattling around, not knowing whether your ass is coming or going—"

He stopped talking just long enough to light up another cigarette and then started right back: "Hey, I was in this same infantry company a year ago, and I can tell you one thing for sure." He took a sharp drag off his smoke. "Being a Lurp ain't *nothing* like this bullshit."

# PART ONE

## THE LINE COMPANY

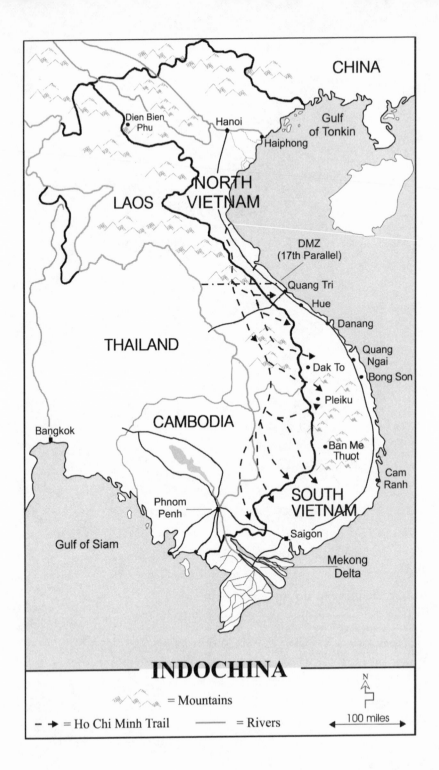

CHINA

Dien Bien Phu

Hanoi

Gulf of Tonkin

Haiphong

NORTH VIETNAM

LAOS

DMZ (17th Parallel)

Quang Tri

Hue

Danang

THAILAND

Quang Ngai

Dak To

Bong Son

Pleiku

CAMBODIA

Bangkok

Ban Me Thuot

Cam Ranh

SOUTH VIETNAM

Phnom Penh

Gulf of Siam

Saigon

Mekong Delta

**INDOCHINA**

N

= Mountains

= Ho Chi Minh Trail        = Rivers

100 miles

# 1

## How It All Got Started

I'D GOTTEN MY DRAFT CARD IN THE FALL OF 1967, WHILE I was going to school at Jefferson State, a small junior college in Birmingham, Alabama, about twenty minutes up the road from where I grew up. I wasn't any too pleased about getting it, but the next day I went over to the army enlistment center and signed up for a stint with the infantry. I thought I might get a different assignment, but the way it worked out I ended up in the infantry all the way. They gave me a couple of months to get my stuff in order—to organize my belongings, that type of thing—and then sent me down to Fort Benning to do my basic training.

Fort Benning is close to where I lived—it's located in Columbus, Georgia, about a hundred miles southwest of Atlanta—but in many ways it was like a whole other world. Fort Benning is one of those big, sprawling military complexes that dominate the countryside and the town, and for me it was a pretty drastic change. Basic training was constant busyness—there was no free time at all, and everything we did we always had to do on the run. Literally, any time we went someplace, we had to run to get there. Even if it was just down to the post office or over to the mess hall. Being from Alabama, I was pretty well used to the heat and humidity, but all that running was enough to make a guy wish he was someplace else.

But eight weeks later I finished up there and moved on to Fort Gordon, where we went through our advanced infantry training. Fort Gordon is located just outside Augusta, and for me it was even worse than Benning. Up there we had to go to a place called Camp Crocket, where they put us through all this advanced training—real experimental stuff—out in these remote, primitive areas, and when it was over, I was actually glad to be headed back to Fort Benning.

I had to go back to Benning for jump school, which lasted for the next couple of weeks, and then after that I was pretty much ready to go. They gave us two weeks at home, then shipped us off to Fort Lewis, Washington, which was basically the jumping-off point for Vietnam.

I waited at Fort Lewis for about a week, and then we finally headed out. We stopped over briefly in Anchorage, then touched down for a minute in Hawaii—not even long enough to see the beach—and then from there it was straight on in to Cam Ranh Bay. That was April 1968.

When I first got there, I was pretty much like everyone else—green and not a little naive—and Cam Ranh Bay didn't do a whole lot to fix that. In a lot of ways it was just like being in the United States, like we'd never left. Of course, it was hot as hell, but the facilities were top-notch, just like something you might find at Fort Benning or Fort Lewis. And the beaches, just to be honest, were magnificent. Like Panama City down in the panhandle. White, sprawling sand, clear—not blue, but *clear*—water. At Cam Ranh Bay it didn't seem like being at war at all. In fact, it actually seemed kind of nice.

The base itself was located along the coast, about a hundred kilometers due east of Da Lat and about fifty kilometers to the south of Nha Trang. It was situated on a peninsula that juts out into the South China Sea, and at the time it was generally considered to be one of the safest and most important bases in Vietnam. The area itself had been used as a harbor for many years, but when the Americans came, we turned it into one of the most massive and modern port facilities in the world. There was an airstrip, a hospital, a ship-repair facility—basically everything you could possibly need to run a world-class port.

Almost all of the new guys passed through there at some point or another. When I first got there, the place was crawling with GIs, with their duffels packed and their shoes shined. The place had an energy to it, almost a tangible optimism. The buildings were clean, and the sand was white. People smiled, and the jeeps were bright and shiny like a fresh spit-shine. There was even a wooden board-walk that ran along the side of the barracks—just *exactly* like Panama City!

Of course, for us it was really just a holding pattern, a place to stay before they shipped us out, but at the time it didn't seem like such a bad introduction to the place I'd been hearing so much about.

That first night there were so many people there that I ended up having to sleep outside, under the eaves of one of the buildings. I found a row of sandbags piled up along the outside wall of one of the barracks and just climbed up there, used my duffel for a pillow, and slept straight through the night—surprisingly at ease for my first night in country.

The next day they started organizing the new arrivals, and before I even had time to think about it they changed my assignment from the 101st Airborne Division and put me in with the 173rd Airborne Brigade. Apparently the 173rd had gotten hit pretty hard—down manpower, somebody said—so they decided I'd better go with them. Of course, to me it didn't really make much difference. One sounded just about as good as the next—and either way I'd still be getting my jump pay.

I sat around Cam Ranh Bay for the next week—the newest member of the 173rd Airborne Brigade—waiting to get shipped out. Then finally one morning, bright and early, just as the sun was peeking over the ocean, they loaded us up and sent us off to join our infantry companies—in my case, Company D of the 4th Battalion. I was kind of glad to be going actually—after all that waiting, I was anxious to see what all the excitement was about—but I knew once we left it'd be a long time before I'd get to see those beaches again. I packed up my bag, climbed on the chopper, and was off to join the company.

The first thing that struck me about the countryside was the size of the mountains. I mean, I knew to expect mountains, of course, but these were *mountains,* not just hills or mounds like I was used to back in Alabama, but real mountains, Blue Ridge Great Smoky Mountain–style mountains—tall and rugged and up into the sky and sprawling out into the distance.

I guess from Cam Ranh Bay the scope and size of the mountains didn't really translate, but riding out across the Central Highlands in a chopper, with the wind in my face and the treetops zipping along below us, I could really appreciate the depth and the size of the countryside. The land was vast, the mountains were huge, and the entire area was blanketed in trees bunched together so thick that you couldn't even see the ground.

The first leg of the flight, to Tuy Hoa, I actually rode in a Chinook, one of those big, tandem-rotor cargo helicopters, but the second leg I hopped on a slick, a Huey-style transport chopper, and from there I could see it all. The mountains, the roads, the wide meandering rivers. The Central Highlands was a pretty rugged place, and from what I could tell they were taking us right into the heart of it.

The flight itself didn't last that long. We flew across the treetops for maybe twenty or thirty minutes, until we spotted a bald patch on the top of one of the mountains, about a mile or so off in the distance. This was the fire support base where we were headed, and within a few minutes the pilot was setting us down in the middle of an empty clearing.

The base was situated on about a fifty- or sixty-acre lot, swept clean of trees and overlooking the highlands for twenty or thirty miles in every direction. It seemed like a perfect place for a base camp, if not the most luxurious—compared to the lush, green landscapes of the Vietnamese countryside, that base camp was nothing but dirt and dust.

When we came to a stop, I climbed down from the chopper, and as I was getting off, I noticed another guy climbing aboard. He was just like me, with his ruck packed and his helmet tight, except that he was headed home. It was kind of odd seeing a guy headed out like that— my own mirror image—but there was no question as to which one of us was on the better end of that deal. When I found out later that he'd been leaving, I pretty much considered him the luckiest guy around.

I stepped away from the chopper and noticed a guy waving to me over at the edge of the clearing, but before I could make it over to him, the chopper lifted off again and sent a swirling gust of dirt and debris flying into the air and, unfortunately, into my eyes.

"Welcome to Vietnam!"

When I opened my eyes, he was standing there in front of me, with one hand extended and the other one pressed against his forehead, shielding his own eyes from the dust.

"Don't worry about it—it happens to everyone. First time I got here I thought someone had thrown sand in my face . . . "

I blinked a couple of times to try and clear up my vision. The chopper moved higher, away from the camp, and as it did the air— and the noise—began to settle.

". . . but you'll get used to it."

I followed him across the camp, trying hard not to trip over all the tree stumps. I guess when they'd cleared the top of the mountain, they couldn't really do anything about all those stumps. There were these sharp little stubs of bushes and trees just sticking up out of the dirt everywhere, and if you didn't keep up with what you were doing, or keep an eye out for those dern little things, you might just get one in the heel—a lesson I'd learn well soon enough.

We continued across the camp—keeping one eye on the ground and one eye out front—to where my platoon was situated. He walked me over to this barren, bunker-looking thing and said, "All right, here ya go"—then patted me on the back and walked away.

Not exactly the welcoming party I was hoping for, but then again, as hot as it was, I couldn't really blame anybody for not rolling out the red carpet. Standing there at that fire-support base, it felt like it must've been about 120 degrees, and the air was just still and oppressive, with no breeze at all.

I stood back and surveyed the layout. The most striking feature about the camp was probably just how dry and rough the terrain looked. It was like you were standing in the middle of a big dirt field—like a cotton field maybe, before the cotton had started to grow. At the edges I could see rolls of razor wire placed along the bottom of the fence that surrounded the camp. And in the distance I noticed a stack of scrap metal, just randomly piled up for no obvious reason.

The bunker itself looked, really, like something a bunch of kids might've built if they'd been *playing* war, like out in the field behind their house or something. It looked like somebody'd taken a big piece of sheet metal, folded it over against the ground, and then coated it in sandbags.

But apparently that was where I'd be sleeping for the next couple of days—or at least until we got going—so I set my rucksack down and went about the business of getting settled in. No point in just standing around sulking.

In looking back on it, I think that fire-support base was probably the first real taste of Vietnam that I had. Cam Ranh Bay was an illusion, and the chopper ride over was only a bird's-eye view, but sitting around that fire-support camp, in the heat and the sun and the dirt and the dust . . . now *that* was Vietnam.

We sat around for two days before another company showed up to replace us—they'd been out in the field and were getting a chance for a break—at which point the real fun started.

Bright and early on the third morning, we saddled up and headed out, one after the other, out through the perimeter and down into the brush.

Now, coming in, I didn't really know what to expect—had no idea really—but once we got going, pushing our way deeper and deeper into the bush, I was pretty sure that it wasn't this. More than anything I was struck by the noise we were making. *Hack hack hack!* Sticks breaking, limbs popping, leaves shredding.

The point-man—whoever he was, I couldn't even actually see the guy, being in single file like we were—was just chopping away at the brush, trying to clear us a path, and the racket he was making—limbs breaking, leaves flying—was just unbelievable. Like I said, I couldn't see him, but I sure didn't have any problem hearing him.

*Hack hack hack!*

I looked back over my shoulder at the guy behind me and gave him a kind of *Are you hearing this?* look—he just shrugged.

So there it was.

I hadn't been on patrol ten minutes, and already I knew that this was no way to be running a military operation. The noise we were making, it was just absurd, but it was also pretty much the way things worked.

As I'd soon find out, walking the bush like that—or "humpin' it," as we called it—was pretty much the norm for us. It would become my daily routine: up in the morning, then walking the highlands in a single-file line that stretched back through the trees and tunneled across the land like a long and noisy train.

And as if that weren't bad enough, they loaded us down with food and supplies that probably totaled near seventy or eighty pounds: a mortar shell, M-60 machine-gun ammo, five hundred rounds of M-16 ammo, C rations, water, a rucksack, a poncho—plus your M-16 and whatever else you thought you might need for the day. Lugging all that stuff around, with the temperature so hot you couldn't walk fifty meters without getting soaked in sweat—it wasn't a comfortable feeling.

And yet despite whatever trouble it was having to carry all that stuff around, it still wasn't as bad as the noise. Above the heat, above the load, above whatever level of physical discomfort you might've had, the worst of it, by far, was the noise. And yet every day, over and over, just as surely as the fact that that sun was gonna rise up over the horizon and make us sweat like a bunch of stinking pigs, there it was:

*Clomp clomp clomp!*

*Hack hack hack!*

*Anyone out there?*

*Here we come!*

When that first day passed and we set up camp for the night, I thought it was basically a miracle that we'd survived as long as we had. If there was anybody out there looking for us—the VC, the NVA, whoever—I knew one thing was for sure: they knew exactly where we were.

Now, the idea behind all this, at least as I understood it, was for us to go out into the highlands and to basically just overwhelm whatever VC (Vietcong) or NVA (North Vietnamese Army) troops we happened to come across. At this point in the war—I got there right after Tet—the NVA had penetrated pretty deep into the South and the VC were solidly entrenched throughout the highlands.

There was a specific concern among some of the higher-ups that the VC and the NVA were trying to cut off the DMZ from Saigon and the lower half of the country—and thus to choke off whatever level of support was being supplied from the U.S.-backed government in the South. This meant that we—we being both the U.S. Army in general and those of us among its members who actually had to perform such tasks—were required to search the land throughout the middle portion of the country, along the coast, along the borders, through the mountains, and clear it of any possible VC or NVA strongholds. Specifically we were required to do this on foot, in a single-file line, with one guy at the front chopping away at the brush with a two-and-a-half-foot machete.

The missions were referred to as search-and-destroy missions, and for many they seemed a sound and logical (if somewhat old-fashioned) strategy. The idea that we could sweep across the land, rooting out the enemy from his mountain hideaway, didn't seem entirely without merit; after all, we did have the backing of the most powerful country in the world, the most modern weaponry, and a constant flow of willing and able-bodied men.

But for those of us who actually had to put it all into action, the theory had some serious and fundamental problems—not least of which was the fact that, in order to destroy something, you had to first of all be able to *find* it. That was the thing that this kind of operation was never fully able to accomplish.

Now, the *searching,* that part we pretty well mastered, but the *finding* seemed to elude us. And really, it was no coincidence. The fact was, whenever we went clomping around through the jungle, all seventy-five, eighty of us, loaded down and packed to the hilt with weapons and supplies, we just made too much noise.

In a country where the enemy could disappear underground—*literally*—trying to move around in a large group like that just didn't work. Whenever we started out through the bush, we were tipping them off just as surely as if we'd sent up a flare.

And the sad thing is, they must've recognized it immediately. They'd been seeing it for years—first with the Chinese, and most recently with the French; to them we must've looked like a bunch of circus performers, coming through town in some freewheeling military caravan. *Come one! Come all! Come see the Amazing Americans! Live and in person!*

They'd been fighting in those mountains for years, and they'd learned to fit their objectives to the landscape. They'd learned to *use* the land, to adapt it to their advantage, rather than struggle against it. That was the smart thing to do, obviously, and for them it was the only way they knew how to do it. It was their history, it was their heritage, and by the time we got there it was practically ingrained in their character.

As it turned out, it was only a matter of time before one of us got hurt. It was just too much of an imbalance: us, out there, trying to maneuver around those mountains, with all our men and our supplies and our noise—*the noise was relentless*—and them, just flitting around like fleas, biding their time, until they found a suitable opportunity to attack. It was about two months later when we got our first serious casualties.

Danny S. was from Philadelphia—he grew up in the city, went to school in the city, and as far as I knew, probably planned to finish up in the city—but to look at him, you'd have thought he'd come straight from the sticks, with his blond hair and his scarecrow body and his oversized shirt hanging down past his hands.

I remember when I first saw him, I thought, *Man, this guy must've gotten his laundry mixed up with somebody else's,* because his clothes were just hanging off of him like they were two or three sizes too big—almost gave me the impression of a little kid playing dress-up rather than an actual, real-life soldier.

But there he was, all 130 pounds of him, and once we finally got to talking, I realized that he was just as likely to get things done as any of us—maybe even more so. He'd walked right up to me, all smiles, hand out, just cool and confident—asked me if I knew where we could get a glass of water, which made me laugh, because I was thinking the exact same thing.

We'd both arrived at the fire-support base on the same day, assigned to the same platoon, and almost immediately we'd hit it off. He was just one of those guys that everybody liked, you could tell, and right off I'd been drawn to his easy manner and his laid-back attitude.

It was a couple of months in when I noticed he'd started hanging around with a guy named Sam S. from Washington, D.C., or Connecticut maybe—someplace back east.

Sam was one of the older guys, one of the veterans. He'd been there for about ten months and was not at all bashful about letting you know it—he'd really seen some things, really been in the shit, he'd say—and for most of the newer guys it actually sounded legit.

I personally wasn't all that impressed, but Danny seemed to like him, and before long they were hanging around like two old friends from high school. They were always together. Whenever we'd stop for a break or to set up camp or whatever, Danny was always right there beside him, listening to his tales and laughing at his stories.

In a way it made perfect sense to try and hook up with a veteran like that—to try and glean a little wisdom off of one of the short-timers—but in this case it didn't exactly work out. Danny was probably a little naive. And Sam, I'm sure, was overly confident. But even then, who can say what causes one thing to happen and not another? I mean, maybe it was a bad decision, but as far as I knew, it just as easily could've been bad luck.

Really bad luck.

We were just outside Tuy Hoa, in the mountains of Phu Yen Province, when it happened. We were humpin' the bush, as usual, and we were in desperate need of some water. Normally we'd just find the nearest stream or river, to refill our canteens, but every place that we'd come across was completely dried up. We were trying to locate a stream that we'd found on the map, but for some reason we just couldn't seem to find it. And I wasn't too sure that it wouldn't be dry once we did.

We moved up to a grassy plateau, near the top of a mountain ridge, and I noticed that our Kit Carson Scout had started acting a little bit funny. A Kit Carson Scout (or KCS) was a former VC or NVA soldier who had swapped over to our side—maybe he'd been captured or given up or whatever, but for whatever reason, he'd swapped over—and was put to work, scouting out the enemy on the other side. This was an invaluable service for us—I mean, who could've known the VC better than the VC themselves?

But that day, as we reached the top of the mountain, I was keeping a close eye on our KCS. That was a habit I'd learned early. A Kit Carson Scout was like a finely tuned barometer: he knew what could happen to him if he ended up getting caught by the VC or the NVA—torture, death, who knows what else—so whenever a KCS got tense, I knew there was probably a cause for concern somewhere in the area. This time he was moving a little more slowly than normal and seemed to have tensed up a bit, like a deer that's caught scent of a predator. I moved over to him and asked him what was up.

"Hey, man, what's up?"

"Boo-koo VC," he said. "Boo-koo" was French—Vietnamstyle—for "a lot," and coming from this guy, I knew to take it seriously.

We moved farther across the plateau, and before long we came across an abandoned VC base camp. Several straw huts lined the outer edges of the clearing, and a campfire was still burning in the center. *Still burning.* There didn't seem to be anyone around now, but judging from the way the camp looked, we knew they couldn't be too far off.

As soon as we got there, the KCS spotted a well on the far side of the camp, and I think we were all probably as glad to have found some water as we were to have found the camp. I don't think I'd had a taste of cool water in three days, and the little bit that was left in my canteen was extremely hot.

We proceeded to search the camp, to see if there was anything there of value. We found some pots and pans, a bunch of rice—basically just necessities. There were also some papers that they'd left behind, but mainly it was foodstuff.

I went over to the well, to refill my canteen, while a bunch of the others continued with the search. Two of the guys had started burning the huts with a long, leafy torch made from a fallen limb.

I was just about to get my first swig of water when I heard the gunfire ring out. A burst of automatic rifle fire, maybe two, three hundred yards away. And an explosion. *Was that an explosion?*

I pulled my canteen away from my lips and looked around at the others, confused. None of our guys would've been anywhere near the area where the gunfire was coming from—it was a pretty good distance away—and it didn't seem like it was directed at us.

We immediately headed out in that direction. Half-running, half-walking, moving fast to see what had happened. We got there in maybe five minutes, and as we approached I could see Danny and Sam, strewn out across the trail.

Danny was unconscious, bleeding bad, from a bullet wound to the head. Sam was nearby, conscious but wounded, and clearly in pain. He'd suffered multiple wounds, one to his hand, one to his chest. Maybe more, I couldn't tell. There was so much blood.

And then, to make it worse, as we approached, the gunfire started back up. *From where? From those trees?* There was no protection.

Chaos erupted as the platoon unleashed a massive explosion of retaliatory gunfire. *Where are they? Where's it coming from? What direction?* I opened up, full automatic, just spraying the plants, spraying the trees. Chaos, leaves flying, the noise deafening.

The area clouded over with smoke. The medic was there, he was bent over Sam. I found myself holding a glucose bag in the air with one hand and with the other firing up the trees with my M-16.

It happened so fast—*Are they even firing back?*—and a medevac had been called, but it couldn't land until the area was secure. *Is the area secure? What's happening?*

I looked back over my shoulder and saw a guy with an M-60 machine gun, another with an M-79 grenade launcher—we were laying down some pretty heavy fire—but were they still there? I couldn't even tell.

A little farther down the trail there was an open field, about half the size of a football field and covered in elephant grass. It was the only place nearby where the medevac could land, so we'd have to carry Danny and Sam down to that clearing before we could get them lifted out.

We started with Danny. We picked him up gently and placed him on a poncho. There were four of us, including our squad leader, Bill Pfister. Each of us grabbed a corner of the poncho and picked him up, cradling him in the fabric like it was a hammock.

We carried him down the trail, and as we neared the edge of the clearing I could see the medevac circling above. Someone had thrown a red smoke grenade out into the field, and the smoke was billowing up above the dark green grass, then dissipating quickly under the force of the chopper.

As the medevac started to descend I saw that we'd be out in the open as we crossed the field. The rifle fire had let up behind us, but it wouldn't take much, just one shot. The chopper hovered gently above the grass, pushing the blades down and away, softly onto their sides. I looked over at Pfister, and I think he must've had the same thought that I did. I could see the concern in his eyes, but he just nodded his head, meaning for us to keep moving.

Pfister and I were holding the front end of the poncho, and as we stepped down into the clearing both of us began to get swallowed up by the mud. The field was a marsh, and the ground little more than slush, and when we stepped off into it, we disappeared up to our waists.

I couldn't believe it. Neither one of us could believe it, but what could we do? We just pressed on through the mud, and the two guys in back followed in behind us. We fought against the weight of the water, the force of the wind. I strained. My muscles hurt. We kept moving.

The chopper was hovering above the grass in the distance. We neared it slowly, water splashing, wind blowing. And all the time trying to keep Danny up above the mud.

We finally reached the chopper, and the medics on board pulled him up. Another group followed with Sam. The medics reached down and pulled him up.

The chopper lifted off and pulled away, then disappeared in the sky. The wind died down, and the grass stood back up. Every muscle in my body ached. My clothes were soaked. I was soaked.

But nobody said anything. We waded back across the marsh, picked up our things, and returned to join the company.

When we got back to the camp, it became a little more clear what had happened. Apparently, Danny and Sam had wandered away from the group, and as soon as they did, they'd been attacked by a group of VC lingering around in the bush. Why they'd done it was anybody's guess, but one thing was definitely clear: they'd made a mistake, one simple slip-up, and the VC had made them pay.

We stuck around the camp for the rest of the day, until the guys at headquarters told us to move out about three o'clock or so. We moved about a click away—a thousand meters—and set up camp for the night. The next morning they sent in a pretty heavy air strike around the entire area—the camp and the place where the ambush had occurred—but of course, when we went back in to check it out, there was no one around. No bodies. No nothing. The place was totally deserted.

So why did they do it? Why'd they wander off the way they did?

Maybe Danny didn't get it. Maybe he didn't want to get it.

But Sam knew. He had to have known. Ten months in? *He knew.* Did he feel immune? Did he think he was invincible? Did he think they were invisible?

Who knows? Does it even matter?

Wasn't it just a matter of time anyway? If not them, then somebody else?

Okay, yes, they made a mistake; they shouldn't have stepped away from the group the way they did, outside of the strength and security of numbers. They were the single calf wandering away from the herd—but what about the herd itself?

Weren't we responsible too? Didn't we draw attention to ourselves? If you're going to walk around with pieces of raw meat dangling from your ankles, why be surprised when the buzzards show up?

When we'd reached the ambush site that day, just moments after we'd heard the gunfire, it was like a bubble had burst. People were yelling, screaming out, in frustration, in panic. I could hear the frustration in the voices, pure and primal, shouting loud, without words. It was chaos. All of the doubt, all of the clawing doubt—the feeling that maybe, just maybe, we were not in control at all. Did we think we were? Did we actually think that we were the ones in control? All our doubts came to the surface as we yelled and screamed and fired our rifles.

And then when it was over, there was silence. Nobody knew what to say, or how to explain it, but the frustration—the pure and utter frustration—remained. Frustration and confusion.

I don't know why Danny and Sam did it. What caused them to do such a foolish thing. Probably we'll never know. All I knew then was that Danny had died and Sam was on his way back to Tuy Hoa on the back of a medevac.

About two weeks after that I stepped in a hole and got a punji stake through the knee. A punji stake was one of those bamboo shafts that the VC liked to use as a sort of leave-behind means of harassment. They were basically just bamboo sticks carved into sharp points, but they could often be extremely dangerous. (Trust me.) The VC liked to scatter them around on clearings and along the outskirts of their base camps—wherever they thought the Americans might be—and whenever you had the misfortune of stepping on one, you could pretty much count on being out for a while.

We were humpin' the bush, as usual, along the floor of one of the valleys, and apparently we had neared the perimeter of a VC camp. I was running point at the time—one of the hazards of the job, I guess—and when we approached the area where the punji stakes were, I just happened to not see them. Usually the VC tried to stick them down in the ground in bunches, at inconspicuous angles, so that when you approached, you'd only see them as sticks or grass or as just a natural part of the terrain. We were actually taught to scan to the left and right, to try and catch them at odd angles, but somehow I missed them—and when I stepped down in that hole, I just fell right on top of one. A frustrating experience really: not only was I wounded in action, but there wasn't a VC in sight.

The injury itself wasn't all that bad, but they decided to send me down to Tuy Hoa to the hospital for a couple of weeks to heal up. I was sitting there waiting for the chopper to arrive, to pick me up and take me to Tuy Hoa, when I noticed a black cloud forming in the distance, just above the horizon.

I couldn't hear anything, but it was such a strange-looking sight that it caught my attention almost immediately: this big, black, amorphous-looking thing, just floating off in the distance. I focused in on it, to see if I could figure out what it was, but I couldn't really make it out, beyond the general, vague impression of a dark, cloud-like body.

Well, soon enough, everybody had noticed it. We were all just sitting there, staring out at this big, dark cloud, trying to figure out what in the hell it was. And even more disturbing, as time passed, it became clear that this cloud, this thing, whatever it was, was growing—apparently as it was moving closer and closer to us.

Suddenly each one of us stiffened—like deer in headlights, frozen by the sound. It was faint at first—subtle, small—but very distinct. I looked over at the guy sitting beside me; his eyes were wide with fear. Apparently he'd recognized the sound too: *bees!*

In the next few seconds the sound of those bees grew louder and louder—*bzzzzzz, BZZZZZZ*—until, just like that, they were right on top of us, a swarm of bees so big it blocked out the sun. People were diving and running and jumping under ponchos and hollering like you've never heard before.

I grabbed up a poncho and hit the ground, balled up tighter than an armadillo. People were scrambling around so fast, you'd have thought the NVA were hitting us with an artillery strike.

I curled up there on the ground and just prayed that those bees would keep on going—I mean, what in the world could you do? If they'd decided to attack, decided just to swoop down and hit us while we were all standing around like that in the open, there wasn't a thing in the world we could have done. With nothing more than a thin poncho and a prayer, each one of us just had to sit there and wait.

Until the bees passed—into the distance behind us, the *bzzzzzz* growing fainter and fainter. Until finally it disappeared altogether.

I poked my head out from under the poncho.

"Are they gone?"

Two weeks later, after my knee had healed up, I rejoined the company on its never-ending march to nowhere. Naturally, things hadn't changed much while I was gone, and when I got back, I resumed my role—hauling my gear, running the occasional point—as though I'd never even left. It was probably about three or four weeks after that—so no more than two and a half months after the ambush—when the next big incident occurred, and I guess you could say that, for me, it was the final blow.

On this particular day we'd moved into a valley, wide open and clear except for some light brush and a low, knee-high grass. Normally that wouldn't have been any big deal, nothing out of the ordinary necessarily, except that, in order to get to the valley floor we'd had to pass right over the top of a rather large—and tall—mountain.

Our CO had wanted to press onward—"Keep on moving, fellas"—so we could make it down to the valley by dusk. I'd been running point that day—by this time I'd been running point quite a bit—and I'd noticed several spots that would've made for a nice, high perimeter. Since I was a private, though, my opinions didn't really carry too much sway with the commanding officer.

As instructed, we moved on over the mountain and down into the valley, where we set up our camp and (contrary to all logic) got ready for the night.

I noticed also on this day that some of the newer guys were acting a little more relaxed than usual. As we'd cleared the top of the mountain the sun had broken through, and admittedly, it was a really beautiful afternoon—or at least it would've been if we hadn't been in the middle of Vietnam in the year 1968—but a lot of the guys were acting like we were out on a picnic or something. They were just cutting up and talking real loud, like there was nothing in the world to worry about.

Personally I was still a little concerned about the choice of our campsite; in fact, I became extremely nervous as soon as I'd found out that the CO wanted us to move down into the valley, off of the higher ground. After four months in country, you started to pick up on certain things, and one of the things I picked up on was that being down in a valley when you could've been up on a mountain didn't make a whole lot of sense. Which was why I didn't mind too much when I found out our platoon had been selected for OP.

OP is short for observation post, which meant we'd have to go outside the company perimeter and establish a sort of second satellite camp. We were basically serving as a nighttime lookout, just outside the main perimeter, in case the enemy decided to come to life at some point in the middle of the night. Our job was to keep a lookout and alert the rest of the company if anything happened; in truth, I really didn't mind the assignment. By this time there were a number of experienced guys in the platoon, and being away from the group like that, we'd get to move to higher ground and find some real cover.

So just before dark we started back to the mountain to look for a place to set up. We walked for about two hundred yards or so before selecting a spot just up the foot of the mountain and alongside a footpath that wound its way through the trees and down into the valley. Pfister and I discussed it, and we both felt like it was the most likely place for the VC to try and access the camp: the dirt was worn clean, the limbs had been cleared—so apparently *somebody* had been using it—and it offered a better view of the valley and the perimeter down below.

To set up our own perimeter we assigned two guys to watch the trail from the rear—this way, if someone approached us from the back, we'd be able to respond in time to defend ourselves. The shift would rotate throughout the night, in two-hour increments, to make sure that whoever was watching at any given time was fresh and alert.

We also established a line of claymore mines just along the side of the trail—again, to protect ourselves in case someone tried to slip up on us or just tried to make it down the trail to the camp. A claymore mine is a hand-detonated, antipersonnel mine that was used pretty frequently in Vietnam; it's easy to carry—not too heavy and not too big—so you could just strap one to your rucksack and not even know it was there. We used them a lot during perimeters—they provided a defense that we could trigger quickly, just in case the VC somehow managed to catch us off-guard.

We set out about a dozen or so of these mines, up and down the trail, and we spaced them out about one every five or six feet so we could cover a pretty good section of the path. We then ran the wires from each of the mines back to a single point so that whoever was on guard duty would be able to control them all—just flip off the safeties, push down on the clackers, and *wham!*—claymores going off, up and down the trail.

Another thing I should point out about the claymores is the fact that they were designed to explode in one direction. They were built in a sort of convex shape that curved outward like a warped piece of plastic so that when they were detonated they'd propel their projectiles (seven hundred steel ball bearings) in one direction, away from those of us doing the detonating. In fact, just to make sure that you didn't get confused, the directions were printed very clearly right there on the front of the mine—FRONT TOWARD ENEMY—and I can tell you, that was one set of instructions you didn't want to ignore.

Basically for us this meant that we could set out the mines in surprisingly close proximity to our own position without having to worry about getting caught up in our own explosive. All we'd get was the back-blast, which was usually just a bunch of dirt and leaves—*a whole lot* of dirt and leaves, granted, but still, just dirt and leaves. This was the standard procedure for this type of setting—by this point I'd set up a number of different perimeters like this, with the guards established and the claymores out—and in general the nights would pass quietly and without event. Most of the time we'd just sit around, watching and waiting—some of us sleeping, two always awake. Of course, we always had to be prepared, just in case, but on this night we had the perfect setup.

About nine o'clock or so, just as the dark of night was beginning to settle in over the mountain and the bulk of the platoon had laid down and shut their eyes, just as things were beginning to seem like they'd finally calmed down, for the first time all day, we heard an explosion.

I could tell from the sound that it was a hand grenade, exploded somewhere down in the valley, just at the edge of the company perimeter. The explosion was followed quickly by a smattering of rifle fire and then by a second explosion, this time closer to the foot of the mountain—and then a third and fourth, in quick succession, pricking away at the edges.

A pause, quiet for just a moment, as the initial assault settled in— and then suddenly, the sound of machine-gun fire, coming from inside the perimeter.

Then quickly, one after the other, we heard the crackling of an M-16, the *woomp* of a hand grenade, and the rattling of an M-60 spitting out its rounds. Someone shot off an illumination flare from inside the camp, and it lit up the valley like a Fourth of July fireworks display. The entire perimeter was a flurry of activity, swelling into a heavy barrage of rifle fire and hand grenades, the sound bursting across the valley and echoing off of the mountains.

I was lying down on the ground, about twenty feet from the guy with the detonators, stretched out on my belly and trying to inch one way or the other to get a better view of the action below. We'd hidden ourselves in some pretty good cover, so I couldn't really see the action all that well without standing up. But I could hear it clearly and followed it by listening to the gunfire.

The initial barrage and the camp's response, that first explosion of activity, had passed, replaced by the point-counterpoint of small-arms fire—the crack of an M-16 followed by the response of an AK-47.

If any of the guys in the platoon had somehow managed to slip off to sleep earlier, before the activity had started, then they were definitely awake now. We were all sitting around, listening intently. Waiting for the action to break. Wondering what would happen.

Eventually, after about half an hour of sniping back and forth, the gunfire seemed to have stopped. We weren't sure, of course, if it was just a temporary pause in the fighting, but it seemed to last longer than some of the previous breaks in the combat. It seemed to be over.

We remained quiet and still, just listening, alert, poised, ready— whatever might happen next, we were ready for it.

The silence remained, still and dark. Then, after maybe five minutes had passed since the last gunshot—it probably wasn't even that long—we heard the sounds of someone running—*people* running! Aha! The VC were coming right up the trail, straight toward the claymore mines!

I couldn't see them yet, but I could hear them, breathing heavy, their weapons rattling, and just as sure as I was lying there in that dirt, they were running right up the trail, just as we had arranged it.

I put my head down against the ground, expecting the blast from the claymores any second. I was probably about fifteen feet off to the side. I hunkered down. The VC approached, running hard, pounding the trail at a full sprint.

Then they were there—*right there,* right there beside me—and then . . . and then . . .

And then . . . *nothing.* They just kept on running, right on past me, and right on through the ambush. Up the trail and over the mountain.

I couldn't believe it. What in the world had happened? It had been the perfect setup, we couldn't have drawn it up any better, and those guys—three of them, I think, maybe more—had run right on through like we weren't even there.

I raised my head and looked over to see who was on guard duty. It was the sergeant who was supposed to have been in charge of the whole thing—a *veteran*—and he was just sitting there with the detonators in his hands, frozen.

"What in the hell are you doing?" It was my voice, but it could've been anyone's. The entire platoon was baffled—and angry. How in the world did that happen? How could a guy just freeze up like that? The guys were so mad, I thought somebody was gonna climb over there and just shoot him right there on the spot.

But it was too late. The VC were gone. And they'd run right through our ambush and didn't even know it.

Incredible.

Eventually we quieted back down—we had to, considering that we didn't know whether there were any more out there or not—and we tried to finish out the night. Personally I could hardly sleep, I was so shook up from what had happened. It was absolutely incredible—the guy'd just frozen up—and as we'd soon find out, it would prove costly.

The rest of the night passed without incident. The sounds of the gunfire were replaced by the sounds of the night, still and quiet.

Just before daylight I woke up and noticed a few of the other guys already stirring. The valley was still dark, but I could see the faint glow of the sun, below the horizon in the distance. Once again things were calm. And once again we were lulled into thinking that things were fine.

I recognized the sound immediately. About three-quarters of the way up the mountain, above where we were set up, the unmistakable sound of a mortar tube. The round hit its target, right in the middle of the company perimeter, and immediately people started screaming, calling out for a medic.

But it didn't stop there. The mortar fire continued. Usually a mortar attack would only include a couple of rounds, but this time, this morning, the assault went on for at least fifteen or twenty rounds. And they were all hitting the camp, just pounding the perimeter with shells.

We were situated near the foot of the mountain, maybe a quarter of the way up, and though we were a pretty good ways from the camp, we still weren't close enough to the VC to be able to do any-thing. All we could do was just lie low and wait for it to end.

I cringed just thinking about it. With every mortar round, I could hear the screams. And I knew—*I knew*—that it could've all been prevented. Setting up in the valley instead of choosing the higher ground. Blowing the ambush, just freezing up when the sappers ran through. That mortar attack should've never taken place, and with every round I was growing more and more angry.

Finally it ended.

We made our way down from the brush and ran quickly to the company perimeter. What I saw there made me sick. All over, there were people wounded, calling out, crying for the medic, calling for help. There were at least twenty, probably twenty-five men, seri-ously wounded and lying around that valley floor. They'd already called in the medevacs, and four or five were approaching in the distance.

The situation had devolved into chaos. I'd never seen so many wounded men in one place at the same time. And the new guys were scared. There was one guy who was so scared that he just stepped down into a foxhole and shot himself in the foot, blew half his foot off with an M-16—thinking he'd be able to get a free ride home, I guess. Anything to get out of this mess. But the CO wouldn't let him leave until all of the others had been choppered out, and even then—I remember this distinctly—the CO read him his rights as the medics loaded him onto the back of the medevac.

Eventually we got all the wounded taken care of—after several trips in and out by those choppers—but there were still the feelings of frustration, and I didn't think they'd be disappearing anytime soon.

Later that afternoon headquarters moved the entire company—or what was left of us anyway—to some nondescript airstrip out in the middle of the province. The mortar attack had left us at about two-thirds our normal strength, so we were going to have to sit around that airstrip for a while until they could find some new guys to fill in.

That's when Pipkin showed up.

"So whatta you think, boys? What's it gonna be?"

Pipkin threw down the butt of his cigarette and stomped it under the toe of his boot, grinding it noisily into the dirt. He'd just finished telling us about the Lurps—for half an hour, maybe forty-five minutes—and though I could only get the basics from what all he'd said, it was clear that he was genuinely passionate about the company.

I looked over at Pfister. He raised an eyebrow at me, then repeated Pipkin's question: "Whatta you think, Bill? Sound like something you might be interested in?"

More than anyone, Pfister understood the feelings I had about the line company. He'd been there in the beginning, and he'd shared my concerns and my worries throughout. He'd listened to me talk when I most needed someone to talk to, and I think that more times than not he agreed with whatever I had to say.

He asked again. Though in truth, I think he already knew the answer.

"So," he prompted, "whatta you think?"

From the first day I'd arrived I could tell that the line company wasn't for me—if it was really for anyone. There were probably eighty or ninety of us, all loaded down in our steel pots and our rucksacks, with all our ammo and our rations. Every time we picked up to go anywhere it was like we were trying to move a house, and all we could take with us was whatever we could fit on our backs.

I saw guys get so exhausted from carrying that weight around that they'd just start throwing stuff down—like a mortar shell—just throw stuff down on the ground and leave it there for whoever happened along to find it. (And of course, you know what happened to mortar shells—they got turned into booby traps, guaranteed.)

Carrying all that weight around was one of the hardest things I ever had to do.

And it was noisy too. It seemed like everything we did somehow attracted more attention to us. Even our rucksacks had these metal frames that clanked around and got caught on the limbs—good for support, but bad for cutting out the noise. And it was a huge production if we ever had to be dropped off anywhere—it'd take either one of those large Chinook helicopters or about twenty of the slicks. We must've looked like the entire U.S. Army, storming in to take the countryside—no wonder they all scattered. I would have too if I'd looked up and seen all those helicopters coming in. There was just no way we were gonna surprise anyone with all that going on. No way.

In the four or five months I'd been over there, we were out in the field almost the entire time and we never *saw* anybody. I mean, there was the occasional glance—like during the claymore fiasco when the three VC had gone running by. But even then, I'd had my head down and mainly just heard them. For us it was like we were fighting somebody who was invisible. They knew *we* were coming—they'd set up a booby trap or wait for us, in hiding, until they decided to strike—but we never even got a chance to get a look at them.

We had one guy sit down on a booby trap, one of those pressure-release types—he didn't even know it was there until he got up and the thing went off. Wounded him real bad. We had several guys step on punji stakes—myself included. And those things could put you out of commission for weeks. Or months even. The way things were over there, I think I was more likely to see a deer out deer hunting than I was to see a VC—and a deer's senses are a whole lot better than a VC's.

I think a lot of our trouble, fighting there in Vietnam, could be seen in those early search-and-destroy missions—to me, they just showed how poorly we understood the situation: our enemy and the terrain. Putting us out there like that had its effects definitely, some even positive, but it was no way to win a war—not in any kind of a long-term way. Large groups of soldiers clomping noisily through the jungle in search of small groups of soldiers. It hardly even made sense.

Earlier that spring, just after Tet—and just prior to my arrival—President Johnson had announced the promotion of General William C. Westmoreland to chief of staff. Westmoreland was the one who was considered the mastermind behind the search-and-destroy campaign—he was the strategy's creator and its most outspoken advocate—so when the announcement came down that he was leaving, a lot of people expected some sort of reevaluation of the strategy.

And maybe there was, but from what I could tell, it didn't make a whole lot of difference. His replacement, General Creighton W. Abrams, took over in June, and my feet stayed just as muddy and just as sore as before he got there. Even though things were likely to change, I had no way of knowing when they would—maybe it'd be two months, but just as likely it'd be ten, or never. I didn't know. And more importantly, did I really want to stick around to find out?

What it came down to for me was the fact that life in the line company was just plain dangerous. I mean, it wasn't simply a matter of inconvenience or incompatibility; being in the line company meant constantly being in danger.

We were working at such a disadvantage that before long I started feeling like a sitting duck. Literally like a duck, just sitting there waiting to get shot. You always hear the expression, but to really know what it feels like, to be in a situation and not be able to do anything about it—well, it's not a good feeling.

We'd trudge across those mountains, our boots heavy with mud, and you just knew you were about to hear a gunshot—that single rifle-shot that might be the last thing you ever heard.

It almost seemed comical, being out there on the water, marching neatly across the rivers and streams: What else were we but sitting ducks?

But it was also very real. And the danger of it was real. I watched, in frustration, as friends were picked off in mortar attacks and night raids, then felt the helplessness as the enemy slipped away and disappeared into the landscape.

When the VC started mortaring the perimeter that morning, there was little they could offer up in resistance—and even less that we could do. It was the most frustrating feeling in the world. Painful. In the deepest part of your gut.

For their part, the line companies did provide a service that probably none of the other companies could have provided: simply by being there, they created a presence that prevented the enemy from settling comfortably throughout the region, that kept the VC nervous and on the move.

The line companies actually had some pretty good men—plenty of them. Of course, we also had a few who were a little suspect, but a bunch of the guys were top-quality people and very competent soldiers. But in the end it just came down to survival.

In such a large group it was pretty much impossible to suppress the noise; even at our quietest, we were still almost a hundred guys walking through the jungle, with equipment clanging—there was just no way to move that many guys quietly.

At the time all this was going on, I was still only eighteen years old, so there were a lot of things I didn't know about and wasn't sure about—but there was one thing I did feel strongly about and that was the fact that the line company was a tough deal. After that last ambush, I knew I needed to make a change.

I looked over at Pfister, who was standing there with an expectant expression on his face—eyebrows raised, his mouth in a grin—and his hands jammed down in his front pants pockets. I knew he'd been considering these same issues for some time, and I also knew that he was aware of what I was thinking—but of course, I couldn't know what he would decide.

I turned to Pipkin. He'd given us the full pitch, so now the only thing left to do was to decide.

"You know, Sergeant, I've been over here for nearly four months now, and I ain't seen the first VC yet." I paused and looked back over at Pfister for a second. *"Four months."*

Pipkin smiled. He pulled out a pencil and some paper and scribbled my name down in a column.

"Bill. Shanahan." He said it slowly, then returned the paper and pencil to his pocket, and stuck out his hand.

"Well, Bill," he said. "Welcome to the Lurps."

The rest of that day was sort of a fog. I wandered around the airstrip, lost in thought, thinking about the conversation, rehashing the words in my brain, and wondering exactly when I'd be hearing from those guys. Pipkin hadn't been all that specific about the time frame, so I was thinking maybe a few weeks, or months even, before I could get transferred out—if in fact I got transferred at all. But the very next morning, after I'd gotten up and gone through the usual morning routine, I got word that the CO wanted to see me. I walked over to his makeshift tent, and just as soon as he saw me he came walking out and said: "Hey, Shan, we're gonna miss you around here, buddy."

I couldn't believe it. Normally the army operated slower than Christmas—hurry up and wait, that was their slogan—but this, this was quick. Real quick. He went on to say that there was a chopper coming to pick me up in an hour—*one hour?*—and that they'd be taking me to a place called LZ English. I didn't have much time, so I rushed back to the bunker and started throwing my gear together.

The guys were all watching me, giving me these funny looks, saying, *"Hey, man, where you going?"*—and when I told them (though actually I wasn't too sure myself), they all wanted to go. They were envious, jealous, whatever—they wanted to get the heck out of there. The CO said, "Yeah, well, y'all aren't invited," and one guy threw his helmet down like a little kid. But really, they were disappointed. I think a lot of the guys liked me, and I'd always had this feeling that they'd sort of depended on me—relied on me to try and keep things calm—me and Pfister.

Not much time. I had my things packed—less than an hour now—and I knew I'd better go find Pfister. He'd decided to stay behind—his tour was short, and he wanted to stay behind, where he felt like he was most needed—but I wanted to see him one last time before I took off for the Lurps.

I didn't have to look far. He'd heard that I was leaving, so he came over to see me off. I was standing there with my things packed when he walked up.

"Those guys didn't waste much time, did they?"

He picked up my rucksack and slung it over his shoulder.

"C'mon. We better get you over there before they change their minds."

We hustled over to the area where the choppers landed—by this time the chopper had already arrived and was kicking up dirt, just like on that first day.

"All right, big man, this is it!"

He handed me my ruck and patted me on the shoulder.

"You're gonna do great!"

With the wind from the blades blowing dust everywhere, I shook his hand—"Thanks, Pfister"—then shielded my eyes and ran toward the chopper.

I thought about the looks on some of the guys' faces when I was packing up my gear—how sad some of them had looked when they'd seen me leaving—but I didn't even know where I was going myself, and I sure didn't know what to expect. I just knew I was willing to take the chance—and to not have any regrets about it.

I threw my ruck on board and climbed in after it. When I looked back out, Pfister was standing there at the edge of the grass, just waving and smiling.

I got myself situated, with my feet at the edge of the door and one hand gripped tightly to the side of the doorway. The chopper slowly began to rise from the ground, and then once we cleared, we banked sharply and accelerated above the mountains. I looked out over the countryside, with the line company disappearing below and the sun just beginning to break above the horizon.

As we passed above a rice paddy I noticed some farmers, in their conical hats, out walking the field. I noticed a cow being led down a dirt path. And a group of girls riding bicycles. It was a new day, and things were just getting started.

# PART TWO

---

# THE LURPS

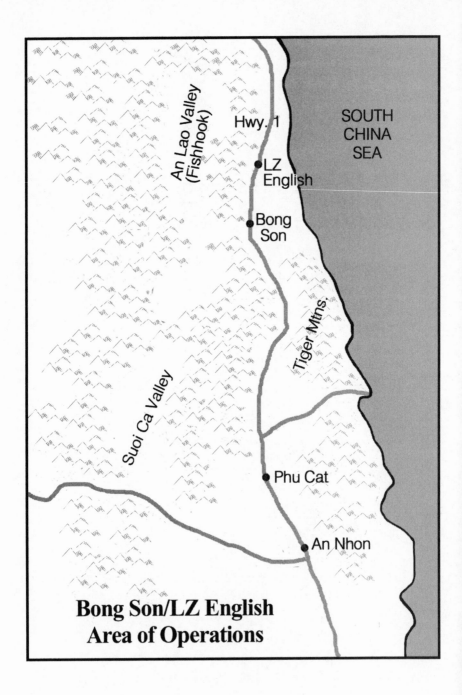

**Bong Son/LZ English
Area of Operations**

# 2

## Back to Basics

L z english was located in binh dinh province, just off the coast, and about half a kilometer to the north of a small town called Bong Son. It was situated adjacent to Highway 1, which was the main thoroughfare through Vietnam—a long and narrow road that ran the entire length of the country, from Saigon to Hanoi, and was the quickest way, as I'd find out later, into Bong Son whenever you wanted to go in on your day off.

LZ English was a pretty well-known location. It wasn't particularly impressive or well fortified in the way that, say, Cam Ranh Bay was, but it was situated in the midst of heavy enemy concentrations and was famous for some pretty intensive fighting. I'd never been there, but I knew the names of the surrounding areas: the An Lao Valley to the north, the Tiger Mountains to the south. And I knew it was supposed to be a pretty remote place.

When I left the airstrip that day, the chopper took me to Tuy Hoa—another coastal town, at the edge of Phu Yen Province—

where we met up with Pipkin and made arrangements to catch a plane from there on up to LZ English. He told me there'd be someone at the base to meet me, then wished me luck and disappeared. "Gotta go check on some of the guys here at Tuy Hoa," he said, "but I'll see you later up at English."

I caught the plane later that afternoon, just like Pipkin had said, and arrived at LZ English sometime around dusk. One of the Lurps was there at the airstrip, waiting for me in a jeep. I threw my ruck on the backseat, then climbed into the front beside him—"So this is it, huh?"—and sat back for the ride.

LZ English was a much bigger place than that airstrip had been— probably a hundred little buildings or so sprawled out among the mountains like a small town. They weren't huge concrete structures—in fact, many were just makeshift tents—but they gave the base a sense of stability, of permanence, that some of the other places had lacked.

Of course, in terms of the basic facilities, it wasn't anything like Cam Ranh Bay—it wasn't nearly the resort that that place had been, with all its boardwalks and white sand beaches—but at the time it seemed just as good. Compared to the airstrip where we'd been staying—not to mention all those countless nights of sleeping out in the middle of nowhere—LZ English seemed like about the best place you could possibly be.

We crossed the base, bumping along in the jeep, kicking up dust along the way. We passed a truck compound filled with jeeps and trucks, all lined up and parked like a used-car lot. Some topless, some like little golf carts, all painted that same dark green and coated in dirt.

We passed a chopper pad just off the strip to the left, and I noticed several guys, pilots probably, hanging around, looking relaxed. Several choppers were lined up at the edge of the pad, still and quiet, their blades tilting at odd angles, as if asleep.

We continued across the camp until we finally reached a hill at the opposite side of the compound. He drove us up the hill and came to a stop in front of a row of small wooden buildings.

"This is it," he said. "Lurp Hill."

Lurp Hill was the area where all the Lurps stayed—it was sort of a barren, open space at the back of the base, with a line of barracks strung out along the edge. It overlooked the chopper pad and the rest of LZ English, and for the guys who lived there it was sort of a home away from home. The quarters themselves were built from wooden frames and canvas tops, and they were posted with hand-made signs: Team Bravo, Team Delta, etc.

I walked into one of the barracks and picked out a bed, then met up with some of the other guys milling around outside; there were about a dozen or so other recruits, all from different companies and all there for the same reason that I was. We were looking for a fresh start, and from what I could tell, they were just as pleased to be there as me—upbeat and alive, and not at all like the tired and downbeat faces I was used to seeing in the line company. About an hour or so later one of the Lurps arrived to welcome us to the base.

"Gentlemen," he said, with arms outstretched, "welcome to the Lurps."

We gathered around in a sort of semicircle to hear what he had to say.

"Now, I'm gonna try and keep this short, since I know some of you guys are still trying to get moved in, but I just wanted to tell you a little bit about the Lurps and what all you can expect from us here at LZ English.

"Over the next two weeks we'll be putting you through Lurp training. I, along with some of the other Lurps here, will be showing you everything you need to know to become a Lurp. This is not the line company, so we'll be showing you *everything*. From square one. Some of it might seem basic, but when you get out there in the field, you'll be glad we did."

He paused and looked us over.

"At the end of the two weeks we will assign you to one of the teams. You'll run a trial mission. A real mission. Not practice. Not simulated. A real, live mission. If you do well, then you might just get to stay. If you don't, well, I'm sorry to say, but you'll have to go back to wherever it is you came from. Which for most of you, I guess, would be the line company."

At that, the guys bristled; nobody wanted to go back to the line company.

"Just because you're here today," he said, "it doesn't necessarily mean you'll be here in three weeks. Making a Lurp is serious business. You'll have to earn it."

We all nodded.

"Once again, gentlemen, welcome to the Lurps," he said. "Your training begins tomorrow."

When he left, the guys all scattered across the hill to get ready for the next day. I just went back in and lay down on my bunk. I'd already gotten my stuff situated, so I was pretty content just to sit there and rest my feet. It was the first time I'd been inside in nearly four months, so I really didn't have a problem with trying to catch up on my rest.

I thought back on what all he'd said and realized why everything was happening so fast. They hadn't even issued the orders to transfer me out of the company—they'd just picked me up and off I went. Apparently they didn't fool around with the paperwork since there was a pretty good chance I might be back there in just a couple of weeks. I was determined, though, not to let that happen. The training, the trial mission, everything he'd told us about—I was absolutely committed to making this thing work.

Later that night, when I finally went to sleep, I actually found myself, for the first time in a long time, looking forward to waking up.

The next morning we started off with a run—a long run—past the choppers, behind the trucks, and all the way over and around by the airstrip. Conditioning, as we would find out quickly, was a fundamental part of the training. For the next two weeks we'd get up and run every morning; then, at the end of the two weeks, we'd be required to do a two-mile course, in full gear, in under twenty minutes. Not that we'd ever have to run that far during a mission necessarily, but it was important to be in top physical condition—they didn't want anybody getting out of breath and making a lot of noise while we were out there in the field.

That first morning we ran for probably forty-five minutes, from one end of the base to the other. And then when we finished, we gathered together to begin what would become the school portion of our training. Every day a group of eight or nine, maybe ten, of the experienced Lurps would call us together and go over the things that we needed to learn to become well-prepared Lurps. Camouflage, ammunition, rappelling, everything was covered in detail, and each day they offered a new and increasingly advanced subject.

That first morning they packed a lot of information in and, from what I could tell, didn't plan on letting up. These guys were professional soldiers, and they took their jobs seriously. It didn't matter if you'd been in country three weeks or six months—if you were new to the Lurps, to them you were a "cherry." They'd be going over camouflage or map reading or whatever, and it'd be, "Hey, cherry, you better listen to me!" or, "You bunch of cherries better listen up!" These guys had been there before, and they knew what it took to do a job and to get out alive. So when they told us to listen, well, that's exactly what we did.

Camouflage. That first morning—and for the next few days after that—they taught us everything you could possibly ever want, or need, to know about camouflage, including how to camouflage both ourselves and our weapons.

They issued us new fatigues, though a lot of the guys opted to go with the tiger-style camouflage that the ARVN (Army of the Republic of Vietnam) wore. The normal, military-issue camouflage was sort of a large, leafy pattern—something you might wear deer hunting—while the tigers had more of a striped pattern, which we thought was better suited for the grassy terrain of the highlands.

A lot of the Lurps wore them, but the problem was, you couldn't actually get them from the U.S. military—you had to go down to Bong Son and buy them there from some of the Vietnamese vendors. I thought they looked pretty good, though, so first chance I got, I went into town and picked up three pair.

They also issued us each a flop hat—one of those light fabric hats with a brim that circled around, like a rain hat—to cut down on the noise when we moved through the brush, and you'd better believe, it was a big improvement over the steel pot I'd been wearing. We also got a canvas rucksack to use—another ARVN product—in place of the more cumbersome metal-frame packs we'd been using.

They taught us how to tape down our equipment with green tape—anything that might rattle or clank or otherwise give away your position. They showed us how to tape down buckles, straps, clips, canteens—anything and everything. Silence, they told us, was critical, and I for one was glad to hear it.

They even showed us how to camouflage our skin—any part that was showing, like our hands or our faces—by applying a mixture of different colored paints, to protect us from being exposed. The best way to do it was first to apply a layer of insect repellent and then to apply the camouflage. They gave us a stick of paint that was a light green color on one end and a deep, dark green on the other.

Rappelling.   Initially rappelling was taught and practiced from a hovering helicopter—one of the Hueys—suspended in the air, about 150 feet off the ground. The instructors showed us how to tie our own Swiss seats, using our own ropes, and they demonstrated the technique by jumping out of the choppers and sliding easily down the ropes to the ground below. It was a tough lesson—made especially tough by the fact that we had to do it without gloves—but it was one we practiced over and over again, until they felt like we'd gotten it just right and it was getting to be second nature.

Later on they built a rappelling tower, designed especially for teaching rappelling, and it was a great addition to the company's regimen. It was about seventy-five feet high, built from long wooden planks—placed one on top of the other, affixed to two large columns—and it presided over the base in all directions, growing straight up out of the dirt and reaching high into the Vietnam sky. There was a small wooden platform on the top where the instructors stood, and once they really started using it, there was almost always someone there supervising the recruits as they tumbled down the face of the tower to the ground below.

Map Reading.  Map reading was taught from a little building down below the hill. We'd all studied maps before—during the advanced infantry course at Fort Gordon, for example—but the Lurp instructors were able to bring it to life, to make it real, in a way that I'd never seen. I guess it was due to the number of hours they'd put in actually having to read a map under real combat conditions, but I could understand layouts and interpret topographies much better than I could before their instruction. Of course, reading maps took on a whole new level of importance knowing that your life would depend on how well you did it, so I put in a little extra time studying the maps and practicing with my compass.

If there was one skill that was absolutely essential to being a good Lurp, it was map reading. If you got out there in the triple-canopy foliage and got lost, that would be big-time trouble. Not only would you have trouble getting out, but you might call in an air strike right on top of yourself. And when you wanted to get extracted, being able to give the chopper pilots the right coordinates could mean the difference between getting out or not getting out—especially in a situation where time was precious.

When we finished with the basics, we moved on to the more advanced training. They instructed us in detail on what the actual missions would involve, the objectives of each mission as well as the procedures and protocol. They went over what would be expected of us, as well as what we could expect from the missions—and on this point, you can guarantee, all ears were at attention.

They started with procedure. Step by step, this was how it was gonna happen. This was the order you could expect, and these were the steps you could count on—we were to consider them the building blocks of the typical successful Lurp mission. First we would get an intelligence report that told us about the area we'd been assigned to cover. Sometimes it was accurate, but just as often it wouldn't be. Things changed, conditions changed—and the enemy didn't always sit still.

The initial report included a map of the area—a topographical map, highly detailed with streams and trails, with the lay of the land indicated by the frequency of the lines; the closer together the lines, the steeper the terrain—and it also included a scheduled time for the team's overflight.

The overflight was the initial preliminary flyover. It was conducted by helicopter and included the team leader (TL) and assistant team leader (ATL). The command and control (C&C) officer also went along most of the time—he was usually a communications sergeant—but either way, it was a small crew, just four or five men, taken up in a single chopper.

The idea was to scout out the land where we would be going and to select an LZ—a landing zone—for the next day's insertion. They usually flew over at very high altitudes in order to keep from tipping off the enemy; this made the selection process a little more difficult, but it was important for keeping the mission concealed. Again, this practice demonstrated a fundamental sensitivity toward protecting the teams—even on the day before the mission, specific efforts were made to keep from giving away our position.

During the overflight the team leader always had the final say. There might be some discussion or some back-and-forth—often it was important to make sure that the pilot could actually get the chopper down into a particular area—but it was always the TL who made the decision.

And sometimes, if the terrain looked particularly generous or if you had a good idea where you'd be on the last day of the mission, you might actually select an extraction point—a second LZ where the choppers would come to pick you up at the end of the mission. But often this might get changed, or the teams might not even stay for the entire time, for whatever reason, so this wasn't as important as selecting the drop-off zone.

Once they'd finished discussing the initial intelligence report and the ins and outs of the mission overflight, the instructors moved on to the mission itself, and to the topic that probably was as important as anything else they would discuss: the mission objective. Or, in other words, what was the point of all this?

Now, for the Lurps the basic objective was simply to gather information. The teams were inserted into known enemy-occupied territory and expected to come out with a record of the enemy's activities from within the region. This was accomplished through a variety of different tools and techniques but was based primarily on the cornerstone of the long-range patrol: trail watching.

Watching the trails—all the interwoven footpaths that wound through the South and represented the major supply and infiltration routes of the NVA—was the simplest and quickest way to find the enemy. The key, of course, was to enter the region undetected and then to establish an observation post, usually on the side of a mountain, sometimes from the top of a tree. To be effective you had to be able to get in without tipping off the enemy that you were there.

Once a team had managed to get inside, though, it was just a matter of watching. Watching and documenting. Each of the team leaders carried some sort of a journal or log, and whenever there was any sign of enemy activity, they would register the movements in the book. Specifically the teams were asked to record certain pieces of information:

1. The location of the sighting (coordinates)
2. The time of day it occurred
3. What they were wearing
4. What they were carrying (weapons, etc.)
5. How many people were in the group
6. How they acted (cautious or relaxed)
7. Whether they appeared to be trained or not
8. A breakdown of males and females

But to look at what was written in one of those notebooks, it probably wouldn't make a whole lot of sense to anyone but the TL—they were usually filled with all kinds of shorthand and codes. A typical entry might look something like this:

1. 15 VC
2. Mov SE
3. 775 586
4. UKN
5. 1315
6. RS

Or, in other words: fifteen VC were moving in a southeasterly direction at one-fifteen in the afternoon. The location is noted by the grid coordinates (775, 586), and the fact that they were carrying rucksacks is noted with the abbreviation RS. The team leader might also have used some kind of a shorthand—like UKN for "unknown"—when the team couldn't determine a particular piece of information, like the types of clothing they were wearing, as in this case. If, on the other hand, the clothing was quite clear, then it might say something like: "*1ˢᵗ Man, White Shirt Black Bottoms— Other 14 Black PJ.*" Or something else, like "*Black PJ, White Hats.*"

And of course, gunfire was also registered, so there might be a note that said something like: "*AK-47—two shots auto—firing W,*" and this would indicate that the trail watcher had heard two bursts of automatic gunfire being fired in a westerly direction.

Basically we were supposed to just document anything and everything that we came across that somehow related to the enemy: any remains or traces or scraps or papers—even rice supplies. Whatever we found or saw or heard we'd put in that book.

After each mission—we were told—there would be a debriefing session. Come rain or shine, that was one of the things we could expect—that after each and every mission we'd be hauled up to the intelligence office to fill them in on the details.

"There'll be a jeep waiting on you at the chopper pad. They'll take you up to S-2. And when you get there, you can expect some detailed questioning. Everything from the insertion to the extraction—the terrain, the VC, everything, from the moment you got there to the moment you left. No stones left unturned."

From there, the information was used to determine brigade-wide strategies, like air strikes and infantry sweeps. Probably they used it to determine what kinds of shells to use, stuff like that. But for us, for the Lurps, it was back to the Hill to get ready for the next one. There was no real follow-up—just get in there, get the information, and get out. Then get ready to do it again.

When the end of the two weeks came, we were all pretty excited about finishing the training and being able to get out in the field. I'd come in at the same time as about twelve other guys, and after all that training you can imagine how ready we all were to finally get out there and put it to work in an actual mission. The only obstacle remaining was the two-mile run; after that, we'd be assigned to our teams and prepped for our upcoming trial missions.

The two-mile run was scheduled for just after sunrise on the fourteenth morning of the two-week training program. That morning we all woke up early and gathered together at the top of the Hill, just in front of our barracks. Normally I might've been a little bit groggy, but this morning, for some reason, I felt energized.

We were required to wear full gear—fatigues, boots, web gear, weapon, and rucksack—and inside our rucksack they made us carry a fifty-pound sandbag. It was already a pretty tough run, with the heat and the humidity the way it was, but adding the weight made it that much more difficult—though, of course, it also made it a lot more realistic.

As we were standing there in a group one of the Lurps stepped forward and scraped a line across the dirt with the heel of his boot.

"All right, fellas, let's line 'em up."

We moved over behind the line, boots shuffling across loose gravel, and got ready to run. The same Lurp who had drawn the line stepped forward and raised his right hand in the air—"Get ready!"—we crouched down into the ready position—"Get set!"— the sound of dirt crunching beneath our feet—"*Go!*"

He threw down his hand, and off we went, galloping down the Hill and out across the base, kicking up dust with every step . . .

—I was already in pretty good shape—I'd played three sports during high school—but after the two weeks of Lurp training—running, climbing, constantly working with our hands—I felt like I was in the best shape of my life—

. . . past the chopper pad we went . . .

—It wasn't actually a race, of course, but I was determined to finish as close to the front as I possibly could—I wanted to make a good impression, and I knew what was at stake—I wanted to show the older Lurps what I could do—I'd been a good infantryman, and I knew I could make a good Lurp—

... past the truck lot, the pack separating behind me ...

—They'd given us fifteen minutes to finish the run—I wasn't sure if everybody would be able to finish in that time or not—wasn't even sure what would happen if you didn't—but I sure didn't want to find out—

... past the airstrip ...

—As I ran past the airstrip, only one other guy in front of me, I noticed a couple of guys wearing steel pots, standing around at the far edge of the strip—they were standing with a couple of Lurps, just laughing and cutting up, probably in on a layover on the way up to Da Nang—one of the Lurps looked up and noticed me running by—he threw down his cigarette, let out a loud cheer, and started clapping for me, like I was a runner in a marathon—the sight of those guys in the steel pots reminded me of just exactly why I was there—I was in no hurry at all to go back to the line company—

... clearing the next hill ...

—I caught sight of the guy up in front of me—he was the only one left—everyone else had fallen back—and I could tell he was running his fastest—his feet were churning in the dirt, kicking up dust—I started running that much harder, and before long I started closing in on him—there was no way I was going back.

When we got our assignments, I found out that I'd been selected to run with a team called Team Golf. The team leader was a guy named Dave Brueggemann, and he selected me and two other guys to run with him and his team on their next mission—a total of six guys in all: me, the other two new guys, and the three guys from the team, including Dave himself.

The mission would be a typical surveillance mission—a trail-watching mission—and for the guys in Team Golf it was just another assignment, one more job like the rest. But for us, the new guys, it meant the difference between getting to stay and having to go back to the line company. For us it pretty much meant everything.

The day before we were scheduled to leave Dave called us together to go over the details. He was a soft-spoken guy from Illinois, and I could tell right off that he was my kind of a leader. He wasn't one of those loud, macho types but rather cool and reserved, which I took as a good sign. His manner was easy and calm. And when he talked about the mission, he did so in a way that seemed not only confident but also relaxed and at ease. Which was just the thing we needed.

"All right, guys. I'd like to just start at the beginning and tell you a little bit about the mission."

He had a map with him, just like the ones we'd studied—with the topography of the land and the roads and the villages all marked—and he spread it out in front of him for all of us to see. It was marked "Hoai Nhon" at the top and broken down into a grid, with the numbers listed vertically and horizontally around the edges. Each square on the map represented one square kilometer, and the map in total represented an area about thirty kilometers squared. The map itself was probably about the size of the front page of a newspaper, opened up and spread out flat.

He showed us a particular section of the map and informed us that this was the area we'd be responsible for watching. It was a smaller section of the map, only about five kilometers squared, but it looked like pretty difficult terrain. There was a valley near the center and a mountain at the edge—this, he said, would be our LZ—and from what I could tell, it looked like a pretty steep slope.

The intelligence report had indicated a large amount of VC and NVA activity in the valley, so our job was to try and enter the valley, undetected, and to watch the trail to establish just what sort of activity was taking place. Dave pointed out on the map how he

wanted us to travel—moving west from the LZ, up and over the
mountain, to a spot on the other side where we could watch the valley floor.

We were scheduled to leave the next day, sometime late that afternoon. Late afternoon, Dave explained, was the best time to accomplish a successful insertion. The closer to dark—without being
completely nighttime—the better. That way the team could use the
fading sunlight as a cloak, as a sort of natural cover, until they managed to reach the relative security of the bush. Naturally there was
no substitute for the protective cover of the trees, but the poor visibility of dusk was a decent alternative.

The drop-off would include four choppers total. Two gunships
would accompany us to lend fire support and scare off any nearby
VC until we could find time to safely penetrate the foliage. There
would also be a C&C chopper, which would fly high above the rest
of the entourage, directing the maneuver from up top. Once we
were safely on the ground, we would communicate back to the
C&C, who would then inform the gunships. The whole operation
would happen very quickly, and from what all Dave told us, its sole
purpose would be getting us in unharmed.

Finishing up his talk, he emphasized one last time the importance
of keeping quiet.

"Out in the field, guys, there's no talking, or at least not in the
way that I'm standing here talking to you right now. Out there"—
and here he lowered his voice—"*you whisper.*"

He looked purposefully around the group, making firm eye contact with each of us. Then he clapped his hands together.

"Okay. Now go on over to the supply tent and get yourselves
fixed up."

The supply tent was situated down the hill from the barracks; we'd
have to go down there before each mission to pick up the proper
supplies and get ourselves ready for the upcoming mission. Which

might be three days, four days, maybe even five. But whatever the situation, and however long we were out there, we'd have to be ready. That meant getting the proper supplies:

**Communication Devices.**    We carried an assortment of lightweight tools and devices for signaling to overhead choppers. A pin flare, a cloth panel, a mirror, a strobe light, and two or three colored smoke grenades. These items were all used to signal choppers, but in different situations. The pin flare was used for nighttime communication, and the cloth panel, color-coded on each side, was for indicating security—orange for caution and red for danger. The mirror was used for daytime signaling, while the strobe light was used at night. The smoke grenades were used during the daytime to designate a hidden LZ. They were also color-coded and could be used to indicate the level of enemy activity in a given vicinity.

Each team had a radio telephone operator (RTO) who carried the radio and conducted any necessary verbal communication, whether with an oncoming chopper pilot or with the headquarters back at the base. The radio was fairly lightweight, but it was still a chore to lug around—so I was thankful I didn't get the assignment.

**Morphine.**    We were each given a Syrette of morphine and an assortment of pills for pain. This procedure would be changed later on, after some indiscretions with the drug supply.

**Food.**    I mentioned before that things in the Lurps were different, and that was even true of the food. In the line company we'd carried the more traditional rations, called C rations, but in the Lurps we carried a new type of meal called Lurp rations.

Lurp rations were basically just dehydrated soups and rice dishes that we could carry without adding much weight and then easily fix in the field. To me they were a big improvement over the C rations, especially for their convenience, and some of them even tasted okay.

There were several different flavors, including beef stew, chicken and rice, beef and rice, and chicken stew. And they were all easy to prepare: all you had to do was add water (hot or cold), stir it all together, wait five minutes, and serve when ready.

Typically the guys would carry enough Lurp rations to have one per day, though some guys preferred allotting for two a day. Each Lurp had to make his own decision about that, taking into consideration how much room and weight the rations would occupy and the fact that for every Lurp ration he'd need to have a corresponding amount of water to prepare it.

During our training they showed us how to separate the different items from the ration kit and prepare them before we left, so they wouldn't make any noise out in the field. The one thing you didn't want to do was tear open that plastic out there in the field, because it could really make a racket.

Water.   Water was critical not only for keeping us hydrated but also for preparing our Lurp rations—without water, our food supply was nothing more than a packet of dried-out powder. If you wanted to fix yourself a hot meal—as opposed to just mixing the water in cold—you could heat up the water using a compressed gas tablet. Each of the Lurps carried gas tablets, which could be broken open to create a small flame that could boil a small amount of water. This quick and easy step was often used to create hot meals.

Ammunition.   As I'd soon find out, the Lurps were often given a fair amount of leeway in determining their own needs and limitations. This was nowhere more apparent than in the weaponry. We were basically able to take whatever we felt we needed and knew we could handle. The trick, of course, was to balance the amount of ammo you took with the food and the water—take too much of one and you wouldn't be able to carry the other—or perform well either. Typically the guys erred on the side of food—better to be short on rations than on ammo. No one wanted to get out in the field and get in a firefight without an ample supply of rounds.

The same was true of grenades. You could carry as many grenades as you thought you'd need—and even claymores, though they were a little bit heavier, so it wasn't likely that you'd try and carry a whole bunch of them. Typically each Lurp carried at least one claymore.

Also, we got to choose how many tracers we wanted to use. I decided to use tracers on every round—as opposed to every third round, which was more common. The more tracers we had flying around, the more people it looked like there were—even though there would only be five or six of us at any given time.

After the mission, if we had any ammo left, they told us we could go out and shoot it up somewhere—just to get rid of it—and then to get fresh ammo for the next mission. They didn't want our rifles jamming up on us when we were out in the field. The shells were held in place in the magazine by a spring, and even though we only used eighteen rounds per magazine—it actually held twenty—it wasn't good to leave the spring compressed like that for a long period of time.

**Rain Gear.**    Nobody really carried any rain gear, but I made a point to carry half a camouflage blanket, just in case.

We started getting ready about one o'clock that afternoon. We put on our paint, taped up our rifles, then headed down to the chopper pad to meet up with Dave and the others.

The communications sergeant was already there; he and Dave were standing over by the choppers, having a conversation. We all stood around for the next few minutes, waiting for the pilots to get the choppers ready, then we climbed aboard and prepared for liftoff. Five minutes later the pilots cranked up the choppers, and off we went. Late afternoon, just like Dave had said.

There were three of us seated on each side of the chopper. Dave and the RTO were sitting beside each other on the left side; the ATL and I were sitting opposite them, on the right, along with one of the other new guys. There were also two door-gunners perched above us, one on each side, sitting attentively, looking out over the countryside.

It was a cloudy day, and there was a hot wind coming in through the doors as we moved across the highlands. The mountains zipped along below us, and the clouds floated along beside us, covering the sky and extending all the way to the horizon. Everything was gray and dark, and the land was dense and black. The trees, the foliage, it all blended together and blocked out the ground. There could've been a thousand VC down there, just standing there among the trees, and we wouldn't have seen a one of them. We could've been flying over them right that second.

After just a few minutes one of the door-gunners reached down and tapped me on the shoulder. We were approaching the LZ.

I glanced over at the new guy to my right. My fellow recruit.

*This is it,* I thought. The test. All the training, the interviews, the recruiting, Pipkin—it all came down to this: who would be able to cut it when we were out in the field.

I glanced over at our team leader, Dave Brueggemann—Bergy, as he was known around camp. For the three of us new guys, it was all up to him. We'd run the mission, but he'd make the decision. Give us each a grade and then tell us our fate. I didn't feel nervous, but I was clear about what was at stake.

One mission, one grade, in or out.

We continued on our path, flying straight and steady, just as we'd been doing, for the next few seconds, until suddenly the chopper banked down hard to the left—I gripped tightly to the panel behind me—and dove directly, nose down, toward a small grassy area on the backside of a mountain. It was about the size of half a football field, but it was surrounded by tall trees on all sides—so banking down into it was a pretty steep maneuver.

We came in fast, and just as it looked like we were about to crash right into the side of that mountain, the pilot pulled up hard and came to a sharp stop, sitting just above the ground, right there in the center of the field. The skids never even touched the ground—they were probably about three or four feet off the grass—but it was a perfect landing, and we all jumped quickly down to the ground.

As I got my footing, I looked back over my shoulder. The door-gunner gave us a thumbs-up, and the slick rose quickly above us. It pulled up hard, clearing the field, then disappeared fast above the trees.

The grass was a lot taller than it had looked from the air, so when the chopper cleared out, it stood back up and gave us some cover from the trees. We moved quickly across the field and pushed our way into the tree line, where we immediately contacted the C&C chopper to let them know that we'd made it in without any trouble. Negative contact.

We continued into the brush, remaining quiet, not saying a word. Moving steadily away from the LZ. There was no talking, just moving, as we constantly, and carefully, ascended the side of the mountain. The sounds of our boots, padding softly across the dirt. The sounds of our shirts, brushing loosely against the limbs. The sound of our legs, moving against the thin undergrowth. We maneuvered along in a single-file line, and as we neared the top the terrain grew more and more difficult, becoming steeper and rockier.

After a couple of hours we reached a point where a particularly thick patch of undergrowth grew out from the side of a steep incline. By this time the mountain had become dark, so Dave decided to go ahead and set up for the night, using the dense patch of undergrowth for our cover. The shrubbery would create a natural cover, while the incline itself would make it difficult for anyone to approach without giving himself away.

Using hand signals, he directed us to climb into the brush. So we pushed our way in, one by one, until we were all surrounded by foliage. The last one to climb in was Dave, and he closed the brush in together behind himself, creating a sort of man-made cove that kept us completely hidden from any possible passersby.

By this point we'd been in the field for over two hours, and the group was remaining incredibly quiet. Except for that brief moment when the RTO had radioed up to the C&C, I don't think anyone had spoken even a single word. All the directions were being given with hand signals, and so far everything had gone without a problem. We'd made it into the LZ without being spotted, and we'd penetrated the forest landscape without happening across any VC.

We stayed up that night until about nine o'clock, just to make sure that nobody had seen us or followed us into the brush. There was no noise. No twigs snapping. No nothing. When we finally felt confident that we weren't being watched, we lay down to go to sleep. As I lay there with my head on the ground and my eyes closed, a light mist began to fall. Cool and wet across my face.

The next morning, when we woke up, we each broke out a Lurp ration and quietly fixed ourselves breakfast. I personally didn't have a whole lot of appetite, but I knew it was important to eat in order to keep up my strength. Keeping your energy level up was always important, whether you were hungry or not.

When we were done, we buried our leftovers—the containers and such—in the dirt, then climbed carefully out of our hiding place and resumed our trek from the day before. We continued across the mountain, pushing slowly and purposefully toward the valley on the other side. The sky was still overcast, but the early morning sunlight was sufficient to light up the ground, which made it considerably easier to maneuver than it had been the night before.

We continued on like that for the next two or three hours, moving first over the crest of the mountain and then down the slope on the other side. Our goal was to find a clearing, some place where we could look down over the valley and on to the trail below, but after almost three hours of looking we still hadn't found one. The problem with the mountain was the trees: they were so tall that we couldn't see over them, and they were growing so tightly together that we couldn't see through them. Eventually Dave just got tired of looking and decided to try something new. Rather than fighting the terrain, and trying all day to find a place that didn't have trees, he decided instead to try and use them to our advantage.

He picked out a spot, right there in the middle of a thick of trees, then handed me his rifle.

"Hold this for a second," he whispered.

He then picked out a tree and shimmied up it like a monkey on a coconut hunt. I couldn't believe how quick he did it—those trees were like telephone poles, and the first limbs didn't start for about fifteen or twenty feet up. But he just shot up that thing, found a limb, and started looking around.

The rest of us watched from the ground as Dave swiveled his head around, looking one way, then the other, until he looked back down at us and gave us the thumbs-up. Apparently he'd found us a clearing.

When he got back down, he told us we'd take turns watching the trail—that we'd each climb the tree with a pair of binoculars, watch the valley for an hour, and then switch. He figured that that was the best way to do it, since it wouldn't make a whole lot of noise—and since we could've been looking for a clearing in those trees for the next three days and still not have found anything.

He explained the setup in detail—always whispering, but describing the situation in enough detail that we'd know exactly what it was he expected of us. He explained that we'd take rotations throughout the day, taking turns with the binoculars, while the rest of us maintained a lookout below.

The ATL got the first rotation, so he took the binoculars, draped them over his shoulder, and shimmied up the tree. The rest of us remained on the ground, and Dave instructed us on how to set up a temporary perimeter. We'd probably be there for the next few days, he said, so we didn't want anyone sneaking up on us.

Always quiet. Always alert.

When it finally came my turn to observe, Dave handed me the binoculars and whispered pointedly, "It won't be long."

He gave me his notebook and a pen to write with, then motioned to the tree with his palms upturned. "All right, go to it."

I eyed the tree for a second to figure out how to approach it. I didn't weigh a lot, and I'd always been able to climb—plus we'd practiced some tree climbing during our training, for this exact situation—but it still looked like a challenge. There were no branches at the bottom at all, and the trunk was just wide enough to make it awkward to get a good grip. I glanced back over at Dave, then shook my head. *Here goes nothing,* I thought.

I slung the binoculars around my neck, then slipped the pen and paper into my shirt pocket and proceeded to dig the heel of my right boot into the right side of the tree. I bounced a couple of times on the other leg, then sprang up against the trunk and proceeded to climb that thing right on up to the top—arms and legs pumping away just like Dave and the others had done.

When I got it going, it was actually pretty easy, and before long I was hovering right there amid the branches and the limbs, where Dave and the others had been sitting all morning.

I turned my attention to the valley.

From down below, you couldn't even tell it was there, but from up above, hanging there in that tree, I could see it in all its grandeur: broad and vast and sprawling into the distance, beneath the dark gray sky. Just as I'd figured, Dave had found us the perfect observation post.

I found a good firm limb about the girth of a softball, and lowered myself down to it. I tested its weight, sitting gently at first, then relaxing and putting all of my weight on it. It seemed fine, so I settled in (still being careful to stay close to the trunk, though) and raised the binoculars to see what I could see.

The valley was covered in grass—or weeds really—but it was shorter than the grass that we'd landed in the night before. Here in the valley the grass looked to be about waist-high, or maybe even chest-high in certain spots, and it gave the impression of an unkempt lawn.

The valley was basically empty of trees, except for a small stand of banana trees and palm fronds that sprouted up in the center of the clearing. The stand looked something like an oasis in the midst of a desert—or an island, set off from the mountains by the grass that surrounded it.

I scanned the valley with the binoculars.

A footpath ran the length of the valley floor, a narrow strip of dirt that disappeared into one side of the trees and exited out the other.

There was a patch of elephant grass at the far end of the valley, against the foot of the mountain on the other side, and it looked as though it might could provide some cover for anyone walking that part of the valley floor.

It was about two o'clock in the afternoon at that point, and there were no signs of any VC. A light rain had been falling off and on throughout the morning, but it had since let up. I opened the notebook and saw that Dave had recorded several VC sightings earlier that morning, several different groups of VC moving along the trail.

I looked back through the binoculars and waited patiently for something to happen. I didn't have to wait long.

A group of four VC—*no, five, there's another one, a straggler*—carrying rifles and rucksacks, emerged from the grass at the far end of the valley. They were dressed in black pajamas—or what we called pajamas—and from what I could tell, they were wearing green flop hats and scarves. They appeared to be totally relaxed. They had their rifles slung over their shoulders and appeared to be having casual conversation, just walking along like they were in downtown Hanoi on the way back from the market.

I eagerly pulled out the pen and paper and started to write something, then decided to watch them some more to see what they'd do.

A jolt of adrenaline went through my body as I sat there on that limb. This was the first time in the entire time that I'd been in Vietnam that I'd actually been the one doing the watching—those guys down there, they had no idea I was anywhere around, and here I was with the five of them, focused just as clear as could be, right there inside my binoculars.

They continued down the trail, just walking along, completely oblivious, until they disappeared behind the stand of trees. At that point I draped the binoculars around my neck and started scribbling into the notebook.

1. 5 VC
2. Moving Due South

For the rest of the afternoon we took turns watching the valley, and we began to notice some patterns emerging. First of all, the activity basically disappeared whenever it started raining. A light rain had continued intermittently throughout the day, and we'd all noticed the conspicuous absence of VC during those periods. It also seemed that most of the activity had occurred either early in the morning or during the middle of the afternoon, around two to five. Over the course of the day I'd personally seen no fewer than fifty VC, usually in small groups of three or four—with one group as large as eight—and the rest of the guys had seen similar numbers as well.

The next day—our third day out—started out the same way. We awoke early and resumed our rotation in the top of the tree, and just as they had done the day before, the VC appeared below, making their way across the valley in small groups, going up and down the trail.

Our RTO reported the findings back to LZ English, and they decided they wanted us to take a more aggressive action. Rather than simply watching the VC, they wanted us to actually try and catch one—*to try and take a POW.*

Now, taking a POW was something that headquarters always encouraged. It wasn't easy, but it had the potential to yield a tremendous amount of intelligence. In this case, they must've figured it was too good an opportunity to pass up, since we'd been seeing VC, on and off, ever since we'd gotten there.

We got the orders sometime that afternoon, just as I was about to go back up the tree—so we ended our observation routine and conferred on the ground about what to do next.

During our lookouts the day before we'd noticed that a lot of the VC stopped inside the trees and took a break, as if they were just sitting around for a while before exiting out the other side—to take advantage of the shade probably.

Dave suggested, and we all agreed, that the stand of trees, there in the center of the valley, would be the best place possible for setting up the ambush. The only problem—or at least the main problem—would be making it across the valley floor without being spotted. We'd have to move from the security of the tree line, there on the side of the mountain, to the bunch of trees out in the center of the valley. We knew that when we made the move, we'd be out in the open for at least a hundred, maybe two hundred, meters.

Dave decided that we should move down to the edge of the tree line and try and make it across the clearing just before dark. It was too late to try and pull an ambush that day, but we could move down to the valley and position ourselves to pull an ambush the next day, probably first thing in the morning.

So we gathered our things and began the descent down the mountain. By this point we'd been in the field for nearly forty-eight hours, and the light rains had finally begun to accumulate on the leaves and in small puddles along the ground. As we made our way down the mountainside the leaves and the undergrowth brushed against us like wet rags at a carwash, and by the time we reached the bottom there wasn't a dry thread anywhere.

The grass at the bottom was actually a good bit taller than it had looked from up above; much of it was nearly up to our chests, some of it even up to our shoulders. The rain had let up, but the sky was still overcast and the heavy blanket of clouds was casting a cool dark gray across the valley. It was only about six o'clock in the evening, but already the land was growing dark.

Dave indicated that we'd wait a little while longer, until the daylight faded away completely, so we stayed put, sitting patiently beside the valley floor, hidden just within the tree line and waiting for the day to end.

After half an hour or so he decided that the sunlight had disappeared sufficiently for us to try and make our move. Given the height of the grass, we couldn't really see very far in either direction, so we had to base our move on timing. If we timed it right, then there wouldn't be any VC around. If we didn't, well, then we'd be in trouble.

We crouched down and, moving one by one, stepped gently into the field. The ground was moist and soft, though, unlike the field where the medevac had picked up Danny and Sam just a month or so earlier, it held fast and didn't swallow us up to our waists.

We took each step cautiously and slowly, being careful not to step on any loose twigs that might snap and draw attention. We stayed low to take advantage of the cover that the grass provided, hunched over at the waist, bent oddly at our knees—it was not a comfortable position, but it was critical for remaining concealed.

The distance from the tree line at the foot of the mountain to the trees in the center was nearly 150 meters. We took our time, moving slowly to avoid stirring the grass and creating some sort of a distraction to anyone who might happen to be standing around.

About half an hour later—maybe forty-five minutes—we finally reached our destination: the stand of trees at the center of the valley. We pushed our way in, being careful not to make any noise, and continued across the undergrowth until we reached the trail, about thirty or forty meters in.

It was worn smooth from the foot traffic, and it looked like it might be slippery from all the rain that had been falling. Most surprising, though, was that it was probably twice as wide as we'd expected. It was at least three feet across and could have easily accommodated two Vietnamese walking shoulder to shoulder. Looking down from the top of that tree on the side of that mountain, it had looked much narrower. But there it was, the very path that all those VC had been traversing for the past two days. Right there at our feet.

After taking a brief moment to contemplate the trail, Dave snapped his fingers, and we continued moving. We eased down to the left, moving parallel to the trail, in search of a proper location to set up the ambush; we stayed a few feet off to the side in order to keep from slipping up and leaving our boot prints all over the mud. After about twenty or thirty meters we found a spot that looked okay. Covered in dense brush, it was just before the trail opened up on to the clearing.

We also needed to find a place to spend the night. It looked a little thicker on the other side, we thought, so we looked for a place to cross that wasn't as wide. It was important not to step on the path directly if at all possible, especially with it being as wet as it was. We didn't want to leave our boot prints everywhere, so we looked for a narrow point in the trail where we could cross without marking it up. When we finally found a spot, we leapt across to the other side.

On the other side of the trail the cover was in fact much thicker than it was on the near side. As we moved away from the trail the brush became denser and denser, but unfortunately it also became wetter and wetter—the land on that side of the trail dipped down, and in spots it was so low that the rain had collected into a sort of marsh.

Luckily we happened across a high spot that was just the right size for six guys with rucksacks. We climbed up on the clearing and lay down for the night.

As I was getting myself situated—as best I could, lying there on the ground with my clothes soaking wet—I noticed that Dave was still up, and that he was scribbling in his notebook. I watched him for a couple of minutes until he stopped and handed me the notebook, open to the page where he'd been writing.

It was dark out, so I couldn't really see the page all that clearly. I sat up so I could get a better look, being careful not to drip water all over it. I saw that he'd sketched out a rough rendering of the ambush site, with the trail and the cover and the way it opened up on to the field and with the mountains off to the side. He'd also drawn each of the team members, with our names marked and our positions designated with little squares—and I noticed that he and I were positioned right in the center of the formation.

At the bottom of the page, just under his drawing, he'd written the words: "Will you spring the ambush?"

Well, I guess the short answer to his question was, "Yes, yes, I'm fine with springing the ambush," but in truth I was a little bit surprised that he'd asked me, and really, I wasn't all that confident about whatever it was I'd have to do. Not that I didn't think I'd been doing a good job—because I felt like I'd been doing a pretty okay job—but I just wasn't sure if I was ready for this. I mean, springing the ambush, on my first mission, it seemed like a pretty big deal.

On the other hand, it also made me feel pretty good to know that he'd asked me to do it, as opposed to one of the other guys—I took that as a sign of confidence, and at that point in the mission I wasn't about to let him down.

I nodded my head in response.

He gave a slight nod back, then took the notebook back and started writing out the plans for the ambush—step by step, everything he'd need for me to do.

Over the next few minutes we passed the notebook back and forth, clarifying the different points and making sure that I felt comfortable with everything that would happen. The way he described it, I got the impression that springing the ambush would be a fairly simple procedure: I'd just pop out of the brush and give the command, and then once the VC caught sight of the team, they'd basically just put down their weapons and come with us. Sounded easy enough. Dangerous, but simple.

I handed him back the notebook for the last time, and he gave me a quick thumbs-up, and that was pretty much it. The only thing left to do at that point was to get some rest and then wake up in the morning and do it.

I lay back down on the ground and tried to settle in for the night. It wouldn't be easy. If I hadn't been anxious before, well, I was definitely feeling it now. And then to make things worse, the rain started back up, but this time it wasn't the light sprinkling that we'd experienced before. It was a hard rain, and it wasn't having any trouble making it down through the upper canopy of those trees.

I reached into my rucksack and pulled out the half camouflage blanket I'd brought with me. I draped it loosely over my face and listened to the rain as it *tap-tap-tapped* against my blanket.

The next morning I woke up, Dave got up and roused the others, and then we quickly got ready to pull the ambush. We all quietly slipped on our rucksacks and reapplied our paint. Nobody said a word, we just went about our business, quickly and quietly. Focused on the job at hand.

When we were ready, Dave gave us the plans he'd drawn up for the ambush. He showed the guys the drawing he'd shown me and indicated to each one of them exactly what it was he'd be expected to do and where he'd need to be positioned to do it. I already knew everything from the night before, but I looked over the drawing again just to reinforce the things we'd talked about—and then I passed it along to the next guy.

One of the interesting things about all this was the fact that Dave was able to brief the entire team using nothing more than those notes and that drawing—there was no talking, just gesturing—and he was able to communicate the entire plan of attack using just those notes. Silence was always an important part of a Lurp mission, but at this point in the mission it was absolutely critical—we were only about twenty-five meters off the trail, and the last thing we wanted was to somehow blow our cover.

The last thing Dave had written in his notebook was the way he wanted us to use the claymores. He illustrated the places he wanted them set up—along the trail in the front but concentrated to the outside of our position—and wrote out the way he wanted them used. He didn't want us to use the claymores unless we got into some kind of trouble.

Since we were trying to take a prisoner, it wouldn't have made any sense to plan from the beginning on using the claymores; once we committed to blowing the mines, we would basically be committing to lethal force—which meant there wouldn't be any survivors around to take back.

After we'd all gone over the plan and were confident that we knew what to do, we started down from the brush. Just as we were about to move, though, we heard some voices coming from somewhere out in the clearing. We couldn't be exactly sure where they were coming from, so we stopped and listened, to try and discern their direction.

We stood perfectly still, listening carefully. And then they disappeared completely, apparently moving away from our position.

Dave gave the signal, and we moved down from our sleeping quarters and started over toward the trail. One by one we stepped down into the marsh, being careful not to stir up the water or to make any unnecessary noise. I measured my steps carefully, placing each foot slowly before the other, as we trekked across the mud.

When we reached the trail, the first thing we did was make sure that the area was secure—to make sure we hadn't inadvertently stumbled upon a bunch of VC, walking down the trail. We hadn't heard any more voices for a while, but you never knew—and it was absolutely vital to be safe.

After we checked the trail for stragglers, we began to prepare the ambush site. One man took the lookout at one end of the area, another man took the lookout at the other, and the rest of us quickly went about the business of deploying the claymore mines. We set them out quickly, in the exact arrangement that Dave had indicated—five mines total, one in the center and two at each end—then ran the wires back to a single man, who would be in control of all five of the detonators.

Once we finished arranging the claymores, we all scrambled around and took our places, according to the diagram that Dave had drawn. The two guys posted lookout stepped back off the trail and disappeared into the brush. Their jobs would basically remain the same from here on out: to watch the trail and signal the rest of us when an appropriate group was approaching. We didn't want to ambush a group any larger than five or six.

Dave and I took our positions in the center of the ambush zone, just off to the side of the trail, about halfway between the two men posted on each end. A small impression ran alongside the trail, about three feet deep and probably six feet off to the side. There wasn't a whole lot of brush between that spot and the trail, but it looked like a good enough place to be in the event that things got messy. If we got in a firefight, it was deep enough to give us cover; it also looked like a good place for actually pulling the ambush.

The other two men were positioned, at a slight angle, just behind Dave and me—one with the radio, the other with the detonators—and between the six of us we covered a pretty good stretch of the trail. Directly in front of Dave and me, I could see a good fifteen, twenty feet without obstruction.

In position there in that low spot, kneeling down at the edge of the trail, I noticed my heartbeat increase. I looked over at Dave, and for a second it looked like even he was a little bit anxious. He noticed me watching him, and he turned and gave me a reassuring nod.

I nodded back at him. This was it.

As I sat there by that trail, even my breathing seemed loud and heavy, and I tried to control it. We were so close that if someone had walked by without seeing us sitting there, I could have jumped out and grabbed him around the ankles, no problem. We were that close.

By this point the light of day had begun to lighten the sky. It was only a matter of time before somebody appeared. We just had to hope that the group was the right size.

About twenty minutes had passed when I heard someone snapping his fingers—that was the signal.

My heart leapt.

I was crouched low in the grass. Dave was to my left.

Time stood still.

I heard voices—Vietnamese voices, loud and casual—they didn't know we were there.

I shifted my eyes, without moving my head, to look for weapons. They were coming in from the right.

The top of an NVA helmet—round and hard. Voices growing louder.

One NVA soldier, with an AK-47 slung over his shoulder.

Then another, just a few feet back, this one with another AK, held loosely in his hand, down to the side.

That was it—I didn't even wait to see if there might be more—I just stood up, with my rifle at my shoulder, and shouted out: *"Dung Lai!"* ("Stop!").

They turned, wide-eyed, shocked—and then instantly started scrambling for their weapons. I don't think they even considered giving up.

I quickly fired three shots in the direction of the first one—he was standing less than ten feet away—but somehow I missed him. Grazed him—*maybe*. He didn't even bat an eye, just kept on reaching for his rifle. This was all happening in a matter of split-seconds, but as I was pulling the trigger I realized that I'd left my rifle set on semiautomatic. A stupid mistake. A cherry mistake.

Almost at the same time that I'd fired, just a split-second after—*BLAM!*—a loud explosion—dust and dirt flying everywhere, in my eyes, up my nose—it blew me back into the brush, completely off my feet—I struggled to see what was happening, but the dirt was stinging my eyes—the ambush zone was nothing but a swirling mess of dust and leaves. I looked over at Dave, and he was worse off than me—knocked on his back, wiping at his eyes with the back of his hand.

I climbed back to my feet, wiped the dust out of my eyes, and tried to assess the situation. The ambush site had started to clear, and lying there in the middle of it all, right smack in the center of the trail, were the bodies of the two NVA—and behind them, a few feet back, were the bodies of two more VC.

I looked back around at the guy who'd been in control of the detonators. Apparently he'd seen what was happening and had blown the claymores, all at once.

Dave had regained his composure after suffering the back-blast from that explosion: "All right, check 'em out."

We scrambled onto the trail and checked the four Vietnamese for papers or maps or anything else of value. The two in the back had been carrying rice, which was now strewn all over the trail.

I crouched down over one of the VC, to check him for papers, when one of the new guys—one of the guys who was being tested like me—just started firing up the first NVA. I wasn't sure what he was doing or why he was doing it—*Is the guy still alive? Did he reach for his rifle?*

I looked over at Dave. He frowned.

The new guy fired off another round, straight down into the NVA's chest, and then it was done.

While all this was going on, the RTO was talking with LZ English. "Hey, Dave. I got some bad news."

I finished checking the VC and ran over to see what was up.

"Just talked to English, and the choppers can't fly—cloud cover's too low."

"Shit."

Dave said it, but it could've been any one of us. Anybody within ten miles of us would've known we were there. With all the noise we'd created with that ambush—the rifles, the claymores—our cover was totally blown.

"All right. We gotta get out of here."

We gathered up our things and made a beeline directly across the tree stand, pushing our way quickly through the brush. At that point we weren't exactly concerned about noise control or anything like that; we just wanted to get away from the place as quickly as we could. Dave had me running point, so I headed out toward the grass—away from the trail and back toward the mountain where we'd been put in three days before.

As we made our way across the grass, we tried our best not to leave a trail—one of the new guys was bringing up the rear, and it was his job to pull the grass back together—but really, the most important thing was just to get away. Funny—all that running we'd done in training, and here we were having to run like this during our first mission.

But incredibly, as we were cutting across the clearing, the rain started back up, which made it even harder than before—with the grass wet, and the rain coming down, it was very difficult not to leave a path. With every step we took, the grass just stuck to the ground like we were dragging a sandbag along behind us.

We didn't want to get too far away from the valley floor—because that was the best and most obvious place for us to get picked up. But we had to find some cover quick, or we'd end up spending the rest of our time having to fend off some very unfriendly folks.

Eventually we broke free of the grass at the far end of the valley and dashed across a small stream that ran along the edge. We'd just gotten across to the other side when I realized what I'd done: in my rush to get us out of there, I'd led us directly across a patch of wet sand—our footprints could be seen just as clearly as if we'd walked through a freshly fallen blanket of snow.

Dave saw the same thing and gave me a frown.

"Uh-oh."

It was still raining, and the water coming down might've washed away the prints, but we couldn't take that chance. We ran back to the bank and covered our tracks as best we could, washing over them with limbs and twigs. When we finished, we hurried across the water and disappeared into the trees.

About a hundred meters in, we stopped.

Dave radioed the command center to tell them what was happening and to see when they'd be able to get a helicopter out there to pick us up. We were all hoping to hear that one was already on the way—the entire team was out of food, and we'd used up almost all of our claymores during the ambush—but unfortunately, the news wasn't getting any better. They said that the weather wasn't expected to break until the next day. That was not what we wanted to hear.

Dave gave them our position just in case—using the map coordinates—and we hunkered down there in the undergrowth, resigned to the fact that this was gonna be one incredibly long day. We sat in a circle, comfortably hidden within the brush, but the rain just kept coming, and the thought of those NVA out there, looking for us, was doing a number on our nerves.

For the rest of the morning the rain continued with little sign of letting up. But Dave continued to check; every hour he'd radio back to the base to see if the conditions had changed enough to get us a chopper. They hadn't. Unless the rain let up soon, we could expect to be out there for almost another twenty-four hours.

Naturally we were pissed off. Dave especially. They should have told us about the weather before we ever pulled that ambush—but we also had plenty to think about without getting too caught up in what they should or shouldn't have done. We had NVA to think about, and our main concern at that point was just getting out of that valley without being found.

We sat quietly and patiently. What else could we do? Dave continued to check back, until finally—*finally*—the weather broke. It was late afternoon, almost dark, and we'd been there all day, but that was just fine with us. To hear that they'd been able to scramble the choppers—now that was music to our ears. When Dave turned and gave us the news, I nodded my head subtly but happily. We were finally gonna get to leave.

About twenty minutes later the choppers arrived, and we climbed on board without incident. As we were lifting off, the six of us let out our collective breath: for the first time in four days we were finally able to relax.

When we got back to LZ English, a jeep was waiting for us at the chopper pad, just like Dave had described. The driver took us down to S-2, where we went over the mission, in every detail, from the first day, when we got dropped off, to the last day, when we'd pulled the ambush and had to sit in those trees for the rest of the morning and throughout the afternoon.

They were very particular with their questions—"What were the VC wearing?" "How much rice were they carrying?" "What were the coordinates of the ambush site?"—and the session lasted for nearly two hours in all.

When we were done, they took us back up to the Hill, where we showered off and hit the hay. Tired but exhilarated.

The next morning Dave found me up on the Hill and asked me to follow him down to the communication center. At the time I didn't really think anything about it; it didn't seem unusual that he'd have something to show me or to talk about or whatever. So of course I followed him down to the bunker to see what he wanted.

The communication center was housed in this old bunker that was left over from the French occupation just a couple of decades before. It was made of concrete, and when you were inside the thing you really got the sense of being inside something solid—as opposed to our barracks, which were just reinforced tents.

When we got there, Dave pulled up a couple of chairs, and we sat down. He pulled out his notebook and started talking.

"Shan, let me just say first of all that I was real pleased with the way you handled yourself out there. I know how rough it can be, the first mission like that, but I thought you did a real fine job out there, handled yourself real good."

My face must've been beaming. To hear him saying that, I wanted to jump up outta my chair and whoop for joy.

"Now, I know you had that one slip-up there with the sand, but hey, if that's the worst thing you ever do, then I think we'll be all right."

"Yeah, I wasn't thinking on that."

"Well, first time out, that'll happen—but, you know, just don't let it happen again."

Of course I knew better than to run through the sand like I had, but for some reason, there in the heat of the moment like that, with all the VC we'd seen and the rain coming down, I wasn't thinking like I should've been—all I was thinking about was getting us away from that ambush site and finding some cover. But I definitely knew better. They'd gone over all of that stuff during the training; they'd even shown us how to cover our tracks and told us how to pull the grass back to conceal a trail. In the Lurps, if you had to detour half a mile around a place to keep from leaving a trail, well, that's what you did—protecting the team was always the most important thing.

"It won't happen again."

Dave flipped his notebook open and pulled a pen out of his pocket.

"All right. Now, Shan, what I really called you down here for was to get your thoughts on the rest of the guys here. I'm trying to put this thing together, and I want to make sure I get the best guys I can, but I also want to make sure that everybody's comfortable with each other. Now, I've already decided I want you to run with us—I talked to the captain about it, and he agreed—so now we just have to figure out what we want to do about these other two guys."

I couldn't hardly believe it. He was asking me for my opinion. I was as green as a gourd, and here he was wanting to hear what I had to say about the team.

"Well, I don't really know, Bergy. What do you think?"

He grinned.

"Well, actually, to be honest, I was a little bit put off with that whole shoot-'em-up deal there on the trail. You know we're not out here to play Clint Eastwood. We're here to do a job."

"Yeah, I know what you mean."

"I mean, if a guy's dead, a guy's dead. There's no point in just filling him full of holes."

I felt a little bit funny about giving him my opinion, since I was so new, but on the other hand, if I was gonna be out there running missions, then I wanted the best guys we could possibly get.

"Yeah, and they were a little bit louder than I'd have liked too," I offered.

He nodded his head in agreement. "I agree. They seemed awful relaxed, didn't they?"

"Well, they did to me. I mean, I think I'd rather have somebody that's cautious and alert. All the time."

He nodded his head again and started writing in his notebook.

The rest of the day I basically just sat around the Hill, resting mostly, chatting some with a couple of the other Lurps. I was excited about making it through the trial mission without having blundered too bad, and my conversation with Dave had just made me feel that much better. I was still tired, of course, from the mission; spending four days out in the rain, in a state of alert the entire time and getting almost no sleep, was a pretty exhausting deal. But hanging around the Hill that day, I almost felt like I was walking on a cloud.

The next morning, when I came out of my bunk for the day, I noticed the two new guys standing there by a jeep that was parked out in front of the hooch. I blinked my eyes for a second and then realized they were packing their gear into the back of the jeep. I couldn't believe it—the very two guys from the mission, the two I'd said were too loud—they were packing their things, getting shipped back out to wherever they'd come from.

It was just like the day the chopper had come and picked me up from the airstrip—one day I'm going about my business, and the next I'm getting shipped out to join the Lurp company. I'd come to realize that doing things with the Lurps was a whole lot different from doing things with the rest of the army, which made you hang around and wait or left you wondering about something for weeks on end. With the Lurps things happened fast—pretty much immediately really. Which was something I was glad to see.

They finished loading up their bags, then climbed in the back as the driver started the engine. He made a slow three-point turn, then straightened it up and headed down the Hill. I figured he was taking them over to the airstrip to get picked up, the same way I'd been dropped off. I watched them until they disappeared, then turned around and went back inside. They may have been leaving, but I still had missions to run. I strapped on my boots, then headed down to the mess hall to get some breakfast.

When Pipkin had come by the airstrip that day, nearly three weeks back, the timing couldn't have been any better. I was already feeling pretty low—running for weeks on end without even spotting a single VC was enough to take it out of even the most gung-ho infantryman—and the mortar attack had all but wiped us out, physically and emotionally. The company morale was incredibly low at that time, and from the way things were going, I couldn't see any signs that the situation would change.

But running with the Lurps was different. That first mission out, I'd seen the enemy—and not just at a distance. I'd stood above him as he lay across the trail, crouched down to him, touched the fabric of his shirt. I'd seen his eyes, as wide as silver dollars, as he'd seen me stepping out from the trees, with my rifle at my shoulder. I'd seen them walking their trails, talking casually, like schoolmates on their way to the gym. I'd seen them surprised, their mouths slack, fallen open. It'd taken almost five months in, but I'd finally gotten a look at the guys we were fighting.

It certainly wouldn't take that long to see them again. When we got back to LZ English, Dave picked out two more guys to replace the two he'd let go. And we started running missions nearly round the clock. We ran four or five in quick succession, and each time out we saw more VC. It'd taken me nearly five months to see the first one, but once I started running with the Lurps, I started seeing them nearly every day—and sometimes more often than I'd have liked.

After a month and a half of running with the Lurps, one of the older guys rotated out—part of the natural order of things—and I became ATL. We didn't pick up a sixth guy for a while, and we ended up running the next few missions like that, with just the five guys. We couldn't have known it at the time, but those next couple of missions would be some of the most active we'd ever run.

# 3

## Getting Experience

From the air the area around Bong Son looked a lot different than it did from the ground. The limbs and vines all disappeared, and the land became a rolling blanket of greens and browns. It was textured with mountains and farms that pieced together like a giant jigsaw puzzle, and the flooded rice paddies that dominated the countryside faded into a matrix of trails and dikes. On foot the area was difficult to maneuver, but from the air it actually looked rather calm, almost inviting.

Dave and I were sitting in the back of the chopper, just taking it all in, when one of the pilots turned around and gave us the thumbs-up: we were nearing the area where we were scheduled to run the next day—a wide cross section of the Suoi Tre Valley—so we'd need to get ready to look for an LZ. Dave had a pair of binoculars slung around his neck, and at that point he started cleaning the lenses with the sleeve of his shirt.

I sat up on the balls of my feet and leaned carefully through the door for a better view. I could see the valley approaching below, and from what I could tell, it looked a lot like any other: a broad valley floor, flanked on both sides by a stretch of rugged mountains. But unlike some of the other valleys, in this one the mountains connected together at the head of the valley and formed the shape of a horseshoe, or the capital letter U turned upside-down. This was fairly distinctive, and it gave the valley a sort of cozy appearance, like a giant amphitheater.

I could also see the trail—which was what we'd be watching—along the left side of the valley; it ran the entire length of the valley floor and disappeared into some trees at the foot of the mountain. The VC had been traveling this path, and it would likely draw the majority of our attention during the mission.

The pilots took us over the ridge at the end of the valley and flew past a clearing on the backside of the mountain. In looking for a good LZ, you usually tried to find a place that was close to your observation post—in this case, the tops of those mountains—but that wasn't always easy to do, and sometimes you ended up having to walk a long ways before you got to your OP. Unfortunately, the clearing that we saw was about the best we could find, and I knew we'd have to walk a good distance the next day when we came back with the team. But that was fine: it was much better to pick out a safe LZ and have to walk than to pick a close LZ and end up in a firefight.

Dave pointed out the clearing to one of the pilots, and they agreed that it looked pretty good. Of course, in truth, nobody really knew what it would be like once we got down on the ground. The choppers flew so high during the overflights that it was almost impossible to get a real sense of what the LZ would be like. But that was just part of the risk, I guess—and since they didn't want to tip off the VC that we were coming, they probably wouldn't ever start flying any lower. We just did the best we could and hoped it looked as good on the ground as it did from the air. Either way, we'd be finding out soon enough.

The pilots turned us around, and we headed back toward LZ English. One more night and we'd be back in the bush.

The next afternoon, about five o'clock, we all piled aboard the Huey and started back to the valley. We were scheduled for a four-day mission, and our job was essentially to watch for VC and determine what kind of numbers they had. There were only five of us, but I think we all felt pretty confident about the mission. We'd run several missions together over the past few weeks—in fact, four over the last two—so we knew each other's tendencies and felt comfortable working together. I'd grown especially fond of Dave Brueggemann: as a team leader, he was extremely knowledgeable, and his experience had a calming effect on the team, even in some of the most difficult situations.

During the flight there wasn't much talking. The guys just kind of kept to themselves, trying to prepare themselves mentally and psychologically for the next few days. In a lot of ways it was like preparing for a sporting event—like a baseball game or a football game—and this was the time when everybody put on his game face.

We'd been in the air for about thirty-five minutes when I finally saw the horseshoe coming up in the distance. We were flying much lower than we had on the overflight, but there was still no mistaking it: the dense foliage of the mountains, the sparse, low grass of the valley floor. It was like an oversized amphitheater, and we were flying right into the mouth of it.

I looked over at Dave, and he nodded his head. This was it. He signaled to the rest of the team, and we all started getting ready.

The pilot flew in hard, over the treetops, and banked down the backside of the mountain. Seconds later, we were piling out of the chopper and onto the ground below. I hit the ground moving, right behind Dave, and we quickly entered the trees at the foot of the mountain.

We stopped briefly, just inside the tree line, to make sure we hadn't been spotted; then we regrouped and headed into the brush. We all knew exactly what to do, so we quickly, and quietly, started up the side of the mountain—Dave in the front and me bringing up the rear—no talking, just moving, one behind the other.

The vegetation at the bottom was pretty thick, but we eventually made it through the undergrowth and into an area where the floor was much cleaner. An hour or so later we reached a point where the trees grew farther apart and the land started leveling off. We were nearing the top, and within minutes the valley became visible through the trees on the other side.

We were able to see it through an opening in some limbs, and from the edge of the brow it looked a lot bigger than it had from the chopper. The valley floor stretched out to the horizon, and the mountains on each side raised up like buildings.

Dave found a flat area without any trees that he thought would make a good observation post—it was covered in tall grass that rose nearly to our shoulders, and it offered an unobstructed view of the valley. Though we'd still need to use the binoculars, we could see the trail clearly, winding through the grass on the valley floor. We broke down for the night and settled in. It was better to go ahead and get our sleep before the action started.

Over the next three days we sat at the observation post, watching the trail through our binoculars—and I can certainly say, we weren't disappointed. During the first day we saw a constant flow of VC, walking mostly in pairs, up and down the trail, and several times we even heard gunfire coming from the valley floor. I saw more VC than I could imagine, and they were just walking the trail as casual as could be, with their rifles slung loosely over their shoulders.

In keeping with our assignment, Dave logged everything we saw in his notebook: sometimes the groups were as large as twelve, sometimes they were as small as two. But over the three days that we were there the traffic remained constant, and it all headed into the trees at the end of the valley floor.

We communicated this back to LZ English, and on the evening of the third day they sent us a coded message saying they wanted us to get a closer look. With all that traffic down there, it seemed pretty clear that there was a base camp of some kind hidden among the trees, and they wanted us to go down and check it out.

Now normally, this wouldn't have been a problem—scouting for NVA was basically what we did—but in this case, with the lay of the land and the number of VC that we'd seen, it seemed a bit more dangerous than usual. If we got down to the bottom and were spotted, we'd have to hump it all the way over the mountain just to get to an LZ—and as steep as it was, that would prove a real challenge. Hiking up after infiltration was one thing, but climbing up with a bunch of VC on your tail was quite another.

Even Dave was amazed at the number of VC that we'd seen, so he sent a second message back to LZ English, just to make sure that they'd understood exactly what the situation was—we'd talked about it and decided that maybe our superiors hadn't fully understood what kind of numbers we were seeing down there— but naturally, when they responded the second time, the message was virtually unchanged: the commanding general wanted to call in an air strike, but he needed to know the size and exact location of the camp first. Well, there was no use trying to change anybody's mind, especially the commanding general's, so we just bit the bullet and accepted the fact that we were gonna have to go down there.

By this point it was beginning to get dark, and the rest of the guys had started eating their rations for the night. We were all lying in a circle, there in the grass, and Dave leaned over and whispered that he wanted to talk to me away from the others. He crawled away from the group, and I followed him into the grass, scooting along the ground, always careful to remain concealed. We stopped about five meters away—just far enough to be out of range of the others—and he started speaking.

"Shan, I just wanted to talk to you about this a little bit." He spoke softly, but I could hear the emotion in his voice. "Now, I didn't want to say this in front of the others, but I'm a little bit concerned about tomorrow. If we get down there and make contact, then there's a chance that some of us might not be coming back."

I'd never heard him talk like that, but I tended to agree with what he was saying—with all the VC we'd been seeing, if we got spotted down there, we'd have a pretty hard time getting out.

"And even if we do manage to break contact, we'll still have a hard time finding an LZ—there's a lot of land between that valley down there and the other side of this mountain—"

He went on like that for a while, slow and serious, and just generally concerned about the mission. We were sitting there in the grass, in a sort of crowded spot of brush, so I leaned back against a tree to try and get more comfortable.

"—You get what I'm saying, Shan? No noise at all—"

It was like a scene from a movie really: Dave the experienced vet and me the fresh recruit—two young kids off in some foreign land about to fight their last fight.

"—We're gonna have to take our time with this thing or we'll all end up down there for good—"

But for some reason I just couldn't stay focused. I guess I was tired, because my mind started to wander.

"—And hey, I don't care if it takes us five hours to get down there, we're gonna have to take our time with this thing—"

I couldn't help but think about the rest of the guys, up there eating their Lurp rations—I hadn't gotten to eat yet when Dave pulled me aside. And about our trek up the mountain from the other day. And about how much more tired I was than normal.

"—Now, the way I see it, it's only five of us, right? So that means that—"

Dave continued talking like that, his voice steady and rhythmic like a metronome, until eventually . . . I just drifted off to sleep.

"Shan!" He gripped my shoulder and shook me awake. "Shan, what the hell are you doing, man? Wake up!"

I opened my eyes and saw Dave's face, right there in front of me, about six inches away. "Shan, wake up, man, what are you doing?"

"What happened?"

"You fell asleep."

"What?"

"You fell asleep, man. What's wrong with you?"

"Oh, man." I sat up and rubbed my eyes. "Sorry about that. I must've hit a wall." We'd been running quite a few missions lately, so I guess it just finally caught up with me—right there in the middle of Dave's talk.

I could see his face in the moonlight, and thankfully he was grinning.

"Geez, Shan, I didn't know what had happened to you, man. You okay?"

"Yeah, I'm fine. I'm good."

"You're not gonna conk out on me now, are you?"

"Oh, no, no, I'm good. I'm good now." I could tell I was gonna be hearing about this one for a while.

"Not gonna try and grab some more Zs, are you?"

Pretty funny stuff, but I guess I deserved it. Falling asleep like that in the middle of our talk. But Dave was a pretty good guy, and he knew he could trust me—I mean, I wasn't perfect by any stretch (falling asleep like that just wasn't good), but at the same time he knew he could count on me—and in the Lurps that meant pretty much everything.

To be successful as a Lurp, you had to work as a team, and to work as a team, you had to have trust. It was the foundation for everything else: with it, the teams operated with a quiet efficiency, and without it, there was nothing. This was one thing that Dave knew well, and whenever he found somebody he liked—somebody he knew he could trust—he stuck with him. And in a situation like this, he also knew when to cut a guy some slack.

We continued talking, and Dave made it clear that we'd try and avoid contact at all costs—even if it meant creeping down the mountain just a few feet at a time. He suggested we change up the order of the team, so that I'd be running point and he'd be following along behind me. This would allow us to communicate more easily and to keep tighter control over the pace of our descent. I preferred the control of the point position anyway, so I told him that suited me just fine.

The second thing we discussed was radio communication. There was a good chance we might lose contact with LZ English when we dipped down into the valley. We were already a pretty good ways away, and descending into the valley would likely cut off our radio communication. Unfortunately, whenever that happened, there wasn't much you could do about it; if you lost contact, you were simply, and absolutely, on your own, without any prospect of fire support or exfiltration. And that's a scary place to be, especially with so many VC buzzing around. So we decided to give a radio check every few minutes as we were making our way down the mountain; that way we could stay in constant contact, and if we did lose contact, we'd know it pretty much immediately. Then maybe we'd avoid getting caught in a situation where we needed help but couldn't get in touch with LZ English.

So that got it covered. The rest would pretty much be up to us and the Lord.

"All right, Shan, let's head back up and get some rest. I'm afraid we're gonna need it."

And I was afraid he was right.

The next morning, about daybreak, we started down the mountain, just as we had planned. I was in the front, Dave was right behind me, and we were moving just as cautiously as any Lurp team could move. I'd go about fifteen feet at a time and then stop and take a look around, just to make sure we hadn't been spotted—or, for that matter, that we hadn't stumbled upon the base camp. I knew from experience that you could walk up on a base camp without even realizing it, and that was about the last thing I wanted to do.

About a quarter of the way down we came across a line of rocks that ran along the side of the mountain, at a slightly downward angle. We'd been walking in some leaves that I wasn't really comfortable with, so I decided to try and walk on the rocks instead, to try and cut down on some of the noise. We moved down along the rocks, one at a time, and then continued on like that.

Each time we stopped we'd give a communication check, and as we expected, the signal got weaker and weaker as we neared the valley. It became clear that we were about to lose communication altogether, so we asked command what they wanted us to do. After several minutes of waiting, they suggested that we relay our communication back through a second Lurp team that happened to be located between us and them.

Well, this was certainly less than ideal, but if that's what they wanted, we didn't really have a whole lot of choice. They contacted the other team and told them to switch their radio over to the same frequency that we were using; we made contact with them and arranged to give a radio check every few minutes as we continued down the mountain. The signal still wasn't great, but it was at least better than it had been before.

We started moving again, slow and easy, until we reached a point about halfway down the side of the mountain. We tried to give another communication check but found that we'd lost all contact. Dave immediately moved us back up, about thirty feet or so, and we reestablished contact with the other Lurp team. They relayed the situation back to command, then a few minutes later gave us word that we were to be extracted—which wasn't exactly a disappointment. Heading into that valley without direct communication was none too appealing to me.

So we climbed back to the top and found a place where we thought a chopper could land. About forty minutes later it appeared in the distance, and just as it was coming in it started receiving rifle fire from the valley below. Luckily nobody was hit, but we climbed aboard quickly and headed back to the base.

After our debriefing, the guys in headquarters were really buzzing about the mission. They were all excited about the VC we'd seen and were apparently pretty eager for us to get back out there. Captain John Buczacki, our CO at the time, called us into his office just a short time later to discuss a possible follow-up.

"Guys, I know you're tired, but the general wants to get this thing nailed down just as soon as possible. Bergy, you got any thoughts on this? Maybe we can try to get you guys back out there in the next couple of days?"

"Well, I think that'll be okay, but one thing I'm a little concerned about is the lack of firepower—if we get down in that valley and get caught up in a firefight, five guys just isn't gonna cut it."

"That bad, huh?"

"Oh, man, it was so many of them walking around down there it looked like a damn ant farm."

The captain paused to consider this. "All right, well, what if we added a second team? You think that would do it?"

Dave looked over at me. "What do you think, Shan?"

"Sure couldn't hurt," I told him. "But I still don't like the idea of getting too close to that base camp."

"All right, then, let me get back to headquarters, and I'll see what I can do."

Well, it wasn't long before we had our answer. By early that afternoon the captain got back with us and told us we'd be going back in two days, just as we'd expected. He arranged for a second team to join us, so Dave and the team leader from the new team would be going on the overflight together the next day—and then the day after that we'd all be heading back to the valley together.

He also informed us of a plan to address the communication problem. They arranged for a three-man radio team to monitor the radio at a fire-support base just a few miles away from the valley. The team would alternate shifts, listening only to the frequency that we were on, for twenty-four hours a day. This would ensure that we'd have constant radio contact, albeit still not directly with LZ English. But it was at least better than having to relay through a second Lurp team.

On the third day back we were all ready to go again, so as usual we piled aboard the Huey and started back to the valley—but this time with the addition of a second team, following closely behind in another chopper.

Dave and the other TL had picked out an LZ on the same side of the mountain we'd entered in previously—opposite the valley—but it was much closer to the top this time, so we wouldn't have the long hump like we had before. It was also large enough to accommodate both choppers simultaneously, which meant we could get in and get off the LZ without having to wait around for the second team to arrive. This was important for obvious reasons: nobody liked the prospect of hanging around an LZ waiting for a second team.

We got there just before dark—the way most of the Lurps preferred—and then jumped off the choppers and moved quickly into the trees. Once inside the tree line, we headed directly toward the mountaintop, walking in single file and keeping an eye out for stray VC. There were eleven of us this time, and I was situated roughly in the middle. We continued this way for half an hour or so until we reached the rim of the mountain, where we stopped to take a break.

There was a layer of dry leaves on the ground—the same type of leaves we'd walked through before—and they created quite a bit of noise as we walked through them. I was probably just being extra-sensitive, but every time I heard somebody crunch down on one of those leaves, it sounded to me like a fire alarm going off—so when we finally stopped to take a break, I was pretty glad to get settled.

We were all just sitting there, resting and keeping quiet, when one of the new guys said he heard something. He was sitting about three people down from me and claimed to have heard something back behind us. I was a little skeptical, since we'd just walked through all those dry leaves and I hadn't heard a thing, but he insisted that there was some noise coming from back in the direction of the LZ.

We sat there a little while longer, and sure enough, not two minutes later another guy started saying that he'd heard something too. Well, this guy was one of the first guy's running mates, so I still wasn't exactly convinced—I just figured they'd gotten spooked for some reason—but given the area where we were running, it was probably better to play it safe.

We sat there for another fifteen minutes or so, just as still and quiet as the trees, and eventually the first guy started saying that now he could see something. Somebody watching us, he said. Well, by this time it was getting pretty dark, so I didn't know how he could see anything at all—and nobody else saw anything anyway—but we all tensed up regardless. We sat there on edge, just waiting for something to happen.

Dave was sitting next to me, and after a few minutes of just sitting there I could tell he was starting to get irritated. He leaned over and whispered, "You see anything?"

"The only way a VC could slip up on us in these leaves would be if he could fly."

"That's about what I thought."

But the way we operated in the Lurps was to give credence to whatever our teammates said, even if we didn't necessarily agree with it, so Dave radioed LZ English and informed them of our situation. Predictably, they decided to pull us out.

Out in the field like that it was generally better to assume the worst—better to assume that you were being watched and make it out alive than to assume you weren't and then get killed—and to resolve your problems when you got back to base.

So we moved back down the mountain, to the same LZ where they'd dropped us off earlier, and waited for the choppers. By that time the sun had completely disappeared below the horizon, so we were going to have to make a nighttime extraction. That was fairly unusual, but the choppers soon arrived and picked us up without a hitch.

It wasn't long before we were right back out there again. We got back to LZ English, and Dave met with the other team leader about dropping the two who had thought they'd seen something. Neither one of us had a whole lot of confidence in them at that point—that valley was pretty well overrun with VC, but we didn't think they'd actually seen anything—so it just seemed like the best thing to do was to give it a try without them.

Also, Dave arranged to pick up a guy named Harry Bell—Bell was a friend of Dave's and a pretty good Lurp to boot. He was running with another team at the time, but he was happy to come along with us—and we were happy to get him. Bell was from Mississippi and he was one of those good old boys who was well liked by everybody. He was a welcome addition to any mission.

Dave and the other TL picked out the LZ, and on the third day back we loaded up into two choppers and headed back to the valley. The new LZ was situated on the right side of the mountain range, near the mouth of the valley floor and on the exterior side of the mountain. Since this was a pretty good ways away from our previous two points, we hoped it'd give us a fresh, and secure, entry into the valley.

We hit the clearing quickly, both choppers coming in together, and tumbled onto the ground and into the trees. We were already close to the top, so we moved directly to the crest of the mountain, took a short break, and started down the other side.

I think by this point Dave was feeling pretty confident, or at least determined, about the mission; he wanted to go ahead and move into the bowl of the valley before we stopped for the night. So we continued on, cautiously but purposefully, until we got about halfway down the side of the mountain and decided to stop.

Unlike the first trip, we didn't find a nice, flat, grassy meadow to sleep on; we found instead a steep, angled slope covered with trees. They were growing up at odd, twisting angles, and they made for a very interesting sleeping arrangement.

The angle of the slope was probably about forty degrees, so when I finally settled in to go to sleep, I placed my feet against the base of a tree to keep from sliding down the mountain. Everyone else did basically some variation on this. At one point in the night I woke up and shifted positions so that I was actually straddling the tree, with both legs just kind of dangling down the slope.

Well, needless to say, this wasn't exactly the most comfortable night of my life, but it was actually pretty safe. With the severe angle of the mountain, there was practically no way that anybody could slip up on us in the middle of the night. In fact, we felt so confident of our position that we didn't even put out any claymores.

The next morning we woke up early and ate our Lurp rations first thing. We knew it was gonna be a long day, so we wanted to go ahead and eat before we got started—once we got going, there probably wouldn't be a whole lot of time for stopping and eating.

I heated some water using a gas tablet, then dug a hole in the ground and buried my scraps in the dirt; even though we were well hidden among the trees, it was still important to try and conceal whatever evidence there might be that we were there.

We waited for just a few minutes, until the sunlight was bright enough for us to see, and then we started moving. We wanted to get in and find the base camp as quickly as we could, but with all the

VC around, it was important not to get overanxious. We moved down the mountain in single file, zigzagging across the terrain in short chunks of land, and within the hour we had reached the valley floor.

A narrow stream ran along the foot of the mountain, toward the area where we thought the camp was located. It wasn't wide, but it looked pretty deep and appeared to be moving pretty rapidly. We needed to cross it to get out of the brush at the foot of the mountain, so we moved slowly along the bank, to look for a shallow spot to cross. We moved for about a hundred yards and finally came to a low point that looked to be about knee-deep.

Dave led the way, and the team followed along behind, crawling down the side of the bank and into the murky water. I grabbed a hold of a branch, so I wouldn't slip, and stepped down into the mud. The water was warm and came up just above my knees.

We crossed quickly, careful to keep an eye out in both directions, in case someone slipped up on us while we were strung out across the water—which was a very vulnerable position to be in.

We got to the other side and continued down the creek, staying close to the embankment and walking carefully along some rocks at the water's edge. We'd been moving like this for about ten minutes or so when Dave spotted an old Vietnamese man crouching down at the stream, about twenty feet in front of us.

He was scooping water into a wooden pail, and needless to say, we came to an immediate stop and didn't move a single inch further. We must've looked like a bunch of statues, just standing there frozen against the bank, but if he'd spotted us, we'd have been compromised for sure—a single shout and every VC in the valley would've been on top of us in a matter of seconds.

He just continued dipping his water, oblivious to the fact that we were anywhere around. A lot of the water was dripping back into the creek, but he eventually filled it to his satisfaction and stood up and left.

He disappeared into the trees, and once he was sufficiently out of view, we all just sort of shook our heads and wiped our brows—just as quickly as that and you're right on top of somebody. We continued down the creek, this time moving more carefully than ever.

The terrain on the valley side of the creek was much easier to navigate than it was on the mountain side. We were able to move along the bank quietly and discreetly because there was none of the leaves and undergrowth that we'd come through before. This gave us some confidence, but we were careful not to move too fast—the slightest misjudgment and we could be in real trouble.

Within minutes of seeing the old man, Dave saw somebody else, about a hundred yards up. He looked to be much younger, most likely a VC, and he appeared to be doing his laundry. He was standing at the edge of the stream—actually a few feet in—with his pants rolled up and holding an armful of linens.

This was definitely a strange sight, and one, most wisely, to be avoided. Dave motioned for us to climb into the brush—there was a stand of trees to our left—so we filed up the embankment and disappeared into the undergrowth. We continued through the trees for about a hundred yards or so and then just slipped right by him as he scrubbed and tugged at his wash. We'd made it by that guy without a problem, but the situation was clearly becoming quite delicate—there were people everywhere now, and with the larger team, there was a greater chance that someone might happen to see us.

We continued in the same direction, with the valley to our left and the stream to our right, moving deeper into the valley, farther into the stand of trees. We were now in a situation where every step had to be quiet, so we moved slowly and cautiously, like a line of sloths creeping gently across the jungle floor.

After an hour or so of this we emerged from the tree line and stood right at the edge of the valley floor. It was broad and vast, much wider than it had looked from the top of the mountain; the clearing was probably five hundred yards across, and if I'd thought it looked big before, it now looked truly immense as we stood there in the midst of it. We'd been watching the valley, off and on, for the past week, but it still sort of took me by surprise when we finally made it there. I stood there for a second and just admired the scene.

By this point the sun was shining brightly in the sky, and it lit up the rice paddies like a bright summer day. The valley had really come to life: people were farming the fields, hunched over the rice in their conical hats; we could hear voices coming from all around us, shouting and laughing, like they were at home in their backyards—which, in a way, I guess they were.

Of course, they didn't know we were there. I suspect they'd have looked a slight bit different if they'd known there were almost a dozen Americans standing there in the trees watching them—but in a way they looked almost unaffected by the war that was going on all around them. This part of the country was definitely considered enemy territory, but it was still striking just how relaxed they appeared.

We were at something of an impasse: we couldn't very well continue without being spotted, and we were so deep into the valley that we couldn't turn back. Dave radioed LZ English, via the fire-support base, to see what they wanted us to do. He sent them a message explaining the difficulty in trying to continue on to the base camp and hoped they'd be able to appreciate the danger in advancing any farther.

The radio signal was strong, but we still had to wait for a while before we could hear back from LZ English. Our message had to be relayed through the fire-support base, and then once it got to LZ English, there'd be another delay while command checked with headquarters to determine what our next set of instructions would be. Of course, we all figured they'd want us to continue on to the base, but we were hoping they'd have a change of heart, based on the message that Dave had sent.

Finally, after about forty-five minutes, the code started coming in. Our RTO was a guy named Ed Zapata, and he motioned for Dave to come over and check it out. Dave scooted over beside him, and they started deciphering code as it came in over the radio. They huddled up together, and finally Dave apparently got what he needed to hear.

"Looks like they finally decided to listen to us," he said. "Now all they want us to do is to pull an ambush."

I had to smile. Pulling an ambush was definitely preferable to continuing on to the base camp, but it was certainly no easy task in its own right—and Dave knew it. The trail we'd been watching was located on the other side of the valley, so in order to pull the ambush we'd have to somehow get across the valley floor. And that wasn't gonna be easy.

The only plausible way to get across without being seen was to move at night, and this was something that we normally didn't do. The Lurp teams often liked to enter at dusk—and to move into the trees and get set up just as it was getting dark—but we generally didn't like to move around too much at night. Naturally we didn't know the terrain as well as the enemy did, so if we were to get into trouble at night, in the dark, we'd be at a serious disadvantage. More typically, we'd just set up a small perimeter and try and stay put at night—this tended to be the safest route—and then do our moving during the daytime.

Dave radioed back and let them know we'd be trying to cross the valley later that night, and that we'd be setting up an ambush, on the trail, first thing the next morning. He also reiterated the need for the radio operators to be listening in on us that night when we started across the valley. We weren't sure whether the VC would have a lookout posted or not—they appeared pretty secure, so it was possible that they might not have a lookout—but we wanted to keep our lines of communication open just in case. If we somehow got spotted while crossing the clearing, we'd be in need of some serious help.

Dave and I talked, and we both agreed that the best thing for us to do would be to wait until midnight or so, to make sure that most of the VC had settled in for the night. There was no way to guarantee that we wouldn't be seen, but we figured the later we moved the better our chances. So for the rest of the day we just sat there, hidden among the trees, waiting for time to pass and hoping that no one would accidentally wander up.

And I can tell you—that was one long day.

About nine o'clock that night the activity in the valley started dwindling down to nothing, and for a couple of hours we just sat there in the moonlight, listening to silence.

Around eleven o'clock Dave glanced over and whispered the command: "Okay. Let's go."

I nodded my head and passed it on to the next guy. And then he passed it on to the next, until we were all prepared and ready to move out.

We started moving in single file, just as we'd done before. The moon was as big and bright in the sky as I'd ever seen it, and it was lighting up the valley like a giant lantern—which was partly good, because it allowed us to see where we were going, but it was mostly bad, since it meant that the VC would be able to see us if they had somebody keeping post.

I stepped out of the tree line and moved slowly into the field. No trees, no dark, no nothing, just a line of Americans, standing out in the open.

We were spaced about fifteen feet apart, and we moved slowly, measuring each step with extreme caution. We crossed through an area covered with grass—similar to the grass we'd slept in that first night at the top of the mountain—and then reached one of the rice paddies about halfway across the valley floor.

The paddies were separated by a series of dirt dikes that were linked together and kept the water-soaked crops from washing away. They were built up about two or three feet above the tops of the rice plants and measured maybe three, four feet across—which gave us a very capable footpath to use in crossing the paddies.

I stepped up onto one of the dikes, still hanging back about fifteen feet from the Lurp in front of me, and moved slowly above the fields. I scanned the valley with my eyes, looking from one end to the other—and praying I wouldn't see any VC looking back at me.

We continued like this, creeping across the valley floor, until we finally reached the trail on the other side—and really, we couldn't have gotten there any too soon for me. Walking around in the open like that, with the moon shining down and the sound of our boots scraping across the dirt, was very unsettling.

But we got to the other side and found the trail we'd been watching from the top of the mountain during our first trip in. It was much wider than I'd thought—more like the width of a small car or three men walking side by side, and it was worn smooth from constant use.

We crossed the trail, being careful not to leave any footprints, and climbed into a thicket on the other side; it was fairly dense, like a briar patch, so we made our way across it and set up a perimeter in a small clearing about fifty feet away from the trail. It seemed to provide us with ample cover and would give us an easy route to the trail whenever we decided to pull the ambush in the morning. So we broke down for the night, spread out across the ground, and went to sleep.

The next morning I was awakened by the sound of voices coming up the trail. They were speaking in Vietnamese, which, of course, I couldn't understand, but from the volume of their conversation I could tell they were quite close.

I opened my eyes to check out the situation and managed to catch a glimpse of two VC moving down the trail. But the other thing I saw was something I definitely didn't expect: the area we'd chosen to sleep in wasn't nearly as well covered as we'd thought—what had previously appeared to be well hidden by the brush was actually not well hidden at all, and two of the Lurps were sleeping right out in the open, with no cover whatsoever.

I reached over and nudged Dave on the shoulder. His eyes popped open, and immediately he recognized the situation. He didn't say a word, but his expression pretty much said it all: *Oh, shit.*

The two of us scrambled around as quietly as we could, waking the rest of the team. They quickly mobilized and within minutes we were all hidden in the trees at the edge of the mountain—but again, we were left just shaking our heads.

Apparently when we'd selected our position the night before, we'd all been fooled into thinking the area was better protected than it was; thankfully, we hadn't gotten burned by it. By then the sun was up, and if any of the VC had happened to look over in our direction, I'm sure they'd have seen us easily.

We regrouped and got ready to pull our ambush—only now, after seeing the area in the daylight, we realized that the ambush spot wasn't nearly as good as we'd thought either. The place where it opened up onto the trail was a bit narrower than we'd realized; it allowed for only four Lurps to front the opening, which was fewer than we'd have liked. But there was no point in turning back now, so we set up our formation and got ready for the next group of VC to come by.

We set up in a formation that looked something like a square: there were four Lurps against the trail, two Lurps to the right, two Lurps to the left, and three more in the back, for rear security. I was situated on the left side of the formation, and within ten minutes of getting set up I heard a group of VC coming up from the right.

I could hear them talking in their regular speaking voices, but I couldn't actually see them yet. Within seconds, however, they appeared around a curve and proceeded toward the kill zone. Casual and oblivious.

There were eight of them in total: six standard-issue VC, with their rifles slung across their shoulders, and two more carrying rice—large bags of rice that looked like they weighed about fifty pounds apiece. They moved calmly down the trail, and as they neared the spot where the Lurps were located I held my breath and waited.

Suddenly the rifle fire burst out like a smattering of firecrackers, and the area in the front clouded over with dust and tracers zipping across the trees. We weren't using claymores—because of the narrow opening in the trail—but almost immediately seven of the eight VC went down, killed instantly by the rifle fire.

Somehow the first one managed to survive the barrage, and he kicked off his sandals and took off toward the base camp like a jet. I have no idea how he did it, but he managed to avoid getting shot—and when he got his feet situated, he just took off running.

Seconds later we were all scrambling out onto the trail to look for papers or maps or anything that might be of value to the guys back at headquarters. We went through their pockets and searched their belongings, but they didn't have anything useful.

One of the Lurps took out a knife and cut open the bags of rice that they'd dropped to the ground, and another one came along behind him and spread it around in the dirt, so the VC couldn't collect it and use it later.

We scoured the scene, then collected their weapons and headed to higher ground, satisfied that there wasn't anything left of value. A couple of minutes had passed since that first shot, and we were already leaving the valley and climbing up the side of the mountain.

The day before, command had said that they wanted us to pull a second ambush on the following day, but I could already tell that that was pretty much out of the question. We were about a quarter of the way up the mountain, and I could hear people just screaming and shouting back on the trail behind us. It was total pandemonium back there, and it didn't take a whole lot to figure out that they'd be coming after us.

We were moving quickly up the mountain, but with all the noise back there, it was none too quick for me. I'd never heard anything like it—and actually I would never hear anything like it again, not in my two years in Vietnam. I think they must've been in total shock—and then angry and panicked and trying to get organized, all at the same time. But I knew they'd be coming after us, and if they had any sense at all, they had to have realized that we weren't too far away. It seemed like things were about to get real unpleasant real quick.

We continued up the mountain, moving quickly through a patch of skinny trees that must've been about thirty feet tall; we ran through them like we were moving through an obstacle course, dodging left and right, but always moving forward.

We eventually reached an area near the top of the mountain that was covered in rocks and provided an excellent location to set up a perimeter. One of the larger rocks, nearly the size of a bus, jutted out from the sloping terrain and created a natural wall that faced outward toward the valley. We climbed onto it and readied ourselves for a possible attack. Dave and Zapata quickly set up the radio and relayed a message back to LZ English that we needed an extraction as soon as possible.

A few seconds later the message came back that we were to make a stand against whatever force the VC sent. We couldn't believe it. With all the VC we'd been seeing down there, now all riled up, it was like we'd just jabbed a stick down in a beehive and they were asking us to hang around and fend off all the bees.

Dave grabbed the radio from Zapata.

"*Who is this?*"

We were still relaying messages back through the radio team, so Dave wanted to make sure they were getting the picture.

"Okay, well, listen, this is Dave Brueggemann—and we need an extraction. *Now.* I'm not saying we mind making a stand, but this is *not* the time for it—this place is about to be crawling with VC."

Dave was speaking quietly, but there was no mistaking his point, or his intention.

"Well, that base camp down there is about to come up the side of this mountain, and if somebody doesn't get us out of here soon, we might not be getting out—"

The location we were in was good for a temporary defense, but it probably wouldn't suffice for any longer than a few hours—if they figured out where we were and we ended up in a firefight, they'd probably try to flank us—which meant they could possibly end up on the ridge above us, dropping hand grenades down on us from right above our heads. Dave knew we couldn't just hang around there indefinitely, so he tried his best to make sure the guys at LZ English understood this.

Thankfully, the next message that came back seemed to take it to heart. "Team Golf, prepare for extraction."

Apparently they'd finally gotten the message, and our general reaction was best expressed, I think, by Dave's response: "Well, hallelujah."

Of course, this did bring up the problem of finding an LZ, but that was just something we'd have to figure out—the fact that the choppers were coming was good enough news for us.

The only clearing that we knew of for sure was the clearing down in the valley—which was okay, but we'd have to somehow slip by the VC as they were coming up the mountain. Dave decided we'd move along the side of the mountain, in the direction of the valley's opening down to the right; we'd move parallel to the trail and then make our descent at a slight angle, back toward the valley floor— this way we could hope to avoid the VC, while also making our way farther away from the base camp.

We started running, in a single-file line, and I made sure to keep an eye out in all directions. I could still hear the VC down in the valley, but there was really no telling which way they might be coming from, and I didn't want any surprises while we were trying to get away.

We were moving pretty quick, and after just a few minutes we'd probably traveled four or five hundred meters. At that point we turned toward the valley and started maneuvering down the slope. We managed to maintain a pretty quick jog, even though the angle of the ground made it difficult to run.

We continued like this for ten minutes or so, until we neared the valley floor, where we were able to pick up our pace again. The plane of the ground started leveling out, and I knew within seconds we'd be moving into the clearing. I was actually starting to feel pretty good about the situation when we emerged from the tree line and burst straight out into the middle of an NVA base camp.

I couldn't believe it. One second we were right in the thick of the jungle, and the next second we were surrounded by a whole village of NVA. We were already running at a full sprint, so we just kept on moving, without missing a step.

A small campfire was burning in the center, and two rows of grass huts ran along the sides. The NVA were all milling around between the huts, and before they had time to cut us down, we just opened up on them.

I had my M-16 in both hands, and I opened it up, spraying rifle fire all around. Some of the guys started throwing hand grenades in the direction of the huts, and the whole place erupted in chaos. People were screaming, grenades were going off, the whole thing was just happening so fast. I know that if running into the camp like that had surprised us, then it must've absolutely shocked them. They were all scrambling around, looking for weapons, trying to mount some kind of a spontaneous defense—but it all happened so quickly, there was practically nothing they could do.

We ran right down the middle of the camp, straight into the trees on the other side, and just kept on going. None of us got hurt, and from what I could tell, the people at the camp were too rattled to follow us into the brush. Of course, it would only be a matter of time before they did get mobilized and come after us, but as it stood, we'd made it through the base camp unscathed.

We continued through the trees like that for another hundred yards or so, and this time when we emerged from the tree line, it was into the valley floor, as I'd expected the first time. We disappeared quickly into some tall grass and created an impromptu perimeter in case the VC managed to get there before the choppers.

We knew it was just a matter of time now. The choppers were on their way, but so were the VC—*and now the NVA as well.* The guys who flew the choppers were absolutely top-quality, so I wasn't worried about them finding us. I just hoped that we'd sufficiently rattled the NVA at the base camp that they wouldn't be able to mobilize quickly enough to get to us first.

I lay there in the grass, with my M-16 at my shoulder, just waiting. I wasn't tired from the running, but my heart was racing with all the adrenaline flowing through me. And thankfully, we hadn't been there long at all, maybe five minutes, when I heard the unmistakable sounds of the chopper blades coming from back behind me.

Two Cobra gunships appeared and flew over us, moving toward the back of the valley. They must've seen a group of VC, because they immediately opened up with their rockets and 40-mm cannon, firing up the trees at the back of the valley floor.

Two slicks followed in behind them and settled down in the grass beside us; in no time, we were all aboard the choppers and glad to be heading back to LZ English. The pilot pulled us up over the trees and turned us back out of the valley. We sped away as the gunships continued raking the valley behind us.

I looked over at Dave, and he wiped his brow exaggeratedly with the back of his hand. I nodded in agreement, then leaned my head against the side of the chopper and closed my eyes for the rest of the ride.

A few days later, back at LZ English, the captain came around and told us that one of the infantry companies was scheduled to sweep the valley with a unit from the Korean division that was stationed nearby. I didn't know if they'd find anything or not—who could say if the VC would even still be around?—but I sure was glad I didn't have to go with them. Three different trips in a week and a half was plenty for me.

For our next mission the captain decided to give us a break—or at least that's what I thought initially. We were given an assignment to watch a trail in the An Lao Valley, but this time we wouldn't be pulling an ambush on the last day, like we normally did. Naturally I thought this was because of our last few missions, which had all been pretty hairy—but as I'd soon find out, there was actually a different reason. We'd been back a couple of days when he called us into his quarters to tell us the news. It was sometime about midafternoon.

"Hey, guys, we're gonna be making a couple of changes for this next mission."

Well, right off, that wasn't such a good start—anytime they wanted to make a change, you could pretty much bet it wasn't because they were trying to make your life any easier.

"I've got some ARVN here that I need to get out into the field," he told us. "So it looks like you guys get the nod."

Our Lurp company was responsible for training some of the members of the 22nd ARVN Division reconnaissance unit; this meant that we were periodically required to include South Vietnamese soldiers in our long-range patrols. I'd never actually had to do it before, but I knew that some of the other teams had, so it wasn't a complete and total shock when he gave us the news—but the next part of the plan, I have to admit, kind of took us by surprise.

"Let's see," he said, as he glanced down at some papers on his desk. "It's four different ones. Doesn't look like they have too much experience—Dave, I guess you and Bill can just take them out for a few days and show them the ropes a little bit, try to get them comfortable out there—"

Dave interrupted. "Uhm, Captain? Now, when you say, me and Bill, you don't mean *just* me and Bill, do you?"

The captain chuckled. "I know that sounds bad, but you won't be pulling any ambushes—it's strictly observational. Three days in, then you're right back out."

That really wasn't much comfort, and from the look on Dave's face, I could tell he was just as startled by this as I was.

"Well, sir, I think I can speak for both of us when I say that, uh, I don't think that's such a good idea." Dave could be quite tactful when he had to be. "I mean, most of those guys don't even speak English."

Now, if there was ever a time when Dave and I were in complete agreement on something, I can say for sure that this was it—two Americans and four Vietnamese didn't sound a whole lot to me like a formula for success, especially with those guys being first-timers.

I'd been running with Dave for only a few weeks myself, so the prospect of just the two of us trying to train four new Lurps didn't really seem too appealing. And even if they'd already had some Lurping experience, there was still the problem of communication— if we got into trouble out there, I really felt like we'd need at least one more American to give ourselves a chance.

But despite our best efforts—and a variety of suggestions—the captain still wouldn't budge; he needed to get all four of those guys out there, and this was just the way he wanted to do it. Unfortunately, it also meant that I'd get stuck carrying the radio, but I guess that was just part of the job—not a part that I cared for too much, but still, just a part of the job.

The next day Dave gathered us all together to go over the plans for the mission. It actually ended up being three Vietnamese and one Cambodian, but that didn't make a whole lot of practical difference, since only one of them could speak English anyway. That was a guy named Sergeant Pao, and he was saddled with the responsibility of translating for us. From what I could tell, that looked like it was gonna be a real chore.

Dave started out giving some fairly basic instructions on things like keeping quiet and carrying rations—just things to do and certain important things not to do once we got out in the field, kind of like a super-condensed version of our training course. Sergeant Pao just stood there patiently, in his tiger fatigues, waiting for Dave to finish so he could translate for the others.

Dave would speak—"Now, out there in the field the most important thing . . . "—and then Pao would speak, repeating in Vietnamese whatever it was that Dave had just said.

I sat there and watched this for several minutes, and I couldn't help but think how inefficient it all was—if we were to get into some kind of a situation out there in the field, where communication had to be split-second, well, this translating stuff was gonna be a serious problem. I could just imagine us out there trying to communicate back and forth through Sergeant Pao, from English to Vietnamese, from Vietnamese to English, back and forth like that—it was painful to imagine. I realized that we were just gonna have to be incredibly careful and make sure that we didn't get into any trouble.

Dave finished up by describing the order in which we'd all be traveling; he'd be running point, then I'd be behind him with the radio, followed by the four ARVN bringing up the rear. He dismissed the group, satisfied that everyone understood the mission, and we all went our separate ways. I returned to my bunk, convinced that things were about to get very interesting. We were set to lift off early the next morning.

The next day everything went about as smoothly as you could possibly want: we left the base just as we'd planned, entered the LZ, and humped our way across the countryside without any problems. The Vietnamese seemed to adapt quickly to the mission, following along in line and being just as quiet as anyone else, and late that afternoon, after about ten hours of trekking, we came across an OP that was one of the best I'd ever seen.

A stretch of rocks provided a perfect cover for watching the valley below, and the ground surrounding the area was covered in thick brush that made a natural buffer between us and anyone who might be trying to get up there to us. It was like a natural OP, nestled into the side of the mountain and protected on all sides by rocks and vegetation.

It seemed like a perfect place to set up camp for the next three days, so we broke down and set up a small perimeter, using the natural cover of the rocks and our ample supply of claymore mines. We placed the claymores in and around the rocks, being careful to plug up any holes, or weak spots, that the rocks didn't cover naturally. You could never fully relax on a mission like this, but given the security of our perimeter, I was actually beginning to feel pretty good.

I sat back and surveyed the setup as Dave crawled over and joined me.

"I'm beginning to feel a little bit better about this," I told him.

"I know what you mean—happening on these rocks was about the best thing that could've happened."

We all went to sleep that night pleased with the day's success. The Vietnamese had done fine—they'd been quiet and cautious, just as we'd hoped—and we'd found a perfect OP, with a natural rock perimeter. So far things were looking pretty darn good. In fact, maybe too good.

That night we heard some noise coming from the valley—distant voices, occasional rifle fire—but it didn't develop into anything significant. The next morning, however, we observed several groups of NVA moving across the valley floor, and just as we'd expected, our observation post proved to be the perfect place for watching their movement. We peered over the edge of the rocks and watched them through our binoculars as they traveled eastward along the trail—or, from where we were sitting, from left to right. They moved in groups of five or six and appeared to be heavily armed, with AK-47s and rucksacks.

We weren't scheduled to pull an ambush—and honestly, none of us wanted to initiate contact anyway—but Dave still wanted to try and hit the NVA before we headed back to LZ English in a couple of days. The only way to do that without putting ourselves in direct danger was to call in an artillery strike—and this was where the mission took its second twist.

Before we left, the captain had told us we'd be receiving our fire support from a navy battleship that was situated just off the coast. We didn't really think we'd get to use it, since this wasn't considered a hunter-killer mission, but based on the lay of the land and the numbers of NVA that we'd been seeing, we thought it looked like the perfect opportunity to call in the artillery.

Now, I'd never been involved with anything like that—we'd always just gotten our fire support from the fire-support bases located around the highlands—but I was sure eager to try. I sent a message back to LZ English in crypto code, describing what we wanted to do, and we all just sat back and waited, hoping to gain clearance from the guys back at headquarters.

The battleship was the USS *New Jersey,* and it was situated just off the coast of Bong Son in the South China Sea. It was being used to hit VC and NVA targets throughout the region, and from what I was told, it could fire several miles inland and still maintain its accuracy. The ship was equipped with multiple 16-inch guns.

Dave wasn't too sure how our South Vietnamese comrades would respond to a direct confrontation with the NVA, so an artillery ambush would enable us to hit the NVA without putting ourselves in any unnecessary danger.

After just a few minutes we received word from headquarters that our plan had been approved: we'd be using the battleship to try and hit NVA targets along the trail. This definitely added some new excitement to the mission, and we all became pretty eager to watch the battleship at work.

We plotted five different points, up and down the trail, approximately a hundred to two hundred yards apart, and we identified each one with a different letter—one was Alpha, two Bravo, three Charlie, four Delta, and five Echo.

Next we had to coordinate with the navy to make sure that everybody was on the same page. I dialed up the battleship's frequency and gave them the first coordinates on the trail. One thing I can say about those guys—not ever having worked with them before—is that they made the whole process extremely easy. We didn't have to wait around or double-talk or haggle back and forth—I just sent them the first coordinates, and moments later they fired up a smoke round about a hundred meters from the trail. We adjusted our coordinates, and in a matter of minutes we had them firing their smoke rounds right on target. I told them to mark the first point as Alpha, and then we continued to mark each of the grid locations and identify them with their corresponding letters.

After we completed this step, the only thing left to do was to establish our timing. We needed to know how long it would take for the live rounds to reach their targets, as well as the amount of time it would take for the NVA to move into the first set of coordinates. The first of these was easy enough: we simply had the navy boys send a live round at one of the targets, and then we measured the amount of time it took before it landed—twelve seconds.

But to answer the second question we had to wait until a group of NVA appeared and then measure the time it took them to move into one of our target locations. This measure was clearly a little less objective, but it was the best way to go about it—and the only way really.

So we waited for a couple of hours, until a group of NVA became visible at the far end of the valley; then we timed their walk until they reached the first grid point, Alpha. There were three of them, all wearing green khakis, and we watched as they moved, apparently chatting with each other as they walked casually down the trail.

Dave handed the binoculars to one of our Vietnamese friends to give him a chance to get a look at the enemy—from probably as close up as he'd ever been—and I'll never forget the guy's expression. It was a strange combination of fear and awe, as if the experience thrilled him and scared him at the same time. I think it must've made him realize exactly how close we were—and you better believe, he knew exactly what would happen to him if those guys ever managed to get to him.

Finally, after about four or five minutes, the trio reached the first grid coordinates. So now we had our second time measured—the only thing left for us to do was wait. Our one restriction was that we couldn't call in the guns on any group fewer than ten people strong, so we'd need to wait until a larger group came through. At that point the largest group we'd seen was only about six or seven people, so there was a chance that we wouldn't get to call in the artillery at all. But whether a large group came along or not, we were definitely ready.

We continued watching the valley for the rest of the day, and as before, we periodically saw a number of different groups moving along the trail. We timed a few more of them, just to verify our first attempt, and they all turned out to take about the same amount of time. The day was coming to a close, and things appeared to be winding down without much ado. But then, just as the sun was beginning to disappear below the horizon and we were all starting to get ready for the night, we saw something that I don't think any of us ever expected to see: out on one of the rocks, just a few meters from the foot of the valley, a Vietnamese couple was out there in plain sight having sex.

Now, there'd been a concentration of activity at one point along the near side of the valley—I think there must've been a cave or some kind of opening down there—and shortly after the sun went down, this guy and this girl just appeared from out of the brush and proceeded to do their business right there on one of the rocks. None of us really knew what to make of it—if seeing them was some kind of an omen, I sure as heck didn't know how to interpret it. On the good side, at least we knew there were two less VC for us to worry about for a while. Eventually, though, they just finished up and disappeared back up in the brush.

Later that night, after we'd all gone to sleep, we heard voices coming from the valley again, and this time I think it really bothered our Vietnamese comrades; they seemed much more restless than they had the night before—they weren't noisy necessarily, but definitely restless. So far things had gone relatively smoothly; I closed my eyes and went back to sleep, wondering whether our good fortune would continue.

The next morning we woke up early and peered over the tops of the rocks at the valley down below. This was our third day out, and we'd still only seen smaller groups of NVA, so it wasn't clear what the rest of the day, or the mission, would hold. We continued watching the trail for several hours, until eleven o'clock or so, when we got our first sign of activity. I was lying across the face of the rock, scanning the trail through Dave's binoculars, when I saw the first NVA appear in the distance.

He entered the valley beyond the point where we'd begun timing the others, and as he continued walking in our direction, another appeared behind him, and then another and another. In all there were fifteen NVA, all carrying weapons, and all walking straight toward our artillery plots.

I snapped my fingers to let Dave and the others know we had a group headed our way. Dave clambered over beside me, and I handed him the binoculars so he could see what was going on. As he looked over the NVA, I switched the radio over to the battleship's frequency and told them we were ready for action. ("Fire mission.") I could hear the battleship radio operator through the radio calling for battle stations, and in a matter of minutes he told me they were ready to fire.

Dave was still watching the NVA through the binoculars, waiting for them to reach the point where we'd been timing the others. I told the radio operator to stand by, and he said to just give him the word whenever we were ready. The way it was supposed to work was that I would tell the radio operator when we were ready, and then the guys on the ship would fire a single live round to verify the target; if we didn't need any adjustment, then I'd follow up with the command for continuous fire and they'd begin the battery. For now, though, we were just waiting on the NVA to reach our trigger point.

There was a low point in the trail, a spot that dipped down below a stand of trees, and the NVA we'd been watching before had typically disappeared behind those trees for about a minute before they emerged again on the other side. We determined that whenever they emerged on the other side, that was the point when we needed to give the command for the artillery.

The group we were watching disappeared behind the trees. Dave stood poised, ready to give the signal, as the rest of us waited. It seemed like minutes going by—five, ten, maybe more—but they finally reappeared, and Dave turned and whispered the command: "Fire."

I immediately spoke the same command into the radio and seconds later heard the boom of the single 16-inch gun, as it was fired from the battleship. I was holding the radio receiver up to my ear, and it sounded through, just as clear as a bass drum. The round was on its way.

Twelve seconds later—though it seemed like minutes—I heard the crackling of the artillery round as it came through the air. No one said a word. We just watched the explosion as it hit directly in the center of our grid coordinates.

I spoke back through the radio: "Perfect. Continuous fire."

No adjustments were needed, and in a matter of seconds the barrage was on. I could hear all the big guns firing at once through the receiver on the radio, and just like that, the valley started clouding over with explosions.

Almost immediately, six or seven NVA went down, and the others jumped off the trail into what looked to be some sort of a stream. The barrage continued, just battering the area for several minutes, until Dave called for a halt in the firing to survey the damage.

The area was clouded over with smoke, but almost as soon as the battleship quit firing, we could see five or six of the NVA climbing up out of the streambed. I again called for continuous fire, and again they jumped down on the side of the trail. I don't know how they were doing it—the barrage from those guns was absolutely brutal—but somehow they managed to find some pretty good cover.

I told the guy on the ship what was happening, and he suggested we use a different type of round, something that would penetrate the ground and then explode—sort of a delayed fuse—to try and clear those guys out. I agreed with his suggestion, and about a minute later the onslaught was on again.

Well, this went on for several minutes, and we were all pretty sure that this new type of explosive had done the trick, when something happened that I don't think any of us expected. The rounds were exploding all over the place, just pummeling the ground, when one of the NVA, shell-shocked or something, just climbed up out of the ditch and started staggering around. He looked like a prizefighter, punch-drunk and wobbly, but somehow he managed to stay up.

The barrage continued for several more minutes, with the guy just standing there in the middle of it, until finally he managed to stagger outside of the grid coordinates. I looked over at Dave, and he was absolutely incredulous. "Call off the guns," he said, and I relayed the message back to the radio operator. A few seconds later the valley got quiet.

A moment of silence passed, the clouds of smoke started to settle, and we all just sort of stared, wide-eyed, at this one NVA. It appeared that we'd gotten the rest of them, but this one guy would just not stay down. He'd fall down, lie still on the ground for a couple of seconds, then stand back up and stagger around the valley some more.

I looked around at everybody else, and from the looks on their faces I could tell they were just as stunned by this as I was. The South Vietnamese, Sergeant Pao, Dave, everybody. We were all pretty much in disbelief.

I contacted the radio operator at the battleship again and told him what was going on. He seemed to understand, and we agreed to use just a single gun to try and target the NVA. They fired a round, and a few seconds later the round ripped through the sky and exploded just behind the NVA.

Dave and I looked at each other. "Okay, try it again."

I got back with the radio operator, and they adjusted the next round. It came in a few seconds later, and again, it missed behind him. I got back with him a third time, and again, another miss.

Meanwhile, the NVA was just wandering back and forth across the valley, zigzagging around with no rhyme or reason.

*Boom!* Another round, another miss.

It was incredible. We'd give the adjustment, then they'd fire a round—and every time the guy would just manage to slip out of range. We chased the guy around the valley for probably thirty min-

utes, with just a single artillery round at a time. Eventually we just
gave up, and the guy slipped off into the trees, gone forever.

But what're you gonna do? We'd already used up no telling how
many rounds of 16-inch shells. And what I'd thought would last for
probably, oh, five minutes had gone on for close to an hour. The
radio operator on the battleship already couldn't believe it; he said
we'd put a good-sized dent in their ammunition supply.

Those navy guys were great—cooperative, friendly, and right on
target with their guns—and even though I knew I'd never get to
thank any of them in person, I told the radio operator I was sure
grateful for all their help. That ambush was a total team effort, and
the guys on the battleship had done a top-notch job.

When the dust settled, I radioed our CO back at LZ English to
give him the good report. The ambush had been a success, and I
knew they'd be pleased to hear it. They told us to stay put: they
were sending an infantry platoon in to get a body count and check
for papers, and they'd need us to give them directions.

About forty-five minutes later they sent word that the choppers
were in the air, and they gave me the radio frequency for the platoon's RTO and the chopper pilots. About five minutes after that I
started hearing the choppers approaching from the south.

I switched over to the slick's frequency and made contact with the
lead pilot. They were moving in at an angle perpendicular to the
trail, so I directed them into a clearing that was within easy walking
distance of the ambush site. The choppers set down gently in a
clearing, and the troops emerged in single-file lines, spreading
slowly throughout the valley. From where we were sitting, we had a
great view of the operation, and the platoon had soon engulfed the
area we'd designated earlier as Alpha.

Within minutes they were moving back toward the choppers; apparently they'd gotten everything they could and were satisfied with
the findings. They filed aboard the choppers and were about to take
off when they started receiving rifle fire from the opposite side of the

valley. The choppers quickly ascended and accelerated away from the valley floor, moving clear of the small-arms fire.

Once they were safely out of range, one of the pilots called back over the radio, "Good job, Lurps. Looks like you guys really did a number on them."

And I guess he was right. What started out as a mission that wasn't supposed to be very active had turned pretty interesting—almost an hour's worth of fire support from a naval battleship and then a platoon of infantrymen flying in for the cleanup. Those guys got to see the damage up close, and I guess it probably looked pretty bad. In fact, with all the activity that had been going on, I'd almost forgotten to worry about our Vietnamese friends, but they seemed to be getting along fine—or at least they weren't getting in the way, which is really about all I'd hoped for anyway. With first-timers like that, you could pretty much consider no news to be good news, just as long as they stayed quiet and didn't get us into trouble.

The rest of the day passed quietly, and we eventually settled down for our last night on the mountain. By then—our third night out— we'd normally have changed positions. We liked to relocate every day or so to keep the enemy from getting a sense for where we were—especially after calling in an artillery strike, since they'd figure that there was a Lurp team hiding somewhere out there and watching. But this time, with the security of our observation post and the amount of time we had left, we figured it would be okay. Just one more night and we'd be back at LZ English.

About ten o'clock that night we started hearing the voices again, coming up from the valley floor, but this time they were much closer than they had been the first two nights. The group of NVA were apparently just down the mountain from us, somewhere along the crease in the terrain where the mountain met the valley.

It was fairly dark out at this point—the moon wasn't nearly as bright as it had been the previous week when we were crossing the rice paddies in the middle of the night—but I could see the rest of the Lurps in silhouette. We were all either sitting or lying down, having eaten our rations earlier in the evening. And as always, we remained quiet.

Hearing voices like that didn't normally bother most of the more experienced Lurps. One of the things you realized fairly early on was that people speaking in loud voices didn't know you were around; otherwise, they wouldn't be talking in their normal speaking voices. But for the Vietnamese who were with us, I think it was downright terrifying to hear those voices. The NVA at the foot of the mountain were no more than a hundred meters away, and judging from the racket they were making, I figured they must've been at least ten or twenty strong.

Dave and I eased over the edge of the rocks to see if we could get a look at the group down below. What we saw made my stomach turn. Standing there down at the base of the hill was a group of NVA, waving probably a dozen or more flashlights around in the dark.

I turned my head to Dave. "As long as they stay down there, we'll be fine."

Unfortunate choice of words. No sooner had I gotten them out of my mouth than the NVA just turned and started heading up the side of the mountain. Fifteen flashlights, all pointed in our direction, and getting closer with every step. Of course, I still didn't think they knew we were up there, but in just a few minutes it wouldn't really matter one way or the other because they'd be sitting right there in our laps.

They were still talking fairly loudly, so Dave called Sergeant Pao over to the rock to see if he could understand what they were saying. He couldn't.

I made contact with LZ English, whispering into the radio just as softly as I could. I let them know that we were facing a pretty serious situation, and that it was developing rapidly into a crisis.

Dave leaned over. "Tell them we need an extraction. Immediately."

The NVA were getting closer and closer, and we were still sitting there in our perimeter. I whispered to the radio operator that we needed an extraction, and he said they were scrambling the choppers as we spoke.

By this point the NVA had moved to within seventy-five meters of our position, and they showed no signs of stopping. They were slowly but steadily ascending the mountain, and within minutes I expected them to reach the brush that was lining the ground around us. We were hanging on to a certain advantage in that, as far as we knew, they still didn't know we were up there, but it was only a matter of minutes before that would change. And once they figured out we were there, they'd be in a perfect position to loft a grenade right over on top of us.

Dave leaned in to give us the instructions: "When the choppers are within five, we blow the claymores."

That's all he said, but that's all he needed to say. We knew exactly what to do—once the choppers got to within five minutes of us, we'd blow the claymores and hightail it to the nearest LZ. Sergeant Pao repeated the instructions to the others, then we all just sat there and waited.

The NVA moved to within forty meters. I was crouched down on the other side of the rock, trying to stay low, but I could see the light from their flashlights dancing across the trees above us. They were about to get too close for me to talk anymore, so I radioed the RTO and told him I couldn't talk, for fear that they might hear me. He understood and said that he'd communicate in only yes or no questions; that way I could respond by just pressing the squelch button: one time for yes, two times for no.

Dave was perched over the rock, watching carefully. I adjusted myself behind the rocks so I could just see over the edge. What I saw was twenty or thirty NVA—and they'd moved to within twenty-five meters of us.

The RTO came back over the radio and asked me if they'd gotten any closer; I pressed the squelch button once for yes. I was holding the receiver up to my ear, and almost immediately after that one of the chopper pilots came over the frequency, saying they were about six minutes away. I peeped back over the rock to see what was happening, and the NVA had moved to within ten or fifteen meters of us—this was getting too close for comfort.

Now, at that point, I had to do something that normally I wouldn't have had to deal with, and honestly I wasn't any too thrilled about it: I had to switch the antennae on the radio—as if things couldn't get any worse, right? Because we were about to take off, I needed to remove the antenna I was using and replace it with another, more mobile antenna.

Over the course of a mission we usually used two different types of antennae: a short, flat antenna that we used while moving and a long, whiplike antenna that we used for longer-range communications. Since we'd been sitting in the same position for nearly the entire mission, we'd naturally been using the longer, more reliable, whip antenna.

The whip antenna folded up to about a foot in length, but when it was attached to the radio and unfurled to its full length, it was nearly ten feet long. This didn't make its removal any easier, as you can imagine, and because the NVA were right there, I had do it in absolute silence.

I slowly unscrewed the long whip, my fingers moving just as quietly as I could make them, and placed it against a stand of bamboo at the back of our perimeter. I knew that the NVA must be very close by now—probably only a few feet away. I removed the short whip from my ruck and quickly screwed it on, being as careful as I'd ever been in my life.

I got it on and looked up at Dave. He gave me a nod. This was it. With the NVA on top of us, it was either now or never.

He was holding the detonators in his right hand, poised for the explosion. I reached over and tapped Sergeant Pao on the knee, he turned and signaled the others, Dave gave us one last look, and then, in a quick fluid motion, he squeezed the detonators together.

The explosion rocked the side of the mountain, dirt filled the air, and in an instant we were off and running.

The plan was for us to blow the claymores and then try to make it to the valley floor—the nearest LZ was about six or seven hundred meters away, down in a clearing amid some trees at the edge of the valley—but as soon as we started running I knew it was gonna be tricky. For one thing, it was really dark—where was the moon when you needed it?—and for another, those NVA back there had to be extremely pissed off.

At least our timing was good—within seconds of firing the claymores, I could hear the sounds of the choppers moving into the valley—*thump-thump-thump-thump-thump*—just over my right shoulder. And in a move that may have saved our lives, the guys at headquarters had coordinated with the battleship to fire flares over the valley once the choppers got there—we were climbing over some brush when they fired the first set. With the choppers circling above, the flares lit up the night sky like a fireworks display, and for a few seconds we could actually see where we were going. Of course, on the downside, any NVA in the area could probably see us too, but at the time we needed that light to make it through the trees.

We cleared the brush and came to a steep embankment that was covered with grass. Dave was leading the way, with me following close behind, and we were moving so fast that Dave just hit the slope running—and when he did, his feet flew out from under him and he started sliding down the bank on the seat of his pants.

Well, I'd managed to stop at the top somehow, and as I was waiting for him to hit the bottom, his rifle went off and fired a round right past my head. That was about the closest I'd come to getting hit, and it was coming from my own TL. What had happened, of course, was that he was holding his rifle out with one hand, and when he hit the slope, he'd just accidentally squeezed the trigger. There wasn't any time to worry about it then, so I just steadied myself and scooted down the slope after him.

We continued running until we finally burst into the clearing at the edge of the valley. Two gunships were already circling high overhead, probably a thousand feet up, to give us fire support, and the extraction chopper was hovering just above the treetops, ready to pick us up.

As soon as we hit the clearing Dave started signaling the extraction chopper into the LZ with a strobe light. It settled down toward the grass, and before it even had time to touch the ground, our four Vietnamese friends were already on board—literally, it was probably three feet off the ground, and those guys were just clambering up in there. Of course, I wasn't too far behind them myself—I think we were all pretty glad to be getting out of this one. I climbed in through the opening in the chopper and quickly sat against the wall. As I looked around at the others, I felt all right—two Lurps, four ARVN, and we'd all done a pretty good job.

A couple of days later I ran into Dave over on the Hill. He was sitting with Harry Bell, and they were cleaning up their rifles.

"Hey, you'd better get that safety looked at—thing's liable to go off." I pulled up a seat and slapped Dave on the shoulder. He knew I was kidding, of course, since we never actually used our safeties—for us, it was pretty much either automatic or semiautomatic at all times.

"Aw, Harry, I damn near took off Shan's head the other day—we went running down this hill, and I accidentally squeezed off a round," Dave laughed. "Damn thing must've gone right by his head."

"Harry, let me tell you, that thing wasn't that far from my head."
I held up my fingers to indicate how close it'd come.

"Course, *you* didn't get run over by all those ARVN—I think I
just about broke my back trying to get out of the way."

"Those guys were moving, weren't they?"

"Aw, man, when I set off those claymores, those guys just about
knocked me down trying to get out of there."

"I don't think I've ever seen anybody climb up into a slick the
way those guys did—darn thing was near three feet off the ground
and those guys were already inside."

"Yeah, I'd say they were pretty glad to get off of that mountain."

"Yeah, well, they weren't the only ones."

The laughter usually came a little easier once you got back inside
the walls of LZ English. Dave and I, we could laugh about it now,
in the safety of the base, but out there, with those NVA climbing up
the hill, you didn't really have time to stop and appreciate the
humor in the situation.

Another thing Dave got a kick out of was me swapping out those
antennae the way I did—sometimes later on I'd hear him telling that
story, saying he'd never seen anybody change out antennae without
making any noise, but that I'd sure done it. The funny thing was,
when we'd taken off running, I just left that antenna sitting there
against the bamboo. Didn't think twice about taking it with me—
for all I know, it could still be sitting there.

But really, things had gone pretty darn well, considering. That
was the first and only time I'd ever have to run with a group of
ARVN, and overall I thought it had gone just about as well as I
could've hoped. We didn't have any serious trouble with our communication like I'd feared. Sitting there in the same OP for four days
probably helped us out; we didn't have to move around too much,
so there wasn't a need for constant communication back and forth.
And the support we'd been given was just about perfect, not just

from the guys on the ship but from the guys back at LZ English too—
getting us out that last night could've ended up as a real disaster, but
they came in there and did it, without a hitch.

By this time I'd been in the Lurps for nearly two months, so I was
beginning to feel pretty good about myself. Of course, I wasn't as
veteran as Dave or some of the others, but I sure didn't feel like a
"cherry" anymore either. I felt like I'd seen enough things that I
could pretty much handle any situation.

Late one afternoon one of the other team leaders, a friend of mine
named Patrick Tadina, came around, and we got to talking about
some of his missions. "Tad," as we called him around the base, was
actually sort of famous for having run so many missions—so many
*successful* missions. As it turned out, I'd soon get the chance to run
with him myself—and if I thought I'd seen it all before, well . . . I
was about to learn different.

# 4

## Things I'd Never Seen

PATRICK TADINA WAS ONE OF THE SENIOR LURPS ON THE HILL. He'd been in Vietnam since 1965, and he'd been in the service since 1962. For much of that time he'd been stationed in Okinawa, Japan, but even then he'd been a part of a reconnaissance unit: at first with the 503rd Airborne Battle Group and then—after they were redesignated—with the 173rd Airborne Brigade. In the summer of 1965, the brigade was transferred to Vietnam, and Tad had been pulling recon there ever since.

He was part Asian and part Hawaiian—born and raised on the island of Maui—and his ethnic background gave him an almost exotic appearance. His skin was dark, near bronze in color, and he wore his straight black hair combed back to keep it out of his eyes.

Physically, he was actually rather small—probably about five-foot-six and 140 pounds—but he was hard as oak and tougher than a piece of beef jerky. One time he got in a fight with a guy who outweighed him by nearly fifty pounds, and he ended up beating the crap out of the guy. But that was an isolated incident—normally he was one of the most laid-back guys on the base. He wasn't one of those hard-core, roughneck types who liked to get into fistfights and drink a lot of beer—he was just a really nice, quiet type of guy. And that's why everybody liked him.

One time when Tad was down in the Iron Triangle—an area just to the north of Saigon that was famous for VC—he found a couple of puppies sitting around at a VC base camp—a brown one and a black one, and probably intended for the next meal's stew—so he just grabbed one of them up, stuck him inside his shirt, and brought him out with them when they left. Probably saved that dog from no telling what. Tad named him Tango, and when he brought him back to LZ English the guys around the base just took to him right off—he ended up becoming something of a mascot. You'd see Tango hanging around the camp, just as content as could be, playing with the guys or eating scraps or just lounging around in the sun.

But he always loved Tad the most—I can remember seeing Tad walking around English with that little black dog padding right along behind him, just a few feet back. And the funny thing was that Tad would even take him along on the overflights; he'd be getting ready for some important mission, and there Tango would be, right there beside him. Tango loved it—he'd sit up in that chopper, with his tongue hanging out, just as proud as he could be.

I guess that was the thing that ultimately made Tad unique. He was different in so many ways: he looked different, he conducted himself different, and out in the field he acted different. But it was that unique combination of being a nice and humble guy and, at the same time, a tenacious and driven soldier that made him seem like such a paradox. Seeing him hanging around the camp with that dog, all quiet and unassuming, was hard to square with all the things I'd heard told about him, the things he'd done out in the field—all the missions, all the kills.

But I guess the best way to describe Tadina would be to describe some of those missions that we ran, because Tad was no more at home than when he was out on a mission. He was a natural. The real deal. And to see him at work—that was something special.

The way the teams operated—or at least the way we did it at that time, when there were still only about four or five teams up on the Hill—was that once you were selected to run with one group, you basically stayed put until something happened to cause you to leave. Team chemistry was such an important element that once you got with a group you were comfortable with, you tended to stick with them for as long as you could.

But even with that general way of doing things, there was still a pretty good bit of overlap, and that's how it was that I ended up running with Tad. Teams would link up, people would get hurt, guys would go on R&R—there were several different reasons a person could end up running with somebody else, and that's basically the way it was with me and Tad. I ended up running with him probably seven or eight times, and I think there was a different set of circumstances for each of those missions.

With Tad, though, there was always one circumstance you could be sure didn't apply: it wasn't that one of his team members had gotten hit. That was part of the mystique of running with Tad—out of all those missions he'd run, he'd never had a single person get hurt. He'd been hit himself a couple of times, but not a single one of his men had ever been hit. Nobody had been killed. Nobody had even been shot.

It was incredible, really. Around camp it was one of those things that everybody knew but nobody talked about—not to Tad anyway. It was kind of like in baseball when a pitcher's throwing a no-hitter. You don't want to mention it to him, for fear of jinxing the streak. Not until the game's over anyway. But we all knew—everybody knew—that running with Tad, no matter how dangerous the mission, no matter how crazy the circumstance, nobody ever got hit.

When I first got the chance to run with him, his ATL was a guy named Kenneth Murray. Murray was a big guy from up in New England somewhere—Connecticut, I think—and though I hadn't run any missions with him yet, I knew him to be a pretty good guy. He was a good Lurp—pretty much anyone who trained under Tad was a good Lurp—and he was a nice guy as well. I'd see him around the base, and he was always real friendly and generous.

His nickname was Moose—I guess because he was so dang strong—and around the base that's always what I heard him called. In fact, I think it was probably the *only* thing I ever heard him called. He was probably about six-foot-one or so, and when he stood there along with Tad, he looked just that much taller. Next to Tad, Moose looked like an All-American tight end.

But I had complete confidence in both of those guys. So whenever I got a chance to run with them, I didn't hesitate to agree.

On the first mission that we ran together our assignment was fairly simple: infiltrate the Suoi Ca Valley, set up an observation post above the trail—probably along the edge of the ridge somewhere at the top of the mountain—and on the last day, if it seemed appropriate, set up and pull an ambush. For us, it seemed like a fairly standard mission—dangerous as always, but still, a fairly typical, and basic, mission.

From top to bottom, Tad had a pretty reliable team, so the mission didn't seem to provide any obvious obstacles for us, outside the normal dangers of being in enemy territory running small-team recon. We felt pretty confident about it going in—but as I'd learn, feeling confident was often the best signal to expect the unexpected.

They dropped us off on the first day in a small clearing near the top of the mountain, on the opposite side from the valley and on the opposite side from the trail that we were scheduled to watch. The insertion went off without a hitch, and by the middle of the second day we'd already established an OP from which we could watch the trail without a whole lot of problems. So we started our observation routine, with each person taking a turn watching the valley through a pair of binoculars.

Now, the Suoi Ca Valley is located about thirty kilometers to the south of LZ English and fifteen or twenty kilometers from the coast of the South China Sea. Though the terrain there was fairly thick, with low shrubbery and a medium-sized canopy, there weren't actually a whole lot of tall trees around, not in the same way that there were in some of the other parts of the highlands. This meant that we could see the valley without having to climb any trees to get a better view. Another interesting point about this particular area was the fact that the valley floor actually opened up on both ends. Unlike some of the valleys that were surrounded on three sides, the Suoi Ca Valley was bordered by mountain on only two sides, with the trail and the river running down the middle between them.

When it was my turn to watch the valley, I took my position near a tree and started scanning the valley floor through the pair of binoculars we were using. None of the others had seen any VC yet, which was actually a little unusual by that time of the day, and before long I found out the reason why.

I spotted movement on the opposite side of the valley—and not just a little bit of movement, like you might see when a couple of NVA regulars come walking down the trail, but rather, some serious, significant movement, as in an entire infantry company, emerging one by one from the edge of the trees. But what was incredible about it was this: as I watched them filing down out of the tree line, I realized, much to my surprise, that it was an *American* infantry company—a group of steel pots, coming down out of the bush, just like the group I'd been running with those few months before. I shook my head in disbelief. This was unbelievable. Somebody had obviously messed up, and it sure wasn't us.

I signaled over to Tad that we had company, and quickly he moved over beside me to get a better look. When I looked back a second

time, things had gotten even worse: apparently somebody had decided
that the valley floor would make a good place to set up camp for the
night, so a bunch of the grunts had dropped off their rucksacks and
started setting up a perimeter right there in the middle of the valley.

Tad took the binoculars from me, and after peering through them
for a couple of seconds, he pulled them away and gave me a look
like *"What the ———?"* He couldn't believe what he was seeing either. He surveyed the situation for a few minutes longer, then decided to contact English to get this thing sorted out.

Obviously somebody had screwed up, and he wanted to make
sure that this infantry company didn't mistake us for a bunch of
NVA out there in the bush. If they didn't even know where they
were—and clearly somebody hadn't been reading their map right—
then there was no telling what they might think to see us come
traipsing down out of the brush. And didn't *none* of us want to get
caught up in a friendly fire situation.

Tad wasted little time in getting English on the radio. It was a safe
bet that those guys in the infantry company didn't know we were
around—normally there wouldn't have been any friendly troops
within miles—and he wanted to make sure they were notified that
we were there.

Tadina talked quietly, but firmly, into the radio, and when he was
finished with the conversation, he put the receiver down and turned
to us to give us the results: "We have to wait here," he said, "while
they try and get it figured out."

Seemed like a reasonable response. So that's what we did. We sat
and we waited.

I looked through the binoculars, back down at the infantry company milling around in the valley; by now the entire company had
appeared, and they were fully involved in the business of preparing
their nighttime accommodations: a cluster of tents now lined the
valley floor, strung up between trees and covered over with camouflage tarps to keep them hidden from view.

It was odd to see them down there, nearly a hundred men, less than three hundred yards away, with not a clue in the world that we were up there watching them. How many times, I couldn't help wondering, had this very thing happened to me while I was in the rifle company—except, instead of a bunch of Lurps looking down at us, it was probably a bunch of VC or a group of NVA, sitting hidden among the trees? How many nights had we set up camp with a group of VC looking down at us? And how many times had we broken open our C rations under the watchful eye of the NVA? For that matter, there could've been a group of VC watching over this company right now—the brush was thick enough and easy enough to find cover in; they could've been hiding there in the trees just as easily as we were.

I shook my head at the thought of it. If we'd been the enemy, sitting there from our vantage point and equipped with, say, a couple of M-60s or a mortar round or two, we could've taken out a pretty good number of those guys.

Finally, after an hour or so of waiting, the guys at headquarters got back with us and gave us the scoop. They said they'd made contact with the CO of the company and that they'd arranged for us to go down there and join them. At that point they'd send out a couple of helicopters to pick us up and return us to LZ English.

Well, that was all fine and good in theory, but Tad wanted to make sure that *all* of the guys down there in the valley were aware that we were on our way. He didn't want any accidents, or some nervous private getting a little trigger-happy when we came walking down out of the grass.

He told the guys at English to relay a message back to the company, telling them to pop a green smoke grenade if they were aware of our presence and expecting us to come down. Sure enough, about five minutes later we saw the green smoke rising up out of the valley floor, from a point right dead in the center of the company perimeter.

Now, unlike most of the other team leaders, Tad actually ran point for his team when they were out in the field—but in this case he was extra cautious and had one of the other guys lead us down the side of the mountain. With his Hawaiian face, he didn't want the Americans down there to mistake him for a VC creeping down out of the trees.

It wasn't all that unlikely either, considering that Tad's weapon of choice was the AK-47—the same rifle that the NVA used. If someone had seen Tad walking down out of the brush, with his AK prominently displayed, they might have opened fire on him, not realizing he was an American. In fact, though, as we were about to find out, that was actually a lot less likely than we might have normally expected—those guys down there weren't about to open up on *anybody.*

So we followed along behind the new point-man in a single-file line—just pushing our way down through all that thick vegetation— and as we were making our way down the side of that mountain I started hearing all those old familiar sounds, the unmistakable sounds of the line company, banging and clanging, digging in for the night. We were still over two hundred yards away, but I could hear the noises just as plain as day, just like those guys were standing there beside me. I followed along behind the others, just shaking my head in disbelief, feeling bad for the guys in the company.

When we reached the valley floor, we made a point to move out into the opening, getting as free of the trees as we could possibly get, to make sure that they could see us clearly—again, trying to avoid an accident. From there we just walked straight on into the company perimeter—crossing the trail we'd been watching in the process—and walked right on up to the company CO and a bunch of the guys who had gathered around to greet us.

I hadn't really thought about it before, but I realized, once we got down there—and once those guys started circling around, checking us out—that we were all still wearing our face paint and our tiger fatigues and had our arms all painted up with black and green paint. To all of these grunts we must've looked like something from out of a movie, showing up all painted over and appearing from out of the trees like that. And in fact, we really were sort of out in the middle of nowhere, so for us to just appear like that out of thin air, out in the middle of known NVA territory—I can see where it must've looked pretty incredible to those guys.

Tad went directly to the CO and started talking to him, but a bunch of the infantry guys intercepted the rest of us and started asking us a bunch of questions:

"Hey man, what do ya'll eat out there?"

"You seen any VC?"

"How long you been out there? You been out there long?"

*"Man, I can't wait till I see some VC."*

I happened to look over at Tad during all this, and I noticed that he was just as serious as could be. That was one thing about Tad: as nice a guy as he was around the base, as cool and laid-back as he was, whenever he was on a mission, there was no question about his commitment to the job. Out in the field he was all business, and to see him standing there, at a distance, talking to the CO, he cut a fairly striking figure: his thin face, those dark, serious eyes—you could just feel the intensity in his eyes, his total attention focused on the mission, intent on the situation and fully living in the moment. Around the base there were times when it was easy to imagine him back home in Hawaii, walking the beach, kicking around in the surf, but out in the field it was another story—there was no mistaking his intensity or his commitment. When I looked over there at him, for a second I saw him as the grunts in that line company must've seen him—and I realized that for them he made a pretty imposing figure.

Well, we stood around the valley like that for probably the next twenty minutes or so, just waiting for the choppers to arrive, but before long something else unexpected happened. We were standing there talking when about ten or fifteen NVA came walking out of the brush, about seventy-five yards away. They were walking down the trail, just as casual as could be, right down the edge of that valley, with hardly a care in the world. And they were loaded down too, with rucksacks and machine guns; some of them even had branches sticking out of their rucksacks for camouflage.

I looked around at the rest of the team to make sure they were seeing what I was seeing. These guys were just walking right by, and that infantry company hadn't moved a muscle.

And then—I remember it like it was yesterday—one of those NVA just threw his hand up in the air and waved at us.

*Waved at us.*

What in the world was going on here? A group of NVA comes walking by, and these infantry guys don't even flinch. I glanced around at the guys on the Lurp team, and they were just as surprised as I was.

Tad went back over to the CO: "Hey, you got company over there." Which was already obvious to anyone who was paying the least bit of attention, but the CO just sort of nodded, not really showing any sign of recognition.

Those NVA were just strolling along, smiling over at us, about as casual as could be. We all sort of waited for a second and then realized that he wasn't going to do anything. Tad approached him again.

"You're not gonna do anything?"

"Well, it looks like it might be an ARVN outfit."

If I'd been sitting down, I swear that would've knocked me off my seat.

I looked over at Moose, and he just shook his head in amazement. These guys couldn't even tell the difference between a South Vietnamese outfit and an NVA outfit—the guys we were supposedly out there looking for, the guys we were supposed to be shooting, the *enemy*.

Well, by this point those NVA had just about disappeared into the trees—I couldn't believe it—and that CO had just let them walk right on by without firing a single shot.

Finally he decided to radio his own commanding officer to find out exactly what the situation was, and when they told him that there weren't any South Vietnamese anywhere in the area, well, he started to catch on.

By then it was too late.

If he'd sent a crew down there looking for them, well, that would've been suicide—those NVA would have set up an ambush so fast that they wouldn't even have had a chance. For a second it looked as though he was gonna do it anyway, but Tad convinced him not to. "No point in getting a bunch of guys killed over it," he said. "What's done is done."

We waited around a few more minutes, until finally the choppers arrived to pick us up. As we were leaving, flying up over the valley floor, with the company perimeter fading away below us, I couldn't help but feel a little bit sorry for all those guys down there in the infantry company. I'd been in their shoes, and at the time I'd had the feeling that there was a better way. Now that I'd been with the Lurps for a while, I *knew* there was a better way.

Our pilot carried us due east for about forty minutes, then veered north over Bong Son and the sprawling Lai Giang River. He hovered in over the chopper pad at LZ English, then set us down, nice and easy, near a row of parked choppers, sitting still and quiet in the Vietnamese sun.

After the incident with the infantry company, command decided to reinsert us fairly quickly, into a different AO (area of operations)—not too far away from our original position, but far enough away that we wouldn't be running into any stray American outfits.

They dropped us off in a clearing on the backside of a mountain, and we quickly crossed to the valley on the other side, moving slowly down the slope, until we reached a point about two-thirds of the way down. As usual, this was a surveillance mission, and though we'd found a spot that was well hidden and not too far from the edge of the clearing, the slope of the wood line was so gradual that we couldn't get an unobstructed view of the entire trail without first climbing trees and gaining some sort of elevation. Once we got ourselves situated and settled into our trail-watching routine, though, we actually felt like we had it pretty easy. There was a little bit of rain, but it was light, and all of the activity we saw was limited to groups of two or three. This was in keeping with the intel report, which had indicated the presence of small clumps of NVA—groups of five or six, but no more than that.

After a couple of days of simple trail watching, we got word from headquarters to pull an ambush; for some reason, they wanted us to go ahead and do it then, rather than wait for the more typical fourth day. To tell you the truth, we were all pretty glad to hear it. Pulling an ambush meant we might get to finish up early and head back to LZ English.

Now, the way the valley was laid out, we could've moved to the edge of the tree line and pulled the ambush from there; the valley floor was covered in brush and grass, and the trail was only about seventy-five yards from the foot of the mountain. But there was also a stretch of trees that grew out across the valley floor—a funny little peninsula that jutted out like a finger and reached across the floor to the edge of the trail. It wasn't wide, but it looked like it might give us enough cover to get close. So we decided to try and set up an ambush there instead.

A lot of the guys actually preferred being up close whenever we pulled an ambush. There were several good reasons for doing it that way, but I think the main reason was the fact that it gave us a sort of psychological edge. There was something empowering about the element of surprise, in being able to beat the enemy at his own game. And a lot of Lurps thrived on that. Of course, there was also a downside—being closer to the enemy was a more dangerous place to be—but in general we were willing to take the risk.

We moved down the side of the mountain until the ground began to level out, and then we made our way to the strip of trees that grew out across the valley floor. We continued like that until we reached the trail about thirty minutes later.

As it turned out, the layout for the ambush was just about perfect. The trees that grew out across the valley floor extended all the way over to the very edge of the trail, so that anybody walking by had to pass directly beyond the tip of those trees. And when we moved back from the trail, we still had a view of the valley floor, clear and open in both directions.

The rest of the valley was covered in yellow grass, maybe waist-high and not too thick, just sort of scattered and dry. The trail was a well-worn path that meandered, more or less in a straight line, down the center of the clearing. It emerged from the trees at the far end of the clearing—150 yards or so to our left—and it passed right along in front of us until it disappeared again on the far end of the clearing on the right.

We set up in an ambush formation, just along the edge of the trail—but still a few feet off, back among the trees, to make sure we had some cover until the action started—and waited. We didn't set out any claymores because we didn't think we'd need any. All we'd been seeing at that point were small groups of two or three VC, and we had no reason to think we'd be seeing any groups larger than that.

That was a fairly bold decision, but it was in keeping with Tad's way of doing things—he was one of the most particular, and careful, of the Lurps, but he could also be quite daring. I don't think he liked using the claymores anyway; I think he preferred the control and intensity of small-arms fire. That preference was in line with the psychological battle going on—there was a certain cachet about using small-arms fire. And Tad liked to use it for all it was worth.

We'd set up our position, and I was sitting there, sort of squatted down in these leaves, trying my best to ignore the mosquitoes that were flying around—it'd been raining, so the mosquitoes had really gotten stirred up—when Tadina decided to climb up a little tree to try and get a better view of the trail. We'd been sitting there for about forty-five minutes and hadn't seen the first sign of the enemy anywhere, so he was just gonna climb up there to see if he could see anything farther out in the distance.

Well, no sooner had he gotten up there than we got our first signs of activity—a single NVA running out of the trees at the far end of the clearing. I snapped my fingers to get Tad's attention, and about that time a second one came running out—and they both dropped to a knee, with their rifles at the ready, one on each side of the trail, about ten yards out from the mouth of the trail as it emerged from the trees.

I looked up at Tad; he'd climbed up this little tiny tree, no bigger round than a maple-syrup can, about fifteen feet up, and he was just peering through the binoculars, checking those guys out.

Shortly after the two point-men had appeared, a second pair emerged, only these guys were walking along at a fairly leisurely pace, real casual. One of them appeared to be an NVA officer of some sort—he had a clipboard with him, of all things—and the other one actually sort of looked like an American. He had a Cau-casian look to him, but beyond that I couldn't really tell what was going on. Then a third guy came out and walked over to the pair of them, and the three of them stood there together in a group, just off to the side of the trail.

I glanced back up at the tree to see what Tad was doing, but by that point he'd already slipped back down—apparently deciding he needed to find some better cover. There was a pause in the action, a stillness across the valley, and for a moment I didn't know what was going to happen. I strained my eyes to see down the trail. And that's when they started to appear.

One by one, a line of NVA emerged from the trees, in a single-file formation. It was the largest group I'd ever seen—marching down the trail, about five meters apart, in a slow and methodical pace, right toward our position. I couldn't believe it—I'd never seen anything like it—but what could we do? They were coming right toward us, and we didn't have time to get back. We had no other option but just to sit there, as still as we could—and to hope that we'd hidden ourselves far enough back in those trees.

I sat there with my body still and tense—as tense as I'd been on any mission yet—moving only my eyes. The NVA came filing down the trail, and as they neared I could feel my heart beating in my chest—this was it, I had to be as quiet and still as I'd ever been. When I became conscious of my breathing, I tried not to move my chest.

The point-man approached—moving now to within fifteen meters or so of our position—and though he was attentive, he appeared relaxed and at ease, which was a good sign for us—he apparently hadn't seen us sitting there in the brush.

As a Lurp, I'd finally gotten to see the enemy that had so often eluded me while I was a member of the line company. I'd gotten a good look at the VC in the last few months. I'd seen them up close, even gone through their pockets as they lay dead across a trail. I'd seen the hard-core NVA, traveling in their close-knit groups, with their twigs and their camouflage and their AK-47s. Only days before we'd seen that group of NVA on the trail near the river.

Over time I'd learned the traits and habits of both VC and NVA—and as far as I was concerned, there was nothing tougher than a group of NVA regulars. Like us, they were professional, fully trained, and fully intent on doing their jobs—and in this case, there was no question that was what they'd do if they saw us. This was a full-size battalion of hard-core NVA.

The first one approached, and I could see him just as clearly as if he was coming down a catwalk. He was wearing a khaki uniform with a pith helmet, and he was carrying an AK-47, holding it loosely in both hands.

He moved to within a few meters of our position—I could hear his pants rustling together—then passed right on by, without missing a step. My nerves were on end, but the fact that he'd passed was a relief—apparently we were well enough hidden that our presence wasn't obvious. We hadn't been careless and left any obvious signs that we were there, and we'd hidden ourselves deep enough in the brush that for someone to have seen us they'd have had to have been looking pretty darn close—but of course, with that many people coming by, we couldn't be sure that they wouldn't.

As the first one moved on by, I started counting them—one by one as they passed—and I didn't stop until I got to 140. Even then, they just kept on coming. There were more of them there in that line than I'd seen anywhere, VC or NVA, and they were so close that if anything had gone wrong—if they'd had any indication at all that we were there—we'd have been dead. We might could've taken out a few, but with numbers like that, they would have wiped us out for sure.

We were so close that I could see the sweat rolling down their faces. And we could hear them talking back and forth, laughing occasionally—if I'd spoken Vietnamese, I could've clearly understood their conversations. Honestly, we were so close, if I'd wanted to spit on those guys as they'd walked by, I could've done it easily. At the nearest point they passed by they were less than five meters away.

After several minutes of just watching these guys walk by, I started feeling my muscles getting tight—I was sitting down in a sort of squat, and it was really straining the muscles in my calves and thighs—and then, to top it off, my feet started going to sleep. Of course, there was no way to relieve either problem. With all the NVA walking by, I couldn't adjust myself without risking detection. So I just sat there and tried to bear it. Didn't scratch, didn't blink, barely even breathed. And I just let my feet stay asleep.

Cam Ranh Bay, April 1968. Welcome to Vietnam!

One of our many nighttime perimeters. Pitching camp for our nightly
bivouac became routine for Dog Company. Bill Pfister is on the right.

The VC base camp in Phu
Yen province where we
discovered the well and
the rice cache. This photo
was taken just minutes
before the ambush.

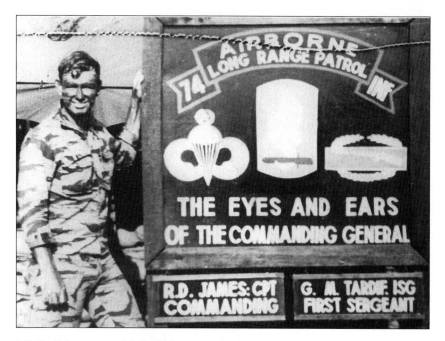

LZ English, summer 1968. Welcome to the Lurps!

Lurp Hill—
my new home-
away-from-home.

By the hooches on the Hill.
I was just happy to be there.

Training at LZ
English. The rappelling
tower was the site for
some of our most
rigorous sessions.

All ready for a mission in my face paint and tiger fatigues.

Dave Brueggmann on the way to the chopper pad. The rifle he's carrying is a CAR–15, a slightly shorter version of the M–16.

A Lurp team just getting
back from the field.

"Chief"

Kenneth Murray

Cameron McAllister

Arthur "Harry" Bell

Kenneth Murray and Patrick Tadina (a.k.a. "Moose" and "Tad").

Pete Campbell's team, early 1969. This was the same team that called in the artillery support to scare off the NVA.

Again with Pete's team just back from a mission.

Left to right: Dick James, G. M. Tardif, Rick Jones, Pete Campbell. This photo was taken in 1969, after the company had made the transition to Ranger status.

Tad and Tango at LZ English. Tango was everybody's friend, but he always loved Tad the most.

Prepping for a mission.
I'd just finished putting
on my face paint.

A typical day in
Bong Son. Note the
military trucks in
the background.

LZ English, 1969. Relaxing in my hooch

Eventually, though, the line of NVA started coming to an end. The one Caucasian-looking guy passed by, and as he did I strained my ear to try and catch a stray remark, a comment, anything, just to see what he sounded like—to see if I could recognize his accent— but I never heard him say a thing. The other two officer-looking guys and the two forward scouts fell in behind the rest of them, and then, just like that, they were gone. Off into the distance.

We still didn't move, though. Not at first. We just sort of let out our breaths in relief—we'd hidden ourselves well, apparently, but still, we were fortunate not to have been spotted. The slightest twitch, a broken stick or twig, and we would've been toast. We didn't have any claymores to collect, so after a few minutes—after we were convinced they were gone—we all just pulled back, disappearing into the undergrowth and getting ourselves a safe distance away from that trail.

Once we'd gotten clear of the trail, Tadina radioed LZ English to let them know what had happened. When we'd first seen how many NVA there were, our RTO had wisely turned off the radio to keep it from squawking or squealing and giving away our position; as it turned out, the guys back at headquarters had thought we'd gotten ourselves into some pretty serious trouble. Which, in a way of course, we had, but our situation wasn't nearly as bad as it would've been if one of those NVA had spotted us.

Tad got them on the radio and filled them in on what had happened—explained why we'd had the radio off and told them in no uncertain terms how many NVA we'd seen. That news apparently caused quite a stir among everybody back at headquarters, including the adjutant general. They'd expected us to find the enemy, but nobody expected us to come across a group like that—that was definitely the biggest group that I'd seen, and it was the biggest group that I'd heard about. So naturally everybody got pretty excited.

The general wanted us to still try and pull an ambush, so we moved back up the slope a little ways and set up our camp for the night. Tad pulled out a hammock and tied it up between two trees so he could sleep up off the ground—the rest of us picked out a small clearing and slept there in the grass. We were all pretty well used to the wet weather by that point, but I have to admit that that hammock was a pretty good idea. When the rain started coming down later that night, the ground got soaked, and us along with it. I think one guy even got a couple of leeches on him.

The next day, when we set up to initiate the ambush, we didn't get nearly as close as we'd been before. If we happened to get a repeat performance from that previous group, we didn't want to be sitting right on top of them, when they came back through.

Now, all the NVA we'd seen before had been traveling from left to right—all of the smaller groups we'd seen that first day, as well as the larger, battalion-sized group we'd seen on the second day—but just a few minutes after we'd gotten situated, the first group of the day appeared at the far end of the trail, moving from right to left.

Like the first few groups we'd seen, this was only a pair of NVA, but they were walking at an odd spacing, about fifteen to twenty feet apart, which could've been an indication that there were more to follow. Tad didn't wait around to find out.

Once the first guy had cleared the tree line by about thirty meters, I heard a loud burst of gunfire coming from just to my left—Tad had opened up on him.

The second guy fell immediately. The first guy slumped forward, like somebody had punched him in the back of the head, and then, apparently having regained his composure, he took off running, at a full sprint, toward the tree line on the other side of the valley.

By the time we got over there, he was already dead. After a frantic few seconds of searching, we found him lying in a thicket of bamboo. Somehow he'd managed to run about seventy-five yards after he'd been shot and before he'd finally collapsed—but by the time we got over there to him and found him lying in the bamboo, he had nothing left.

When we got back to LZ English, we had the longest debriefing I'd ever been a part of; they wanted to know every detail, every stitch and sound, every weapon and sandal. They kept us there for nearly two hours, and by the time we were done they'd gotten all the information they could squeeze out of us—and we were all pretty exhausted.

They took us back up to the Hill, and after I'd taken a long, drum-temperature shower—for me, that was always the first priority after we got back from a mission—I just lay back on my bunk and closed my eyes. We'd had a pretty eventful week, first with the friendly rifle company and then with the NVA battalion, and I was feeling pretty tired.

If one of my complaints about being in the line company had been that we never got any good looks at the enemy, I definitely couldn't say the same about the Lurps. After sitting by that trail, with all those NVA going by, I felt like I was sitting right there in the middle of them.

And really, I was feeling pretty fortunate to have gotten out with as little trouble as we did. When we were sitting there in that ambush and saw those first two NVA coming out of the trees, we wouldn't have made it out if we'd opened up on those guys without waiting to see how many there were. That was actually one of the few times when we sat in an ambush and didn't fire a shot. But of course, we had made it out, and I guess that was just part of it—call it luck, good fortune, God's will, whatever, but we'd been in another tough situation and come out of it unscathed.

A few days later I heard that a fire-support base to the south had gotten hit by a group of NVA; nobody knew for sure if it was the same group, but I couldn't help but wonder—and I also couldn't

help but wonder what headquarters had done with all that information we'd given them.

In any case, I didn't have time to worry about it. Tad came by
later that afternoon and told me we'd gotten our next assignment:
we were going to the Fishhook.

There was a guy from New Mexico named Reyes—"Chief" we
called him—and I'd gotten to be pretty good friends with him while
I was there at the base. He was an American Indian, and he had a
sort of comical personality. He always had an interesting way of
looking at things, and an interesting way with words.

After Tad came by and told me about our assignment, I started
down the Hill to see the supply sergeant, and on the way down I ran
into Chief out in front of his hooch.

"Hey, Shan, you 'bout to head back out, man?"

"Hey, Chief, how you doing?" I said. "Yeah, Tad just stopped by.
Said we got another mission lined up."

"Oh, yeah? Where you going?"

"Well, it looks like we're headed to the Fishhook."

Now, somehow Chief had picked up the Vietnamese habit of rat-
ing everything as either a 1 or a 10. All the locals used to rate things
as either a 1 or a 10 to indicate what they thought about it: a 1 meant
that something was good, and a 10 meant that something was bad.
When I told Chief about the Fishhook, he was quick to respond.

"Ooh, Shan." He pulled his head back and whistled. "That's
number 10, man. Fishhook's definitely number 10." He shook his
head slowly.

And I knew exactly what he meant.

The Fishhook was one of the most notorious areas in the entire
region. It was known among the Lurps as extremely dangerous and,
even worse, just plain scary. There was something about the area—
the tall canopy, the empty floors, the dim lighting that filtered down
through the leaves—that gave it an almost ghostly appearance. The

Fishhook was haunting and shadowy, and it was one of the few places that people just really didn't want to go to.

The Fishhook was situated about twenty-five kilometers to the northwest of LZ English, at the far end of the An Lao Valley. The An Lao was a major river that ran north to south and twisted along the northern border of Binh Dinh Province, just to the south of Quang Ngai. At the far end of the river, amid the sprawling mountains and the towering trees, there was a curious little bend that looped back around and then turned back straight; it didn't form a complete U-shape, but it did loop around, and for a short bit the river seemed to run back on itself. From the air it looked, of course, like a big, muddy fishhook. I don't know who had first called it that, the Fishhook—that was just the name that I'd always heard it called—but when you flew over it in a helicopter, the name seemed absolutely perfect.

The terrain there was unlike any other I'd seen—I'd been there before, one time with Dave, and I was struck by how tall the trees were. The upper canopy was probably a hundred feet high, and the limbs were interwoven so densely that they blocked out the sun and cast an eerie glow on the entire region. I don't know what kind of trees they were, but they were extremely tall, and they made our insertions and extractions extremely difficult. Another problem was how completely the trees obscured any possible view of the enemy's trails; while many of the trails throughout the highlands could be seen from the air, by helicopter, those within the Fishhook were completely hidden from view—and thus, so was the enemy.

Because of the dim lighting, the floor of the Fishhook was unusually free of brush—which meant it was also unusually free of cover. For a Lurp team, cover was about as important an issue as there was; without proper cover, things could get dangerous really quickly. The whole point of a Lurp team was to move around without being detected. That's why it didn't matter that we might be completely outnumbered—since nobody knew we were there, we were always able to maintain the element of surprise. But with no cover, with a limited ability to disappear into the landscape, well, that changed the dynamic. Out in the open, we were just as vulnerable as the next guy.

But the biggest variable of all about the Fishhook—or at least what I was most concerned about—was the presence of the Montagnard tribesmen. Unlike some of the other areas we ran in, the Fishhook was densely occupied by these indigenous tribes that lived throughout the Central Highlands. The Montagnards were groups of native peoples who lived in a completely primitive and basic way and found themselves in the very midst of a complex and modern war. They weren't Vietnamese—they were an entirely different ethnic group—and politically they were neither Communist nor capitalist. They were just a bunch of people who were doing what they felt like they had to do to survive the war, and unfortunately that meant that they were susceptible to influence—from *both* sides.

Apparently the Special Forces had recruited and trained scores of Montagnard men, though I wasn't entirely sure what for or to what end, but I'd heard that the VC had managed to get some of the Montagnards under their thumb as well—and unfortunately, a lot of those Montagnards were living in the Fishhook. It wasn't uncommon to hear about these guys tracking Lurp teams around the Fishhook whenever they were out on a mission, and I didn't look forward to sharing the experience.

The Montagnards lived up in the mountains of the most remote parts of the highlands, and in general, they tried to keep to themselves. They lived in these simple grass huts that were built up on stilts, about eight or ten feet off the ground, and they got into them using these little wooden ladders that they would pull back up into them at night or whenever there was trouble. The men wore these raggedy-looking loincloths, and they used to chew on this tobacco-like stuff that made their teeth black and gave even fairly young men an older, grizzled appearance. (I'd learn later on that it was betel nut.) They hunted with crossbows and spoke in their own curious-sounding language, not Vietnamese. (Not that we could've understood them either way.) I'd run into them from time to time when I was in the line company, and in general, they hadn't given us any trouble at all. In fact, I'd done some trading one time with one of the Montagnard women—for some trinkets and bracelets and such. But I'd heard enough stories to know better than to try doing that out there in the Hook.

Apparently, from what I'd heard, the VC operating in the area would force the Montagnards—probably by threatening their families—to track you around and then report back to them, alerting them to your presence. And they would just follow along behind you, picking up on all the subtle little clues you didn't even know you were leaving behind. You might have thought you were doing a good job covering your trail, but to some of these Montagnards it was like you were walking across clean carpet in a muddy pair of boots.

Now, at that point Tad had a pretty experienced team—the five of them, plus myself—so most of them had been to the Fishhook before. Tad had been there several times, and Moose had been there a few times as well. But nobody was really looking forward to going back. I think more teams got chased out of the Fishhook than any other area I knew about, and those who did usually didn't want to go back. It was the worst place a Lurp team could go. When Chief said it was number 10—well, that pretty much summed it up perfectly.

Our mission was to observe the enemy's activity for three days and then wait for our orders for the fourth day. In general, we usually pulled an ambush on the fourth day and then prepared for extraction, but in this case we couldn't be sure what would happen. The Fishhook threw you so many curves that you never knew what the situation would be, or if you'd even still be there on the fourth day—a whole lot of teams got chased out before then.

We left LZ English at about six in the evening, escorted by two Cobra gunships and one C&C chopper. This was a fairly typical departure time, to try and take advantage of the approaching night-time, but it offered little relief from the sun and the heat. Even though we'd waited until late to leave, the temperatures were still in the nineties, and the air, as it whipped in through the open chopper door, was heavy with moisture.

The flight to the Fishhook usually took forty-five minutes or so, and this time it was no different: after thirty-five or forty minutes, Tad gave us the signal that we'd soon be approaching the drop-off point. I hadn't gone on the overflight with Tad—he and Moose had done that the day before—but he'd shown us all on a map where they were planning to drop us off. They'd picked out an LZ that was just to the left of the river—not too far from where it turned in the shape of the fishhook.

Now, most of the time we liked to use an LZ that was up on the side of a mountain, somewhere up high that didn't make us an easy target for any VC or NVA that might happen to be lingering around. But this time Tad had picked out an LZ that was down in the valley, down along the bed of the river, and though I was a little bit nervous about it, I also had a great deal of confidence in his decisionmaking. Even when it might not look like it, or if it was a little bit unconventional, Tad always knew what he was doing.

Our pilot took us over the rim of a mountain, flying wide open, just over the tops of the trees, and then quickly, suddenly, dropped straight down to the valley floor. I just about lost my stomach—it was like being on a roller coaster—but before I had time to even think about it, we were already out and moving. The chopper never even touched the ground, and in an instant it was gone—up and away.

We moved across the ground, toward the tree line, and in the absence of the helicopter, all I could hear was the sound of our clothing brushing up against the grass. There in the valley the ground was covered in dense elephant grass that rose above us in a rich, green umbrella. I tried my best to cover the trail behind us, pulling it back together as we pushed our way through, but as tall as the grass was, it just sort of angled out beside us, leaving a shoulder-width rift all the way to the trees.

Normally I felt better once we made it off the LZ, but there in the Fishhook the trees weren't much of an improvement. The ground was so stark and barren that, even though you were out of the valley, you still felt like you were out in the open. Anywhere else we'd slip off the LZ to find some cover, but there in the Fishhook there was hardly any cover to be found.

We stepped out of the elephant grass at the edge of the valley and made our way slowly into the trees. Just as I remembered, the floor below the trees was largely free of undergrowth, and as we pushed our way up the side of the mountain it became easier and easier to walk—one of the few advantages of the Fishhook.

Tad was running the point, and as he crept along the mountain floor, we followed behind him, one behind the other. We gave ourselves about five meters a piece, and we moved softly and slowly.

I was pulling rear security, so as we moved I was constantly monitoring the ground behind us, trying to make sure we didn't leave any tracks. I was also keeping an eye out all around us, scanning the area to each side, looking as far into the trees as I could see—and there in the Fishhook, with the terrain the way it was, you could actually see for a pretty good distance, sometimes as far as two hundred feet. Which, of course, was the double-edged sword: if we could see that far, then naturally our enemies could too.

Every seventy-five feet or so Tad would come to a stop. He'd listen. We'd all listen. To the trees, to the wind, to the silence. The sounds of the Fishhook. Haunting and still. We knew they were out there, but we couldn't hear a thing.

For the next hour or so we continued moving along the side of that mountain, gradually working our way up to higher ground. We moved at a slight angle, hedging closer and closer toward the top of the ridge, careful to maintain a state of constant alert the entire time.

The mountain was always about ten degrees cooler than most other places. This was partly due to the altitude—the mountains up there were some of the tallest I'd seen—and partly to the fact that the canopy blocked out so much light. Walking around in the Fishhook was like walking around in the shade, or inside a building.

Eventually, as the sun finally settled below the horizon and the last bit of daylight faded away, Tad picked out a spot where we'd set up for the night. It was a clean little area, in a clump of trees, along one of the steeper parts of the mountain; even if someone realized that we were there, they'd still have a hard time slipping up on us without tipping us off.

As we all got situated for the night, I positioned myself, as I sometimes did in these situations, with a tree between my legs and my body on the high side of the trunk. It was bad enough worrying about the enemy without having to worry about sliding down the side of that mountain in the middle of the night. The rest of the guys got settled, and before long I drifted off to sleep. We'd made it in okay and managed to make it through the first day; now we just needed to get some rest for the rest of the mission.

I woke up early the next morning and fixed myself a cold Lurp ration. The night had been pretty quiet, but I still didn't feel comfortable enough to boil water. No reason to take any unnecessary risks, and those gas tablets would sometimes put out a slight odor—plus, it just seemed like an extra step in the process. I ate my rations while I was still sitting there with that tree between my legs; again, there was no reason to make any unnecessary noise, and it was just safer to keep still. Before long the entire team was awake, and after we'd all finished up with our breakfasts, we slipped on our rucksacks and headed out.

We worked our way farther up the side of the mountain, pushing slowly along the steep terrain at a slightly upward angle. We hadn't seen any signs of enemy activity yet—no voices, no footprints—but we knew they were out there. We stayed in a constant state of alert. We moved cautiously, carefully balancing our bodies along the steep slope, taking small but sure steps, and pushing against the tree trunks with our hands for support. The terrain there was difficult, but as always, we had to remain cautious: if we happened across the NVA, we wanted to do so without being spotted.

We continued along the side of the mountain like that for another thirty or forty minutes, until we came to the first, and most definite, sign of enemy activity we'd seen. As we were clearing a particularly steep part of the terrain, we came upon a trail—the widest and most well worn trail I'd ever seen. And from the looks on the faces of some of the others, it must've been the widest they'd ever seen as well.

From the looks of it, this was a major infiltration route, and probably had been for years. It looked as though hundreds, if not thousands, of NVA had been traveling this path, infiltrating the valley and probably bringing in supplies, since no telling when. The dirt was packed solid from all the traffic, and it was at least eight feet across, easily wide enough to accommodate a small truck. And the amazing thing was that, back there in the Fishhook, with that dense canopy, you couldn't have seen it from the air if you'd flown over it twenty-five times.

I glanced around at the rest of the guys, and they were all just standing there wide-eyed. This was one of the most amazing, and scariest, things to see—a clean trail like that, as wide as a road, out in the middle of practically nowhere. It was as sure a sign of enemy activity as any we'd see.

I looked up and down it as far each way as I could. It appeared to just wind around the side of the mountain, though naturally, from where we were standing, we couldn't be sure exactly where it went.

Tad just whispered under his breath, "Damn."

Apparently this one impressed even him—and he'd pretty much seen them all.

He decided to move us down the trail a little ways, just to see if we could get a better take on the situation. We didn't normally make a practice of moving up and down the trails, but in some cases it might be considered okay. And like I said before, Tad had a way of doing things that was a little bit different from how most of the others did it. In any case, we all had confidence in him—just so long as we didn't sit on that trail any longer than we had to.

I stepped gently onto the trail and followed along at the back of the line—I can remember now that as we were walking down through there, with the canopy high overhead and the sunlight trickling down on us, it was almost like a dream. I could see the other five Lurps up ahead, and they were each moving so slowly and so gently—it was almost like we were floating.

I was pulling rear security, so I made a special point to cover over any boot prints I noticed on the trail—leaving boot prints all over the place was one sure way to give ourselves away. But we were very careful, and from what I could tell, we didn't appear to be leaving any signs that we were there.

After about 150 yards, Tad decided he'd seen enough. He pulled us back into the trees a ways, down toward the area we'd just come from, and radioed back to LZ English. He described the situation, with the trail we'd found and how significant it looked and how heavily traveled it looked, and after a brief wait, they sent us a message back in crypto code saying they wanted us to pull an ambush. *On the trail.*

Well, needless to say, none of us were any too thrilled with that order. Pulling an ambush there on that trail would draw in every NVA in the entire region—and from the way things looked, there were plenty of them. Not to mention the fact that if we initiated contact, we'd have one heck of a time getting out of there!

Tad got back on the radio and tried to explain the situation again. This wasn't your ordinary, everyday little footpath, he told them. And any enemy activity we saw was likely to be extremely large.

Regardless of how surprised the enemy might be by an ambush, or how shocked they might be once we made contact, if they out-manned us ten to one, it just didn't make any sense to draw attention to ourselves.

"And besides," he said, "if you look at the map, you can see there aren't any LZs out here."

And he was right. Finding an LZ out there in the middle of that dense jungle would've basically been impossible.

So then someone suggested we just go ahead and do the ambush and they'd try to get us out using McGuire rigs. But that wasn't really any better. A McGuire rig was this special rope assembly that they liked to use whenever they couldn't get a chopper in to pick you up the normal way—it was designed for areas just like this—but it wasn't the kind of thing you wanted to depend on after you'd just pulled an ambush. The rigs were awkward and cumbersome, and they didn't exactly make for the quickest, or safest, getaway.

They were basically just these long ropes, probably two hundred feet or so, with loops at the end. During an extraction the chopper would hover over a stationary point just above the trees, drop a number of these contraptions down to you, and then, once you got yourself fastened, lift you up off the ground and take you to safety.

Of course, they didn't actually pull you up into the chopper, like with a winch. They just lifted you straight up off the ground and flew you through the air. The helicopter itself would rise straight up into the air, being careful to stay directly above the same point and pulling you up into the air with them—and then once they'd cleared the trees, they'd start moving forward, with you and the Lurp team just dangling there in the air below them, hanging at the ends of your ropes.

The McGuire rig was actually used fairly frequently—or at least more frequently than you might imagine—but it was a method of last resort and a highly undesirable way to go in the wake of a fire-fight. You're just hanging by a rope in midair, slowly rising up through the trees; with a platoon of NVA closing in on you, it'd be worse than dangerous—it'd practically be target practice.

This was assuming, of course, that the chopper pilot would be able to find you in the first place; as I said before, with the dense upper canopy there in the Fishhook, visual communication with the pilots was extremely limited. And even if they did find you, pilots and crews were often put at extreme risk by a McGuire extraction. In a normal extraction the chopper would swoop in to the ground and you'd hop aboard, but the McGuire extraction was a slow process that required patience and coordination. The chopper might have to sit and hover over one spot for several minutes, becoming a potential target for enemy gunfire.

So when the folks back at LZ English suggested we use the McGuire rigs, none of us really saw that idea as much of an improvement. Tadina sent them a coded message back and told them exactly what he thought about it, and thankfully, after a few minutes, they decided to rescind the idea. I'm not exactly sure what Tad said, but to call his tone unfriendly would've been an understatement—he was pretty hot about the whole thing, and I'm sure he wasn't mincing any words in letting them know it. But whatever his language was, it definitely worked: a few minutes later they decided to have us scout out the area instead.

We moved down the side of the mountain and started scouting around a ravine that twisted down through the trees toward the valley. Everything was still quiet at that point, but as always, it could change quickly in a matter of seconds. We maneuvered quietly away from the trail and started looking for signs of VC. We were now into our second day, so we figured we'd be getting some action pretty soon—though as it turned out, we just didn't know what kind.

We scouted around for another three or four hours—by this time it was nearing midafternoon—until one of the guys signaled to Tad that he needed to stop. Apparently he'd started feeling sick, and as we were climbing around the side of that mountain, he'd realized he wasn't getting any better.

We came to a stop, and Tad radioed back to LZ English to fill them in on what was happening. They told us to sit tight for the night and to see if it passed, but it looked as though he'd contracted some sort of malaria, which isn't the type of thing that just goes away.

He seemed to be running a fever, and he said he was beginning to feel weak. And plus, with the heat and humidity as bad as it was—and all the equipment he was carrying around—he definitely didn't need to be out there trying to finish out the mission—especially in the Fishhook, which required your full attention and focus.

They mentioned the possibility of sending a chopper out to pick up just him, but that didn't really make any sense, since a chopper would compromise our position—if anybody in the area saw a helicopter, just sitting there hovering over the trees, it wouldn't take a whole lot to figure out that there was a Lurp team there.

So finally they said they'd just take us all back, which really was the only possible option anyway—this guy needed to get back to camp, and there wasn't any good way to come and get him and not get us. This was just one of those things that happened from time to time, something that occurred independent of the mission but had an effect on it nonetheless—like the weather or the light. Of course it came as a surprise, but getting sick like that—especially in a hot and humid tropical country—was just a natural part of it and something that you had to deal with.

So Tad gave them the coordinates, and an hour or so later we could hear the sounds of the choppers approaching from the south.

As they got a little bit closer, Tad popped a green smoke to indicate our position to the pilots—but as soon as he did, the wind just took the smoke up and pulled it through the trees about a hundred yards away.

Well, a couple of minutes later Moose decided to try his, and he had roughly the same amount of success—he tossed it on the ground in front of us and the wind just took it up and pulled it down through the trees—pretty much everywhere but where we wanted it to go. *And now we had two of them going off.*

We stood there for a few minutes more, now pretty much fogged in with smoke, until eventually Tad decided to use a pen flare, and thank God, the pilots were actually able to spot it down through the canopy. There were two different choppers, and within seconds the first one was hovering directly above us and dropping rope ladders down through the trees. Now, a rope ladder was a little bit different from a McGuire rig, but the principle was basically the same: they would drop the ladders down to us and then pull us up off the ground and carry us to a safer spot. We wouldn't actually be climbing the ladders, we'd only be using them to hang on to when the chopper lifted us into the air.

So the first chopper dropped the ladders down, and we quickly secured the sick man to the ropes. There was room left for two more, so Moose and one of the others climbed on and tied themselves in.

Tad and the RTO and I stood below as the chopper lifted the three men straight up through the trees, slowly at first, then gaining speed, straight up off the ground and then up and away, through the canopy at the top of the trees. A few seconds later a bunch of leaves and twigs came raining down on us, from where they'd broken through the top of the canopy.

We stood below, waiting patiently, and soon the second chopper appeared, hovering over the exact same spot as the first. They dropped another batch of ladders down to us, and we quickly attached ourselves, intertwining our bodies with the ropes like ivy up a tree.

Finally, once we were secure, Tad gave them the signal to pull us up. Slowly at first, pulling the slack tight in the ropes, then lifting us just off the ground—we hovered briefly, like we were floating, and then quickly the chopper started pulling us straight up through the trees. Straight up toward the sky, like an elevator.

As we neared the tops of the trees—that upper canopy where the limbs hung over and the leaves grew together and blocked out the light—the chopper pilot began to slow down—for what reason I have no idea—and then came to a brief stop. And we still weren't out of the trees yet. We were a good ten feet short of clearing the treetops.

There was a brief pause, just long enough for me to realize what was about to happen, as we sat there motionless.

I could see the C&C director—a guy we called Bagpipes—peering down at us through the side of the chopper. They were a pretty good distance up from us, probably about eighty feet or so, but I could see him clearly, and I didn't like the expression on his face.

Tad started waving his hand at him, signaling for him to pull us up farther. Bagpipes starting hollering to the pilot for him to pull us up. I just gripped onto that rope ladder like a vice.

Too late.

The chopper started moving forward. Again, it moved slowly at first, but then quicker—and as the pilot accelerated the chopper started dragging the three of us through the tops of those tress, crashing through the leaves and the limbs, just breaking it up and sending leaves and debris flying everywhere.

I was just hanging on to that ladder as tight as I could, using every ounce of energy and every single muscle I could muster; I was gripped around that ladder with my entire body, and it was all I could do to keep from falling off.

I had my eyes only half-open—the trees were giving us a pretty good beating, so I had my head buried down in my shoulder to try and dampen the blows from those limbs—but from what little bit I could see, we were shredding up those leaves pretty good. I can only imagine what we must've looked like—leaves flying around, limbs going everywhere, and the three of us Lurps just bouncing around at the ends of those ropes.

But finally, after dragging us through the canopy top for a good seventy-five to a hundred feet—*finally*—the pilot pulled us up over the trees. Away from the limbs and into the sky. I breathed a sigh of relief, but until we were back on the ground, I wasn't about to let go of my grip. I was hanging on to that rope like my life depended on it—which, based on the way that pilot was flying, I was pretty much thinking that it did.

Back at LZ English, we stood down just long enough to get ready to go right back out. The guys at headquarters were interested in getting us back out there to finish scouting around that trail we'd found, so we didn't exactly have time to linger. Of course, the first thing they did was tend to the guy who'd gotten sick—I think he ended up having to go to a hospital up in Japan—but after that they arranged to send us right back out. And after a couple of days down, that's exactly what they did.

The first time in, we hadn't seen anybody, which actually was a bit of luck—with a sick man on the team, we were fortunate not to run into any trouble—and the second time in, it started off the same way.

They dropped us off at a different LZ, a little farther up the valley, and unfortunately, we were having a difficult time finding a way to get back over to the trail. It had started raining, so the leaves were slick, and those steep slopes were becoming difficult to maneuver without making more noise than we were accustomed to.

After several hours Tad decided we'd move around to a more gradual slope that ran down the side of the mountain, but by this time it had gotten late, so we decided to set up camp for the night and try again in the morning.

I lay down that night on the ground, and just as I had done before, I pulled out my blanket and covered my head to keep the rain off my face. We'd managed one more day in the Fishhook and still hadn't seen any NVA. But I knew that was bound to change. Like I said before, in the Fishhook it was always just a matter of time.

The next morning we woke up as usual and, after fixing a quick breakfast of cold Lurp rations, resumed our efforts from the previous night. We maneuvered around to the finger that Tad had picked out for us, the one that ran down the side of the mountain, and began a slow ascent toward the trail at the far end of the valley.

We continued like that for an hour and a half or so, careful to remain quiet, but still intent on making our way over to the trail—after the previous day's difficulties, we felt like we needed to make it back to the trail before the day was out.

But then, for reasons unclear to the rest of us, Tad came to a stop and kneeled down to the ground. In the Fishhook he would come to a stop periodically anyway, just to evaluate our settings and to make sure that everything looked okay, but something about this was different.

He motioned back to the rest of us with his hand, then whispered back. "Something about this doesn't feel right," he said. "I've got a feeling we've been spotted."

Well, right then and there, I can tell you my nerves stood up on end. I was already pretty alert, but when Tad said he thought we'd been had, well, it was like a jolt of adrenaline just shot through my body.

Nobody in the outfit knew the enemy the way Tad did. Nobody else knew the land or the sounds or the smells—he told me once that he could actually smell whenever the enemy was around, something about their food or something—so when Tad told you that he thought something was up, well, you could pretty much count on it.

He motioned for us to follow him behind this small clump of brush, and as we gathered around behind it he whispered quickly, "I think someone's following us."

I started looking intently back down through the trees, peering out from behind the brush, with my rifle at the ready. There was a small ravine that we'd just come through, and I was staring just as hard as I could to see if I could spot anybody. The ground was dark and the leaves were wet, and being in the Hook, I could see for a long, long way.

And then, in an instant, he was there.

I'd been staring so hard, I couldn't believe I'd missed him, but there he was, just as plain as day, right in clear view. And he'd been there the whole time. Only, I hadn't seen him, because he blended in with the land.

A Montagnard tribesman.

It was like when you're out deer hunting and all of a sudden you notice a deer standing there that's been there the whole time but you just haven't seen him—well, that's the way it was with this Montagnard. He was right there in the open, down on one knee, with his hand along the ground.

Nobody said anything. We all just watched him.

He looked like he was about fifty years old, but from what I knew of the Montagnards, he just as easily could've been thirty-five. He was wearing a small cloth around his waist and nothing else. His skin was dark and his hair was black. He moved his hand across the ground and looked thoughtfully in our direction. He was like an Indian from one of those old Hollywood Westerns, checking for tracks—only this guy wasn't an actor. He was the real thing.

I don't know if Tad had heard the guy or what exactly, but somehow he knew he was back there. Maybe it was just a feeling, like a sixth sense or something, telling him that something wasn't right, but whatever it was, he sure as heck knew that that guy was back there.

The Montagnard stood up slowly and started moving toward our position. When he got to the edge of the ravine about forty meters below us, I think he realized he'd been had. I never made eye contact with him, but he must've seen us at that point—and he took off down the ravine, back toward the bottom of the mountain. Not running exactly, but not exactly waiting around either. He knew the jig was up.

Eventually we made it over to the big trail we'd seen the first time in, and we set up an observation post and watched it for the next day and a half. Unbelievably, we never did see any NVA, but we did hear quite a bit of noise at night—footsteps, gunfire, the occasional voice.

After the third day they decided to come get us—sitting there by that trail, in one spot for so long, it wasn't really very safe. One of the guys at headquarters suggested picking us up by rope ladder, but after what we'd been through last time, we decided to look for a proper LZ instead. We humped back down to the valley and after another day and a half of walking found ourselves a sufficient LZ. We radioed the coordinates back to LZ English, and within the hour they flew back out and picked us up.

On the way out our chopper drew sniper fire from the trees. *And good riddance to you too!*

Running with Tad was a constant learning experience. The way he ran his missions, the way he did things, he was always finding himself in new and unusual situations. Call it a nose for action, I don't know, but for some reason he just always ended up in the midst of some sort of unique or interesting situation. And for me it meant seeing some things I'd never seen before—like the NVA battalion we'd spotted near the Suoi Ca Valley and the oversized trail we'd found out in the heart of the Fishhook—and with each new mission I was growing more and more confident and learning new and important ways to deal with situations out in the field. In a way it was sort of humbling to realize how much there was to know and to see and to learn, but running with these guys—first with Dave and then with Tad—I knew I had some great teachers to rely on.

When we got back to LZ English, we went down to headquarters and went through our usual debriefing session. They were particularly interested in hearing about the trail we'd found, though I'm not really sure what ever came of it. It didn't seem like the kind of place where a rifle company would be very effective.

After we finished, I started back to the Hill to get a shower and some rest, and as I was dragging myself up there, I noticed this big swaggering figure coming down from up by the barracks. I stopped dead in my tracks and just sort of shook my head in surprise—he hadn't seen me yet, so I called out his name.

"Bill!"

I waved my hand at him so he'd see me.

"*Bill!*"

It looked like it took him a second to recognize me—I was still pretty dirty at that point—but then he realized who I was and started jogging down the hill to meet me. I must've had a big ol' grin across my face, because as soon as he got down there, he started smiling like a kid on Christmas. I set my rucksack down and grabbed his outstretched hand.

"*Bill Pfister*—I can't believe it, man! How you doing?"

Right there in the middle of all that, tired and rundown, still wet with sweat from being out in the field, I run into one of my best friends—and I can promise you, after ten days out in the Fishhook, there was no better sight in the world.

"Shan, you look like hell, man."

"Yeah, I know," I said, "but I feel great."

# 5

## Friends and Neighbors

DURING THE TIME I'D SPENT WITH THE LINE COMPANY, BILL Pfister had been our squad leader, but he'd also been much more than that. He was the one person everyone had relied on. He was a friend and comrade, and he'd helped us get by when the going wasn't going so great: he talked with us when we needed to talk, he saw me off when I left, he was even the one who introduced me to Sergeant Pipkin—in a very real way, he had helped me get out of the line company. And when I left, he was the one person I'd hated to leave behind.

He'd stayed in the line company because he felt a sense of responsibility toward some of the younger, less experienced guys. He knew they looked up to him, so he wanted to help them learn the ropes and make it through their tours. But even so, there had to be a point when enough was enough, and when I saw him walking down the hill that day, I figured he must've finally reached it.

"Hey, what can I say? That line company hasn't changed a bit," he said. "It's just like it was when you left."

It didn't surprise me to hear him say that. The line company hadn't shown any sign of being flexible when I was there. I had no reason to think it would have changed after I left. He went on to say that he'd needed a change and felt like the Lurps would give him the best opportunity to find it.

"I figured I'd better come up here and see what all this Lurp stuff is really about," he said. And I for one was glad to hear it.

Bill Pfister was a good infantryman and a better friend, and I knew I'd get a kick out of having him around. But his decision to join the Lurps was significant for another reason as well. When I'd made the decision to leave the line company, Pfister had made the decision to stay, and though I'd never really regretted my choice, the fact that Pfister had stayed behind had always caused me some small element of doubt. He was the only person I'd truly respected in the entire outfit, and he had chosen to stay. But now that he'd decided to come on board, my one lingering doubt had finally been put to rest.

"Well, Pfister," I said, "I think you're doing the right thing. We can always use another good Lurp around here."

I patted him on the shoulder again.

"And I can always use a good friend."

After we got through talking, I went on up to the Hill and got cleaned up, then I caught back up with him over by the chopper pad. I took him around to introduce him to some of the others— he'd already met a lot of the Lurps, so I took him around and introduced him to some of the support personnel, the guys he'd be seeing and working with around the base.

Besides the Lurps, there were a number of guys at LZ English who we interacted with on a daily basis, guys who kept it going, doing the communications work and the transportation work and all the other odd jobs that needed doing in the 173rd. These were the skilled craftsmen—mechanics, engineers, artillerymen—who did the hard work of improving the facilities, repairing the equipment, bringing in supplies, and protecting the base from attack. Some of these guys we saw on a regular basis, and over the course of time they became as familiar to us as any other Lurp.

There was a guy from up north named Rick Hanbury who ran the communications center. He was the one we called "Bagpipes" (or "Pipes" for short). He used to play this set of bagpipes that he had, and after playing those things around the base, he became pretty well known to everybody—I don't think there was anybody there at LZ English who didn't know who he was. And from what I knew, there wasn't anybody that didn't like him.

He was a colorful character, with a bushy mustache and a twinkle in his eye, and as he did with nearly everything else, he always liked to play his bagpipes in the most dramatic fashion. Whenever we were getting mortared, for instance, he'd crawl out from the radio room where he stayed and stand up on the bunker playing those pipes, just huffing and puffing and making all kinds of racket, with mortar shells exploding all around him. One time I happened to be down there when he climbed out onto the bunker to play, and about ten seconds later he came diving right back in.

"Damn," he said, "that's not mortar, *those are rockets.*"

Bagpipes was something of a fixture at LZ English, and as far as the Lurps were concerned, he was one of the most important guys there. Being in charge of the radio shack, he had to monitor the radios and make sure the communications were always clean for the teams out in the field. For us, that was hugely important: without proper communication, you were out there by yourself, without any way to call for help. So making sure we were able to communicate was paramount for a successful mission.

He also supervised the infiltration-extraction exercises, so he made a whole lot of trips in the C&C chopper, overseeing the drop-offs and making sure the teams got on the ground okay. Whenever there was a rope or ladder extraction, he was always the one in the bird, looking down on us, getting things done. He was very reliable in that respect: he didn't mind putting his own life on the line to come out there and save a few of ours, and among the Lurps that garnered a tremendous amount of respect.

One of the photographers for the 173rd was a guy from Malaysia named Ralph Dixon. He was an inquisitive guy who used to come around the base every now and then, and whenever he was there he always liked to go out on some of the missions with the Lurps. He was especially interested in running with Tad, and Tad didn't seem to mind, so they'd go out together—just like on any other mission, without any extra precautions or security or anything—and when they got back, he'd always be about as excited as a kid at a carnival.

He used to carry around all this sophisticated photography equipment—a nice camera with a zoom lens and everything—so his pictures were always top-quality. And whenever he got them developed, he'd bring them back around and show us. I'd always look at them with some of the other guys—we'd pass them around and listen to him tell the stories about where they were taken and how they'd happened—and I was always impressed with how clear and detailed they looked. Dixon managed to capture every blade of grass and every scared expression. And his pictures always seemed to be taken from right in the middle of the action.

One time, though, he'd taken some pictures of an ambush as it was actually happening—it was a series of frames he'd taken by holding the camera up and mashing the button down, *click-click-clicking* them off, rapid-fire—and a bunch of the photos were all blurred in a sort of swirl of motion, where he'd lost his nerve during the attack. Of course, we laughed over it a little bit when he got back, but we all respected him for getting out there and doing it. That was more than a lot of people would do.

Some of his pictures ended up in a magazine that the brigade used to put out called *Sky Soldier,* but we also used them for a little more practical purpose—some of the pictures of the enemy were so clear and objective that the guys at headquarters liked to use them for intelligence. No matter how descriptive we were with our reports, we still couldn't match the detail of a photograph.

The supply sergeant was the guy who stood between us and our supplies. In the early days we didn't have a supply sergeant to help us get our equipment—we just had the supply tent and a bunch of eager Lurps—but once the company started expanding, we finally got someone to help us out, and having a supply sergeant became something of a constant. Every time we had to run a mission, we'd have to go see him to get our supplies—so we ended up dealing with him pretty much all the time.

When I was there, there were actually a couple of different guys who served as supply sergeant, but the one I remember the most was a guy named Webb. He was a sharp guy with short, dark hair, and he ran that supply tent the way a librarian runs a library: strict, orderly, and not a thing out of place. He knew just what went where and how much of everything was left at any given point in time. And he wasn't one to put up with a whole lot of waste either.

He used to give me a hard time whenever I'd come back in with leftover ammo—"Shan, you know I'm running low around here, man, why don't you use up that ammo you got left?"—but he'd always end up getting us whatever we wanted anyway, and it made our missions a whole lot easier.

It was probably a thankless job, running that supply tent—I think he used to get a little stir-crazy sitting in that tent all day, fooling around with those supplies—but it was about as important a job as any other. Because he was retrieving the supplies and making sure we had the proper equipment, we could leave the base and concentrate on doing our jobs, knowing we wouldn't run out of ammo or not having to worry about food or anything like that.

The commanding officer, or CO, was always the most prominent figure in the company. He was the one who made the decisions and gave the company its sense of direction. He set the tone and established a vision for how the company should operate and how the missions should be run—and ultimately he was the one held responsible for its results (for better or for worse).

When I first got there, the CO was a guy named John Buczacki. Buczacki was a hard-nosed commander, with a strong sense of purpose, but he was also creative and flexible in the way that a good Lurp commander should be. He oversaw the first hunter-killer missions, and he nurtured the company through a period of growth and experimentation. He was the CO when the company was still just a small group of volunteers, scratching to make a name for itself, but he was also there as the company started to mature. By the time he left, the company had developed into a tight-knit unit with a first-rate record and a good number of experienced team leaders—which was definitely good news for his successor, Captain Dick James.

Captain James assumed command in December 1968, and before long he'd made his own mark on the company. He understood the basic need for the Lurps, and he pushed us hard to fulfill our various responsibilities. But he was also a conscientious leader, and he sought to balance that broader military perspective with the need to protect his men and look out for our safety. He wasn't afraid to pursue an objective, but he never did it at the expense of his men either. This quickly made him a favorite among the team leaders, who generally shared his aggressive-but-safe philosophy. And he soon became a powerful influence on the rest of the company as well.

A third company commander was there during my time as well, but he didn't arrive until sometime in late 1969. His name was Captain John P. Lawton, and he definitely didn't have any trouble making his mark on the company. Captain Lawton was a tough guy who had won several medals prior to joining the company, and once he got to LZ English, he continued to be a demanding and action-oriented leader. Captain Lawton was a CO who didn't mind getting down in the trenches with the teams—he'd actually put himself out there, at his own personal risk—and as a result the teams often had some pretty remarkable missions.

In general, there were probably about five hundred men at LZ English at any one time, so there was always something going on. That was one of the benefits of having so many people around—whenever we were there on stand-down, we could always find something to do to help us pass the time while we prepared to go out for that next mission.

The most popular activity was probably going into Bong Son. It wasn't very large, but it was big enough to give us a temporary distraction—shops and streets and vendors, the general hum of village life. Like most Vietnamese villages, it wasn't modern at all—the streets weren't paved, and the primary mode of transportation was the bicycle—but it was always teeming with people, which gave us the feeling of getting away for a while, even if we were just a couple of miles from the base.

We used to go into town on our days off, usually for a couple of hours in the afternoon. We'd wander around the shops for a while, then head back to base. It was close enough to walk, but we'd usually ride in on the back of one of the trucks and then ride back the same way.

I liked to go into town and look at the people. Sometimes I'd buy things, but most of the time I'd just wander around down there, watching the vendors, watching the salesmen, watching the Americans haggling for goods. There was such a confluence of cultures down there—with the base so close, there was almost always a bunch of our guys in town wandering around the streets. You'd see these Vietnamese, with their conical hats and their bundles of rice, right alongside a bunch of Americans in their green army fatigues, an M-16 in one hand and a canned drink in the other.

Of course, if we were too tired or didn't have enough time or just didn't feel like going into town for whatever reason, we could always just hang around the Hill and see what was going on around there. Sometimes just sitting around the base, writing letters or catching up on your sleep, was about the best thing a person could do to get himself going again. It was usually pretty calm, and you could almost always count on somebody being around to help you pass the time.

A lot of the guys liked to keep up with how the other teams were doing—how many VC they spotted, how many kills they got, that kind of thing—and back at the base they'd always compare their results. This actually developed into a lively competition, and I can remember a few of the guys even placing bets over how they'd perform. One guy might place a bet, for instance, saying that your team couldn't last three days without getting chased out—that kind of thing.

Some of the guys liked to play basketball, and a lot of the guys liked to drink—whatever we could think of to pass the time, we'd do it. Some of the guys liked to mess around with Tango, the dog—they'd play with him or sometimes take him on trips.

Some people liked to write letters, but I personally wasn't one of them. I tried a few times—writing letters to my mother, my grandmother, my friends—but I realized pretty quickly that I didn't have anything I could say. I wasn't comfortable telling them about the things we were doing—I didn't want to worry them any more than they already were—and besides that, I wasn't sure that they'd believe me anyway. Some of the things we were doing would have probably sounded outlandish to the people who weren't there.

Sometimes we'd play cards or we might get up a game of football if we had the time. And sometimes we actually had fun. All of the Lurps tended to get along because, regardless of personalities or whatever differences we might have had, in the early days we were all in the same boat—having the same experiences, pursuing the same goals, and often sharing the same sensibilities.

For a lot of the guys those friendships served a larger purpose as well: in addition to helping us pass the time, friendships helped us to keep it together mentally. Without those friendships and the support they provided, it would have been all but impossible to keep up the company morale and maintain our focus. Running those missions over and over was a pretty tough deal, and if you didn't stay sharp, both physically and mentally, it could really take a toll.

Even under the best of circumstances, a Lurp mission involved several consecutive days of being at a heightened sense of alert. So if you ran missions back to back for several months in a row, without keeping yourself fresh, it was inevitable that it would wear on your nerves. The stress, the exhaustion, the fatigue—we had to have some way to keep ourselves up, to keep ourselves fresh. And for most of the guys our friendships were a way to do that.

Having those friends was like having a safety net, a big web of like-minded kin who were always there to break your fall—if you were down or afraid or confused or just plain tired, your friends were always there to pick you up. Being so far from home, we all needed something to keep us afloat, and for most of us our friendships did that. Those guys were the closest thing to a family we had—they *were* our family—and they made what was normally a hard life just a little bit easier.

But unfortunately, not everybody felt the same way—or at least not to the extent that I did. Some of the guys couldn't deal with it. They couldn't cope with the stress and the constant pressure of running missions, so they ended up trying to calm their nerves in different ways—which more times than not meant turning to drugs.

In Vietnam drugs were something you could get your hands on easily and without much hassle. They'd been a problem in the line company, and they continued to be a problem at LZ English. They were less of a problem with the Lurps, though any problem in the Lurps was usually amplified because of the close-knit nature of our work—a single team member with a bad habit could have serious repercussions for the entire team out in the field. Even the slightest mistake could compromise a mission—or worse, get somebody hurt.

The most popular drug was probably marijuana. I'd seen it a lot in the rifle company, and I knew a couple of guys who had it with them at all times. I don't know exactly how they got it, but I know it couldn't have been very difficult. One time when I was still in the line company, we'd walked straight through a field of it, just growing out in the middle of nowhere. I don't know if it was growing wild or what, but it was just a big field of these tall green plants, and we marched straight through the middle of it.

Opium was another drug that people smoked. I heard about these guys who used to go down to the opium dens in downtown Bong Son and get high. The Vietnamese had these places where you could go in, just like a store, and buy up as much of this opium as you could handle. I used to see a bunch of the grunts down at this one place in Bong Son, coming out after a session of smoking that stuff— they'd be stumbling around, just as high as a kite, and wouldn't even know where they were, which I guess was exactly the point.

The problem with all of this was the fact that some of the guys couldn't leave it behind. I don't know if they were addicted or what, but they couldn't just do it and then go back out, clean and sober, straight and sharp. They got to where they'd take it out with them—their drugs *and* their habits. They may have started out just trying to relax or to escape, but some of them got to where they couldn't leave it behind—and their drug use became a problem in itself. Imagine being out in the field with a Lurp team and knowing that one of your teammates is hurting for a hit of opium. It's not a good feeling, I assure you.

And then, in addition to that, there was the compounding problem of morphine out in the field. We'd carry enough morphine on a mission to provide each guy with one injection. In the event of a gunshot wound or some other sort of casualty, the morphine was an essential part of the treatment. Without it, the pain could be devastating. Now normally, of course, we didn't have to use them, and we'd just bring them back to camp when we were done. But as you might imagine, the easy access led to abuse.

For people who were inclined to use drugs, or who got themselves in a situation where they needed to take drugs, carrying around a supply of morphine was a pretty powerful temptation. In the early days we used to each carry our own needle and tube—the morphine came in a sort of toothpaste tube that you'd just attach to the needle and roll up—but after an incident of abuse they realized that this wouldn't work and changed the way we did it: they had the team leader take care of the morphine for everybody. They fastened them all together, and the TL had to account for them when he got back to base.

I don't know what it was that caused certain guys to react in one way and other guys to react in another, but I guess it was inevitable that some people would turn to drugs to help them get by. Drugs were so readily available, and we were living one of the most high-pressure lifestyles a person can lead. One time I asked a friend of mine about it, a guy who was fairly well known for being a habitual drug user, and he explained it like this:

"It helps me to relax," he said. "It helps me settle my nerves."

"But I don't see how you can make a good, split-second decision out there if your mind's all clouded over with drugs."

This guy was actually a good Lurp, so it bothered me more than usual that he felt like he had to use drugs to get by.

"Well, you may be right," he said, "but I got to do something to keep me relaxed. And if I don't do that, then what else is there?"

Unfortunately for a lot of the guys who got themselves into trouble like that, the military didn't really do anything to help them out. I saw guys get shipped back to the States with no mention of drugs or anything like that—in Vietnam one week, back in the States the next, and not a single thing done for the real problem. I saw some good guys, some good infantrymen, get messed up that way. The army could've given some of those guys medicals or something, but I guess they didn't want to go through the trouble.

Turning to drugs, or even alcohol, was a pretty typical way for guys to try and cope with the stress and strain of combat. It wasn't necessarily common, but it wasn't altogether uncommon either, and for many it provided the quick escape they really were trying to find. But there were a couple of guys at LZ English who managed to try something a little more creative. When they decided they couldn't cope with the pressure and needed to get away, well, that's pretty much exactly what they did. They just up and went away.

There were two guys—a Private X and a Private Y—and they'd never been comfortable with where they were. They weren't happy with the company, and they didn't like the direction it was going. By every possible measure, they were unhappy, and they eventually decided they'd reached a breaking point.

One night they went into Bong Son, and when it was time for them to get back, they didn't show up—which wasn't completely unheard of, but it was still a little bit unusual. Most of us just assumed they'd shacked up with a couple of girls and would show up the next day, but once the next day rolled around, they didn't appear then either.

Well, by then it was clear that something was seriously wrong, so the guys at headquarters decided to put out a search party. They had a couple of teams scour the countryside, in and around Bong Son, across the ride paddies, and even into the mountains. But several days later there was still no sign of Private X or Private Y, and shortly after that we were told that they were now being considered deserters.

It seemed such an unlikely thing to do. I mean, even if you wanted to leave, where in the world would you go? It wasn't like you were back in the States and could just disappear among the people—here an American GI walking across the highlands would look about as inconspicuous as a double cheeseburger at a soup shop. And that was assuming you didn't get killed by VC in the meantime.

And how bad did it have to be for a person to decide to just up and leave like that? I couldn't really understand it. Even though I knew what they'd been going through—because everyone in the outfit was going through the same exact thing—I didn't know what had caused them to react that way. To me it just seemed crazy. I mean, if you've ever heard the saying "out of the frying pan and into the fire," well, that's exactly the way this seemed to me. No matter how bad it was at LZ English, running missions, it was bound to be worse once you got out in the field by yourself. At least whenever we were in the field running missions, we had the support of an entire American army base at our back—but these two were just out there, completely by themselves.

Several weeks passed, and these guys still didn't show up. Around camp we all just figured they'd either been killed or managed to shack up with a Vietnamese family that had decided to keep them hidden for some reason. I figured they'd turn up at some point, maybe down in Bong Son or somewhere nearby, since it didn't seem likely that they'd get very far, with all the hostile territory that surrounded us and all the anti-American sentiment that seemed to be everywhere.

Finally we got word that they'd been captured, which didn't really surprise us—or upset us much for that matter. We figured that if they'd decided to leave like that, they deserved to be captured. But then came the part that shocked us all. They hadn't been found nearby in Bong Son, or even out in the Central Highlands somewhere—they'd been found at a bar in Bangkok. *Thailand.* Some six hundred miles away.

Over the next several days their story began to filter back—apparently these guys had actually walked to Bangkok. I don't know how they'd done it, but they had made the trip on foot, from the coast of Vietnam to the streets of Bangkok—which meant they'd had to cross over Laos as well. It was unbelievable that they'd made it without getting killed, and when I first heard about it, I told Dave that I'd love to hear how they'd done it. But none of the guys back at English really expected to see them again. Once they found them over in Bangkok, we figured they'd just ship them back to the States and take care of it over there. But as it turned out, that's not exactly what happened.

One afternoon about a week later I was sitting around with Dave when one of the guys from headquarters came up and told us these guys were being shipped back to LZ English. Apparently they needed a place to keep them before they transferred them out to a military prison to be placed on trial. Of course, I couldn't believe it. We hadn't seen these guys in several weeks, and now it looked like we'd be holding them as prisoners.

Sure enough, the next day our CO had us build a small makeshift jail out in the center of the yard. We took a bundle of razor wire and bent it into a circle about fifteen feet across, then placed two small tents, made from ponchos, at either end. It was primitive and ragged and just barely large enough to hold two men.

A few days later I went on a mission with Dave and the rest of Team Golf, and when we got back, Private X and Private Y were sitting right there in the middle of that circle.

Now, I saw a lot of things when I was over there, but I can tell you that the sight of those guys sitting inside the razor wire was one of the most difficult. I think seeing them like that shocked even the most hardened Lurp in the outfit. I mean, nobody really sympathized with those guys, but at the same time, they seemed to have fallen to such a low place, sitting there in the sun like regular prisoners.

For the next two weeks Private X and Private Y just stayed inside that fencing, right there in the middle of LZ English, beneath the hot sun—at this point the temperatures were reaching the hundred-degree mark nearly every day—without any exercise or interaction. A guard was posted outside the site twenty-four hours a day, and I heard that he was told to shoot to kill if they tried to get away. The rest of us were given strict orders not to talk to them, to not even wave or otherwise acknowledge that they were there.

During this time the teams just continued running missions, and whenever we got back, we'd always have to walk by that razor-wire circle. It was bad for them, but it wasn't a whole lot of fun for us either. Then one day we returned from a mission and saw that they were gone, and where the fencing had been, well, there wasn't anything there. Somebody'd cleaned it up and taken the razor wire away, just like it had never been there—just like it had never happened.

Pfister, as it turned out, was a great Lurp—a little bigger than most, but active and bold in the exact way that a Lurp needed to be. Plus, he took to it like a natural. After being in the line company for so long and being constantly frustrated by their inability to find the enemy, he felt like the Lurps were a breath of fresh air. Pfister thrived on the fact that the Lurp teams were actually able to find the enemy and, when appropriate, initiate contact. That may sound like a small thing, but to anyone who'd been in that line company for so long, trust me, it was no small accomplishment.

He started running a lot with a team leader named Cameron McAllister. He and Mac were kind of similar: they were both big guys, and they both had these big, bold personalities. A couple of times when Mac was short a man, I ended up running missions with them, and that was kind of neat, getting to run with Pfister again. But even running with the closest of friends, you were still running missions, and they were still dangerous. We ran two together that were some of the most memorable I ever ran.

A GI Joe type from Omaha, Nebraska, Cameron McAllister was big, stout, and linebacker-tough. He was a little bit older than the rest of us, probably about twenty-seven at the time, and he was one of the most daring and aggressive team leaders around. If some of the guys were dealing with the war by cowering away from it—turning to drugs or whatever—Mac's response was basically just to embrace it. This guy was about as hard-core as they came, and he thrived on the constant face-to-face contact with the enemy.

He'd been in the Lurps before, on a previous tour I think, and he'd come back for a second round during the time I was there. They'd given him his own team right off, because of his experience, and once he got rolling, he accounted for a whole lot of enemy kills. He was one of these guys who liked to shoot first and ask questions later—if at all—which meant you could usually count on getting some serious action whenever you ran with him.

Physically, he looked a lot like that old World War II comic-book hero Sergeant Rock. He was broad-shouldered, thin-waisted, and muscled up like somebody had drawn in his muscles with pen and ink. I don't know if he played football when he was growing up, but I'm sure he was a good player if he did.

I remember especially how strong he was. One time when one of his men had been shot, the choppers flew in and tried to get the team out using the rope rigs. As they were trying to leave, the injured man's D-ring broke, and Mac just grabbed him around the waist and carried him right out of there—one hand around his waist, the other gripped tightly around the rope.

That was really incredible, but just like Mac—he was big, strong, and always right in the middle of the action.

The first of those missions that I ran with Pfister was a surveillance mission into the An Do Valley. This mission started out with a bang and ended up the same way. It was also one of the few missions that I got to run with Chief, which was usually a pretty interesting experience in itself.

The mission started off with the chopper pilot going through his usual maneuvering around, up above the mountains and down over the treetops, trying to throw off any enemy that might happen to be in the area—and then eventually moving in to the LZ that Mac had picked out the day before on the overflight.

The LZ was situated on the side of a mountain, about halfway up, in a clearing that was covered in brush. Unlike most of our drop-off points, this one wasn't situated on a plateau—usually there were flat areas around that you could find and use for landing—and it was angled down at a pretty steep slope. Unfortunately, this meant that, while the helicopter hovered over the position, the guys on the near side of the chopper were only a few feet off the ground and the guys on the far side were nearly twelve feet off the ground.

I saw immediately as the pilot flew in and pulled up sharply that Pfister and I were on the high side, but of course, there wasn't really anything we could do about it. Jumping off the high side was just one of those things you had to do—I'd jumped that far a dozen times before, but still, it looked like a long jump down.

I glanced over at Mac, who was sitting on the other side. We had a rule that when one guy jumped, we all jumped, so as soon as I saw him disappear out the door, I nodded to Pfister, and we bailed out the other side.

But no sooner had I cleared the door than my feet flew up over my head and the weight of my rucksack flipped me completely over onto my back. I hit the ground with a thud, and the air shot out of my lungs.

A second later I looked up and saw Pfister peering at me, with a funny look on his face.

"Hey, man, you all right?"

He thrust his hand down to pull me up, but I just lay there for a second, trying to get my breath back.

"Mmmm."

I tried to tell him to hold on a second, but I think it came out as more of a moan.

Pfister smiled.

"Come on, man, we got to get off this clearing."

This time I took his hand and let him pull me up. The rest of the guys were over in the tree line, so we went over to join them, Pfister in front, me hobbling along behind.

Apparently when I bailed out, I'd jumped right on the top of a small tree, and my rucksack caught on a limb. It had thrown me completely over onto my back, and when I'd hit the ground, the breath was knocked out of me.

When I got over to the others, Chief just gave me a funny look and sort of shook his head. When I got close enough to hear him, he leaned over toward me and whispered in my ear: "Infiltration number 10."

It wasn't exactly the most auspicious beginning to a mission, but after a couple of minutes I was fine, and we all headed into the brush.

We moved over the ridge of the mountain, and after a couple of hours or so of sniffing around, we set up our laager site for the night and went to sleep. We heard some gunfire about midnight—a couple of individual rifle-shots—and even saw some lights flashing from down below. But beyond that, the rest of the night was quiet, and we slept without incident.

The next morning we decided to get a little bit closer to the valley so we could get a better look at the area we'd seen those lights coming from. Mac was running the point, so he led the way along the ridge of the mountain, then angled us down a ways, moving gradually closer and closer to the valley floor.

About halfway down we stopped to do a communications check and discovered that the mountain, rising up behind us, was blocking our signal. We couldn't get anything. Zero.

We moved back up the mountain a bit to try and make contact so we could establish some sort of plan to maintain communications. The guys at headquarters decided to send up a Hawkeye, which was the small prop plane we used to use for recon and surveillance support. It would pass overhead every three or four hours and radio down to us to make sure we were still doing okay.

Naturally this wasn't an ideal situation for us. Not having radio communication shifted the burden fully onto the Lurp team; in the event of an emergency, we were totally on our own—at least until the plane flew back over. But you had to be flexible to run Lurp missions, and after doing it for a few months, I'd come to expect a certain amount of compromise.

We continued like that for the rest of the day, moving a little more cautiously and using the Hawkeye to maintain communication. When nightfall came, I was pretty relieved to get the additional cover of the dark.

The next morning—the third day—we got word to go ahead and try and pull an ambush. The plan was for the plane to remain in the vicinity, just flying off in the distance a little ways, so that when we pulled the ambush we'd be able to communicate back to them that we needed an extraction.

Before moving the entire team down to the ambush site, however, Mac wanted to go up with one other guy to scout around; he wanted to find us a good spot to set up the ambush without having to worry about dragging the whole team all over the valley. He asked Pfister to go along with him, so Chief and I and the other two Lurps—Minor Hopkins and Scotty Norwood—stayed behind to wait. We started setting up a small perimeter there in the brush as Mac and Pfister disappeared into the trees. Then just sat and waited.

Well, we hadn't been sitting there five minutes when all of a sudden all hell broke loose from down in the valley—the exact area that Mac and Pfister had been heading toward. It sounded like M-16 fire, just opened up and bursting out across the valley.

I looked over at Chief. His eyes were wide.

We'd just had a commo check, but the RTO quickly got the Hawkeye back on the radio and told him we'd just made contact. We rushed down through the brush, toward where the noise was coming from, but by the time we got there the gunfire had ceased and the smoke was already clearing.

Mac and Pfister were standing there calmly at the edge of the clearing with their rifles at their sides. Lying there in the grass, doubled over at the waist, were two VC. Both shot, both dead.

We contacted the Hawkeye and told them to arrange for an extraction; shortly thereafter, the choppers arrived to carry us back to the base.

On the way back I looked over at Pfister and noticed his unusually calm expression. He didn't say anything, but at that point he didn't really have to. His look pretty much said it all: being a Lurp ain't nothing like being in the line company.

After we returned to the base and finished debriefing, we went back to our bunks as usual, ready to shower off and hit the sack for some much-needed rest and relaxation. But this time, when we got back to the Hill, it wasn't the same comforting scene we were used to.

I walked into the hooch and saw my footlocker turned upside down at the foot of my cot, and my belongings—my stationery, my letters, my socks, everything—strewn across the floor in a jumbled mess.

I looked around and saw that everyone else's was the same way—clothes spilled everywhere like a neat little tornado had come in and systematically hit each footlocker.

I tossed my stuff on the cot and walked out to see if I could find out what had happened. Harry Bell was walking past with a group of Lurps, so I motioned him over.

"Hey, Bill, what's up?"

"Hey, Harry, what happened to all our stuff? I just got back and my clothes are all over the floor. Looks like a tornado hit."

"Oh, yeah, they did that to everybody. Went through everything." He shook his head. "Came through over the weekend. Looking for drugs."

Apparently, over the weekend, while we were out in the field, one of the new guys had shot himself in the head while playing Russian roulette. I'd heard stories about him before I left. He'd play the game with this Smith & Wesson pistol that he had, with a bunch of the guys standing around watching—just trying to show off or draw attention to himself for some reason.

I don't know if he'd gotten high on drugs or what, but apparently, while we were gone, he was playing this game one night, and instead of using the same Smith & Wesson that he normally used, he'd gotten hold of a different pistol, a Colt, I think. From what I heard, the cylinder in this new pistol rotated a different direction from the one in the Smith & Wesson. Before, when he'd done it, he'd been able to remember where the round was in the chamber. But that night he'd either gotten confused or just didn't realize what the problem was, and he ended up shooting himself, right there in the middle of the base, with five or six guys looking on.

Well, obviously when the guys at headquarters heard about it, they assumed he'd been doped up on drugs—not incorrectly, I shouldn't think—and by the time we got back from our mission they'd already gone through all our things and just dumped them out on the ground.

They did that all over the Hill, rooting around for marijuana and opium and whatever other kind of drugs they might've been hoping to find, though from what I heard, they didn't really find anything. But either way, I guess the fact that one of the guys had actually gotten killed like that was just the thing to trigger a crackdown. Something like drug use is easy to ignore sometimes until somebody gets hurt.

Even so, I'm not sure if the crackdown corrected the real problem—which was that some people just didn't make the adjustment to combat. Vietnam was a tough place to be, for many reasons, and all too often the military didn't want to address that. Like I said before, for some guys being in Vietnam was just too much to handle; it could often be physically and psychologically exhausting. We got R&R, of course, but still, the pressure of our normal routine and everyday surroundings built up and had a cumulative effect—and for some of those guys there was nothing that friends or vacations or even drugs could do about it. They just couldn't cope.

On our second mission I went with Mac on the overflight, and we picked out an LZ about two-thirds up on the inside slope of the mountain. We knew from a previous Lurp team that we'd probably lose communication again—that team had been there a few days earlier and lost communication when they dipped too far down in the valley—but we felt like we could find a spot near the top of the ridge that would give us a clear view of the valley without interfering with our communications.

The next day, when we got there, we managed to get in and get up to the top of the mountain without any problem, which was just as we had hoped. This was a mission designed strictly as an ambush mission—a hunter-killer mission. We wouldn't be doing any reconnaissance or scouting around; we were just supposed to go in there and set up an ambush for the VC that were known to be traveling the valley. A river ran down the center of the valley, wide but shallow—it was nearly a hundred yards across at its widest point but only waist-deep, even in the center—and previous Lurp teams had discovered a heavy flow of enemy traffic in and around the river.

Mac was carrying an M-60 machine gun, and once we got to the top, he set it up and directed it toward the valley below. Carrying an M-60 like that was pretty unusual—almost never done really—but the circumstances of the mission were such that it seemed like an appropriate exception to make. We wouldn't be humpin' much—we weren't planning to anyway—and we knew we'd be pulling the ambush from a fairly long distance. Normally the M-60 was considered too heavy and cumbersome to try and lug across the jungle—Lurp teams needed their mobility—but in this case, Mac was willing to haul it along.

We selected a clearing at the top of the mountain where the brush was low and the trees were sparse. We lay down in the grass, one beside the other, and waited patiently for the VC to appear. We were a pretty good ways away from the trail that disappeared into the river—probably four or five hundred yards—but the position was safe and our view was unobstructed.

About thirty minutes later a group of VC appeared at the other side of the river, walking down the trail in a single-file line. At that distance we couldn't make out many details, but we could clearly see that they were armed and, from the way they were conducting themselves, well organized. They proceeded down the trail in a slow and orderly manner, each walking about five meters behind the man in front of him.

When the first one reached the edge of the river, he stopped briefly and then pushed his way into the water, proceeding awkwardly into the waist-high water. The rest of the group continued along behind him, still being careful to remain spaced out, one after the other, as they stepped slowly into the water.

The last one in line appeared from the trees and walked tentatively down to the water. As he slid down in the mud, with his rifle over his head, we could see that there were fifteen of them in total. By this point the first one had nearly reached the other side—our side. They were spread out across the river like fresh laundry drying in the wind, and at that point I knew we were getting close.

I glanced over at Mac—he was eyeing those guys the way a grizzly eyes salmon. I double-checked the setting on my rifle, then eased it down to my shoulder. Mac positioned himself behind the M-60, which was set up like a tripod; one of the others slipped around beside him and got ready to feed him the ammo. When we were all set, Mac gently nodded his head.

There was a brief pause. No noise, no motion. I focused in on the line of figures standing awkwardly across the river.

And then suddenly, I heard the *crack-crack-crack!* of the M-60 from just over my left shoulder. I pulled back on the trigger of my rifle—the others followed suit—and the previous silence was replaced with a literal explosion of sound.

The valley rocked as the figures in the river thrashed about. A couple of them dropped immediately, others tried to run, their progress slowed by the waist-high water; if you've ever seen someone trying to run in the shallow end of a swimming pool, you can imagine what they looked like and how hard it was for them to run. It was like we'd caught them in an ambush and they had weights on their feet. They splashed around, they ran as hard as they could, but by and large they were had—out in the open, with tracers raining down all around them.

Mac was sitting behind the M-60, and he was firing that thing just as fast as he could get it to go. He had the tip of the rifle tilted upward to make sure the rounds could cover the distance—we were so far away that the rounds were literally dropping down on them in a downward trajectory. At one point the ammo got hung up, but Mac didn't stop—he just pushed the other Lurp out of the way and started feeding the belts in himself.

One of the VC at the front of the line managed to get near the bank on our side of the river, and it looked like he was about to clear the water, but for some reason—and I have no idea why—he decided to turn around and head back in the other direction. I guess he wasn't thinking straight at that time, but it seemed crazy—he just turned back and headed back in the opposite direction, the direction they'd come from. But what was most amazing about this was the fact that he actually made it out: he crossed the river once, under a hail of machine-gun fire, and then he crossed it again—who knows why.

This went on for a full fifteen minutes—the longest ambush I'd ever been a part of—and by the time we were done eight of the fifteen VC lay strewn out across the river, dead. I think we'd have gotten them all if we'd been a little bit closer, but as it was, we'd gotten over half of them—and exhausted our ammo in the process. We'd carried over eight hundred rounds of ammo for the M-60, and by the end of the ambush I think we'd used it all. And I was nearly out of M-16 ammo myself.

The smoke cleared, and the quiet of the valley returned. Mac slapped his hand on the top of the M-60 like he was petting a dog.

"Now that," he said, "was an ambush."

Then he got back on the radio and contacted headquarters with the news. They immediately sent out an infantry platoon to inspect the damage; they appeared quickly, two sets of choppers flying in from the north and settling in on the sandbar that crawled out into the river. As the choppers sat still over the sand, chopping up the water and sending sand and debris flying into the air, two dozen men emerged and dispersed throughout the river, all wading slowly, with the water up to their waists. We could see the shadowy figures, moving along like ants, just as the VC had done moments before, pushing against the current, splashing across the water. They inspected the dead VC, and then, just as suddenly as they'd appeared, they reentered the choppers and took off.

As the guys from the line company waded around in the river, I glanced over at Pfister, just to catch his reaction. He didn't notice me; he was staring intently at the scene down below. He had told me back when he first arrived at LZ English that he'd been ready for a change. He knew that he'd done all he could do with the line company and that he couldn't accomplish any more without moving to a different company. He had recognized when it was time for a change, and after a while I guess I did too.

When we got back from the mission, we went through the debriefing as usual, describing the various details of the mission: the lay of the land, the number of VC we'd seen, the timing and condition of the ambush, etc. It was a fairly unique mission for a couple of reasons: the distance from which we'd pulled the ambush—usually we were right there in their faces, but this time we were four or five football fields away—and the fact that we'd taken the M-60. Both of those elements had made the mission somewhat unusual, so when we went through the details, the officers all sat around listening intently. In fact, they were so pleased with our results that they gave us an extra four or five days off.

But even with the success we'd been having out in the field, I knew that my time with Mac was only temporary. I ran a few more missions with him after that, but I wasn't interested in becoming a full-time member of his team. I felt more comfortable running with guys like Dave and Tad, who placed a premium on things like noise maintenance and team security. Mac took a straight-ahead, take-the-bull-by-the-horns approach, and I was more comfortable running with guys who were more cautious and laid-back.

After the debriefing I went up to the Hill and took a shower, like normal, then returned to my hooch to catch up on some sleep. I was sitting on my bunk when a friend of mine named Pete Campbell popped his head in.

"Hey, Bill, you just get back?"

"Yeah, I just got back from a mission with Mac."

"Oh, yeah? You guys get any action?"

"Oh, you can't run with Mac and not get some action."

He laughed at that, because he knew it was true. Mac was famous for finding the VC.

"That guy's a bulldog, isn't he?" he said.

"Oh, man," I said, "the captain was so pleased he gave us some extra time off."

He laughed again.

"Well, look, I won't keep you," he said, "I know you want to get some rest, but whenever you get some free time, I want to talk to you about running some missions. I'm trying to put this new team together, and I need to get an ATL lined up. I figured you might be interested?"

Well, I guess it was like Pfister had said: sometimes you just know when it's time for a change.

# 6

## As Veteran as It Gets

Pete Campbell was a smart, sensible guy from New Hampshire, with an All-American face and a wry sense of humor. He was easygoing and likable, with a sort of John Wayne quality. He was probably about six-foot-two and 175 pounds, with dark hair and an athletic frame, and he was polite and mannerly, without seeming prudish or square. The kind of guy you might set up with your sister or loan money to.

He arrived in Vietnam at about the same time I did, in April 1968. He'd been attending the University of New Hampshire when he decided to join the army and volunteer for Vietnam. He was pretty unique in that respect. Most of the other guys had been drafted and had no real interest in either the army or the war. But Pete was different—he was patriotic. He actually cared about things, and he felt a sense of responsibility toward both his country and his fellow Americans.

In Vietnam he followed a path similar to the one I'd taken. He started off as a rifleman with the 2nd Battalion, Charlie Company, in the 173rd Airborne Brigade, and like me, he'd quickly recognized the problems inherent with the larger company activity. In the larger companies there was no sense of control, or even influence, for the individual soldier, who never knew what was going on, where they were going, or what they were doing. And what was worse, they nurtured very little loyalty to the company. For Pete, and for most of the others who ended up volunteering for the Lurps, the most appealing option just seemed to be to get out—or in other words, *anything else but that.*

Pete's first exposure to the Lurps had come when Charlie Company responded to an emergency situation with a Lurp team operating just outside the Tiger Mountains. One of the teams had gotten hit, and the infantry company was called in to provide cover while the choppers came in to extract the team. There had actually been two guys killed, which was fairly unusual for a Lurp team, and the experience had left a definite impression on Pete. Prior to that he wasn't aware that there might be an alternative to the rifle company.

A little while later, while they were back at the rear, a friend of his suggested he sign up for an interview with the Lurps. They were sitting around a fire-support base somewhere when his buddy told him he was planning on trying to join the Lurps. At that point Pete didn't have any real intention of doing it too, but after thinking it over for a while, it started to sound like a pretty good idea. He and his friend volunteered for the interview, and before he knew it, just like that, he was in—but the friend whose idea it had been didn't make it. That's just the way it was sometimes—even though the company was eager for new members, not everyone got in. A few weeks later Pete was shipped off to LZ English, where he joined the others and started his training. That was June 1968.

I would get there a little bit later, sometime in late summer, and run with Dave Brueggemann basically the whole time, though I'd run a few missions with Tad and Mac, helping them out whenever somebody went on R&R. And there was nothing wrong with that—getting to run with Dave was one of the best things that could've happened to me. He was patient and understanding and cautious—everything that I could've wanted in a team leader. He helped me learn the ropes and taught me a good deal of what I learned about running missions and staying alive.

But after running with him and the other guys for so long, it seemed like it might be a good time to make a change. Those guys were all veteran Lurps—back on their second and third tours—while I was still on my first. Dave had already been there for a couple of years before I even got in country, Mac had been there on a previous tour and then come back, and Tad—well, Tad had been there basically from the beginning. But Pete was one of my contemporaries; he'd gotten to Vietnam at the same time I had, and he'd joined the Lurps at just about the same time too.

Plus, we seemed to share a similar philosophy when it came to running missions. We were both cautious and professional, and we paid a particular amount of attention to the details. Taping the equipment, reading the maps—these were the things that kept us alive and allowed us to make it back each time, so we could go out and do it again. We were careful and particular, we used the terrain, we used the cover of night, we knew when to take risks, and just as important, we knew when not to. We wanted to do a good job, but we also wanted to come out of there alive at the end of the day. We both felt that a good Lurp team used smarts as much as muscle, and we both believed in the importance of strict noise control.

We also had similar views about combat. When you made contact running a mission, it was either kill or be killed. If you had any reservations about pulling the trigger, you probably wouldn't be around for very long. This was especially true of the areas where the Lurp teams operated. All of the areas we operated in were considered hostile—enemy territory—so you could pretty much assume that anybody you saw out there would kill you if given the chance. Neither one of us was just out for blood, but we understood what it took to survive—which often meant pulling that trigger.

That was one lesson you learned quick—if you didn't already know somebody who had been killed before you went over, then you'd know somebody soon enough. I think Pete had one real good friend that was killed in Vietnam, and his roommate from college was seriously injured.

So when he came by to ask me about joining his team, I was definitely interested in hearing what he had to say. I'd been running with Dave for several months at that point, and it seemed like it might be the right time to move on. It seemed to me that I'd seen pretty much every possible situation, and I felt like I was ready to put that experience to work for another team—for a new team. I was ready to step out, to make my own mark.

Pete had been running with several of the veteran Lurps around the Hill—Dave among them, and also a guy called Doc Potter—and he was ready to form his own team. The next day he came back by, and we discussed the new team—his ideas, my ideas, and everything else we needed to discuss for me to be able to make a decision about joining his team. We even talked about getting Pfister to run with us.

Later that afternoon I went by and squared it with Dave. He wasn't exactly happy about it, but he okayed the decision. "If that's what you want to do," he said, "it's fine with me." Then I went back over to the Hill to finalize it with Pete.

"Hey, Shan, you talk to Bergy?"

"Yeah, I just got back. It's all set," I said. "I'm in."

My first mission with Pete was actually something of an event. It was supposed to be a typical surveillance mission—a trail watch just to the south of the Tiger Mountains—but because the AO was located so close to the coast, they decided to have us try and infiltrate the area by boat.

This wasn't unusual, but it wasn't exactly typical either, and it certainly wasn't the easiest way to go about it. A boat insertion required a great deal of coordination and was always susceptible to a larger number of variables—weather, drift, waves, etc. My personal preference was definitely a helicopter insertion, but in this case the guys at headquarters had made up their minds: we were to be inserted by boat.

The plan was to drop us off by chopper at a point along the beach, to the south of our AO. We would then link up with a navy ship, which would transport us up the coastline to our destination. If things went according to plan, the ship would drop us off there, and we would just slip ashore and carry out the mission. Naturally, though, it didn't exactly happen like that.

The helicopters dropped us off at the beach, just as they'd planned, but from there on out everything that could go wrong pretty much did. The ship arrived and anchored about 150 yards offshore. They sent in a smaller boat to pick us up, but as soon as it got close the surf swamped it and it sank. We ended up having to take a raft out to the ship, and by the time we all got there just about every one of us was seasick.

To make it worse, when the ship drew close to our drop-off point, the navy guys told us they wouldn't be able to get the ship any closer than five hundred yards. That meant we'd have to take a second raft, which we soon discovered was too small for the team. So next thing you know, we're all out there in the water, swimming along beside it, trying to hang on to the edges—with two of us trailing along on a spare piece of balsa—and none of us able to get the thing to make any progress toward the beach.

We ended up floating around out there for the rest of the night until we finally linked back up with the ship and they pulled us back on board. To top it off, as we were all trying to climb back onto the ship, somebody's M-16 went off and shot a hole in the side of the raft, sinking it and taking half our equipment with it. The perfect ending to a perfect mission—and not exactly the kind of start I was hoping for with the new team.

But before long we got it going, just like we'd been running missions together our entire lives. Pete ended up being as good a team leader as I'd figured he would be. He was fantastic at reading a map, he was great with crypto code, and he never took any unnecessary risks. But above all, he used his head. He never let us do anything crazy or reckless, because he was always thinking, always had his head in the game.

Pete reminded me a lot of Dave Brueggemann—an eye for detail and a cool head, even under some of the most difficult situations. Cool, particular, and extremely professional—just the kind of character you wanted in a team leader. A good Lurp, with good basic skills, but also a cool temperament.

When they added Pete's team to the ones that were already running missions, that made a total of seven teams altogether. Our new team had a core group of guys who ran together, and over the next few weeks we grew closer. We developed the trust and chemistry that was necessary for running good missions—and for staying alive. For me, the decision to run with Pete had been a good one. I had been ready for a change—and as it turned out, not long after that the company changed too.

After Captain James arrived at LZ English in December 1968, he oversaw the growth of the company into a much larger and more highly visible unit. It had already gone from being referred to as an LRRP unit—short for long-range reconnaissance patrol—to an LRP (long-range patrol, or Lurp) unit. They dropped the reconnaissance part as the Lurps grew into a more active outfit and went beyond the realm of simple information gathering, as the original name had suggested.

In January 1969, it became apparent that another change was needed to reflect the growing use of the Lurps throughout Vietnam— not just within the 173rd but also within the 101st, the First Cavalry, the 4th Infantry, etc. The use of the Lurps had become a significant trend, and the army decided to recognize their importance by tying them all together under a single umbrella organization. On January 1, 1969, they created the 75th Infantry to do just that.

The 75th Infantry had been a unit at Okinawa in the wake of the Korean War, and it traced its history back to the 5307th Composite Unit, which had served throughout Southeast Asia during World War II. Reactivating the 75th gave the Lurp teams a common parent organization as well as a common history. Each company was given an alphabetical moniker, and on February 1, the Lurp company at LZ English, which to that point had been known as the 74th Infantry Detachment (long-range patrol), was renamed Company N (Airborne Ranger), 75th Infantry.

The transition, incidentally, coincided with the advent of the Tet holiday. Tet was the big Vietnamese holiday that the NVA had used the previous year to launch a surprise attack, and the folks at headquarters were intent on preventing a similar episode this year. They decided to implement a companywide Ranger screen by placing Ranger teams extensively throughout the region to detect any possible enemy uprising and squash it before it got started. These were the first missions we ran after changing to Ranger status—the first missions we ran as Rangers rather than Lurps.

The guys at headquarters gave us an intel report that indicated the presence of an NVA hospital along the southern end of the An Lao Valley, just to the west of Bong Son. That was about fifteen kilometers to the southwest of LZ English—an area that was generally considered pretty hostile. I'd run there a few times before with Dave, and we'd seen a number of NVA nearly every day we were there.

The next day Pete and I went on the overflight to check out the area and pick out an LZ to use the next day. Like the rest of the land around there, the area was dominated by mountains—huge, bulbous, hulking mountains that grew up out of the earth and left wide, flat valleys in between. These particular mountains were covered in thick vegetation, so it wasn't hard to imagine an NVA hospital hidden somewhere in their midst.

Our chopper pilot remained fairly high above the valley—standard procedure for an overflight like this—but we were able to spot a footpath running along the edge of the valley floor. It meandered across the wide, grass-covered opening to the right of the river, then disappeared near the back of the valley, into the thick trees that grew up and over the mountains. Though we couldn't be sure, we figured there was a good chance that was where we'd find our NVA hospital.

We selected an LZ, gave our findings to the pilot, and headed back to English, ready to brief the others on the next day's mission.

The LZ we picked out ended up being a little bit closer than we'd realized. In fact, when we got there and started to land, I really had second thoughts about landing so close. The spot we'd picked out was a treeless area, just over the backside of the mountain, and from what I could tell, we wouldn't have far to go at all to find an adequate observation post. Normally we'd have a pretty good ways to hump before we found a good place to set up. But from what I could see, this place was practically right on top of it.

Our pilot flew us in quickly and pulled to an abrupt stop, just a foot or so above the ground. He hovered like that, just floating in the air, as we tumbled out of the back and onto the dirt below. The area was covered in tall grass—probably waist-high—but as the chopper pilot hovered, the blades of the chopper spinning around like a fan, it lay over, flat against the ground like a welcome mat, or a carpet, welcoming our arrival. We walked quickly across the grass toward the trees nearby. As we walked, and as the chopper rose up over the LZ, the grass sprang back up behind us, covering the clearing in a thick, lush field of green.

It always happened quickly. One second you're sitting there on the chopper—just riding along with the warm air blowing in against your face—and then the next second you're out on the ground, moving toward the trees, with the chopper behind you and no telling what in front of you.

When we reached the trees at the edge of the LZ, we regrouped to make sure that we'd all made it out okay and hadn't been spotted. The insertion was actually one of the most dangerous parts of a mission—getting off the chopper, there was always the possibility that you'd landed, just by accident, right on top of a group of VC. Or that they might have a group of guys out watching the LZ, waiting for this exact thing—a group of Lurps doing a helicopter insertion. And of course, the lack of cover made it especially nerve-wracking—any group of VC in the area would have a clear shot at you until you reached the trees.

Standard operating procedure was to stand there for about ten or fifteen minutes, just waiting to make sure we were secure, but in this case we'd been standing there for only five minutes, maybe less, when we saw a group of NVA emerge from the tree line on the far side of the LZ.

There were three of them, and we could see them standing there, just as plain as day, in their light khaki uniforms and tall, round pith helmets. Pete immediately tried to make contact with our chopper on the radio, but for some reason—apparently lay of the terrain— he couldn't reach it.

Obviously they'd seen us, so we were already compromised. If we could get the chopper on the radio, we could shoot these three guys here and then have the chopper come back and pick us up. But not being able to get back in touch with the chopper, we had ourselves a bit of a situation. And what was worse was the fact that if these guys knew we were there, it wouldn't take long for everyone in the entire valley to know we were there.

The only thing to do was to try and lose them. Pete instructed us quickly on the plan, and we proceeded to disappear into the trees in a quick but purposeful single-file line.

About two hundred yards later we doubled back around. The idea was to double back enough times until we lost the NVA. And sure enough, when we doubled back around the first time, we could see those three NVA, walking through the trees in our direction, following along behind our path.

When we saw them the first time, we stopped, became completely still, and let them pass quietly by, never knowing we were sitting there, within twenty-five meters, watching them.

We repeated the maneuver four more times—moving at about two-hundred-yard intervals and then doubling back on our tracks—until eventually we lost them.

But even so, it wasn't exactly a great way to start off a mission. And unfortunately for us, there were now at least three NVA out there who knew we were there. When we were completely satisfied that we were in the clear, we proceeded over the ridge of the mountain toward the valley that we were scheduled to observe. It was time to find a place to set up our observation post.

We set up an OP on the opposite side of the ridge and watched VC and NVA moving along the trail for the rest of the afternoon. The movement was thick and constant, and at one point we called in an artillery strike on a small group of NVA moving across a stream. Results: negative.

When the day finally started to wind down, we found an appropriate place to set up our nighttime perimeter, and we proceeded to laager in for the night. There was a patch of thick brush right up against the side of the mountain—vines and undergrowth that formed a sort of web of vegetation—so Pete suggested we try and use that for our nighttime cover. One by one, we got down on our stomachs and crawled under the lowest part of the brush, right into the middle of the vegetation.

It was important not to leave any indication that we'd been there—that was always an important part of any mission—so we tried not to disturb the outward appearance of the brush. We always tried to cover our pathway behind us, with leaves and branches, and in this case, once we were all inside the brush, we tried to seal up the entranceway—with twigs and vines and whatever else we could find.

By this point it was beginning to get dark, which meant we'd soon have the cover of night to conceal us as well. Even though we usually liked to hit an LZ at dusk, so that we could make it off the LZ and into the brush just as the daylight was starting to fade, this time we'd gotten there considerably earlier, so we'd had to wait it out. Now the nighttime was nearly upon us, and we were all beginning to feel a little bit more secure. We'd just gotten settled when the sun started dropping below the horizon.

A few minutes later Pete got out the map and a penlight and started reviewing the area around our position. I pulled out one of the camouflage blankets and draped it over our shoulders to conceal the light. Out there in the field even the smallest amount of light could be seen from far away.

To be a good Lurp (now Ranger), you had to be good at reading a map, and fortunately for us, Pete was particularly good at it. He could read those gradients and pick out a spot just like he'd been doing it his whole life. That was very important to the rest of the team because if we didn't know the exact location we were in, we could start getting in trouble in a hurry, especially if we were to call in artillery. But we trusted Pete completely on that: if Pete said that this was where we were—and he'd pointed it out on the map—then, by Joe, that's where we were.

He reviewed the map quietly and quickly, then turned off the light. I put the blanket back in my rucksack and got ready to go to sleep.

It was extremely humid that night—more so than normal—and I was already soaking with sweat. It was still early too, so most of us still had the paint on our faces. After a while it might wear off, or wash off with the sweat, but right then, sitting there in the brush, everyone was still painted over—and in the waning twilight I could see their faces, painted over, in their blacks and their greens.

I took out a bottle of insect repellent and reapplied it to my face, using slow and deliberate motions, being careful not to make any noise. After I covered my face, I applied the warm liquid to my arms—first the left, across my forearm and hand, and then right—slow, deliberate, and without sound.

After six months of running missions, I was beginning to feel comfortable with all my experience. Call me a Lurp, call me a Ranger, call me whatever—either way, I was someone who could get a job done.

I leaned back against the brush, being careful not to make any noise, and just lay there and listened. I listened for two hours but heard nothing out of the normal. And then after listening for another hour or so, and still hearing nothing, I finally dozed off to sleep.

The next morning we all woke up a little before sunrise. I remained still, lying quietly in the brush, listening for anything unusual, as I'd done the night before. The daylight slowly began to penetrate the canopy, and eventually Pete, who was also awake, broke the silence.

"Shan." He whispered quietly, but there was an emphasis in his voice, as if to make sure I was awake.

I rolled my head slowly toward him to see what he wanted.

"Hey, Shan, you want to go ahead and eat now? Or do you want to move out and eat later?"

I was always a little bit nervous about sitting in one spot for too long. I felt more comfortable when we were up and moving around. I felt more in control that way.

"I think I'd feel more comfortable if we went ahead and got moving."

He took a moment and looked around. I could tell that wasn't what he'd wanted to hear. He looked back over at me.

"Well, Shan, I'm starving."

I just shook my head with a smile and broke out my chicken stew.

Even though we hadn't set out any claymores, this was about as good a place as any to set up camp. We were so well hidden, back up in that brush, that I didn't really feel like we could be spotted. So even though I was anxious about getting out and getting on with the day's events—and also about all those NVA from the day before—it was probably just as well that we went ahead and ate. Plus, it was a great place to bury any trash or leftovers we might have.

Pete got out one of the compressed gas tablets that we all carried and boiled some water. When he was done, he let me have the water he had left over, and I used it to fix my rations. Lurp rations were more for function than taste, but I'd gotten to where I was actually starting to like them, especially the chicken stew. I apparently ate so much of that chicken stew that Pete had started giving me a hard time about it—making fun of me because I was always trying to trade for it. But, hey, what could I say? That chicken stew wasn't bad.

When everyone finished, we buried our leftovers and crawled out from under the brush. I covered our tracks, then pulled some limbs back over the entryway and fell in with the others as we headed back down toward the valley. Even before we left, we'd noticed that there was already some activity down there: several groups of NVA had appeared and moved along the trail, and one group was even carrying somebody on a stretcher.

Once we'd gotten away from the LZ and managed to make it through the first night without any trouble, it always seemed like the mood changed, the dynamic changed—instead of feeling vulnerable and open, I always started feeling like we were back in control. Rather than feeling like we were the ones being hunted, I started feeling like we were the ones doing the hunting.

On this mission there were six of us: five regulars and one recruit. The new guy was on his trial mission, to see if he'd be able to make the cut. For the mission, he was assigned the duty of RTO.

As we moved across the side of the mountain, edging slowly toward the valley below, I could see the new guy up ahead. He was quiet and cautious, walking slowly and being extremely careful not to step on anything that might make any unnecessary noise. But he also seemed anxious. Nervous maybe.

Of course, that was only natural. If you were a new recruit out on your first mission, you had to worry about not only the dangers of the mission but also the fact that you were being judged. If you didn't make the cut, then you'd have to go back to the rifle company or wherever it was that you came from. It was definitely a trying time.

We continued down the side of the mountain, looking for a spot to set up our next observation post. We'd covered over a few hundred yards since we'd left our OP, and as we moved along we were expecting the valley floor to appear any second through the trees just off to our front. What we weren't expecting, however, was for a second trail to appear right there at our feet. We'd been walking for about an hour when we came upon it.

"Hmph."

Pete stepped up to the edge of the trail. The rest of us cautiously came up next to him and stood there for a moment, quietly looking it over.

"Another one," he said.

It was a small trail, only a couple of feet wide, but it was very distinct—well worn and probably recently used. It was situated about halfway up the mountain, and it ran parallel to the trail down in the valley.

The upper canopy there in the trees was so thick that we hadn't seen it on the overflight—and in fact, there was no way we could have seen it. That upper canopy was so dense that we could've flown over it all day and still not have seen this trail. Thankfully, though, nobody was on it when we happened across it. Otherwise, we might've really been in a mess.

As it was, Pete decided to just jump across and continue down toward the valley. Since it was so narrow, we leapt across without a problem, being careful not to leave tracks or any other indication that we'd been there.

We continued on down the mountain until we found a second spot that offered a proper view of the trail down in the valley. Of course, we had to climb a tree to get it, but it was still good enough for our purposes.

We stopped and set up our usual observation formation, with one guy in the tree, scouting the valley floor with binoculars, and the others down on the ground, keeping the area secure. Coming across that second trail had really thrown us a curveball. Now we had two trails to worry about—one behind us and one in front of us. It wouldn't necessarily mean trouble, but it did give us at least one more thing to worry about.

When it was my turn to watch the trail, I took the binoculars, slung my rifle over my shoulder, and shimmied up the tree. By that point I'd gotten to be something of an expert at climbing those trees, so I just shot right on up there and found myself a good limb to sit on. Once I got situated, I wiped off the binoculars, got them adjusted, and started checking out the valley.

The trail that we'd been watching ran along the opposite side of the valley, on the other side of the stream that trickled down the middle of the valley floor. Looking through the binoculars, I thought it looked a little bit wider than the one we'd just crossed—it was probably three or four feet wide—and from what I could tell, it was very well worn.

I panned down to the left and saw the crook in the trail where it twisted around and disappeared into the trees. It was definitely a major thoroughfare, and based on the activity we'd been seeing, I knew it wouldn't be long before I'd see some movement.

I'd been sitting there for only a few minutes when the first NVA appeared—a couple of couriers walking slowly along the trail, followed shortly by a second pair not two hundred yards behind them. Within minutes a third group appeared, this one much larger—I counted six—and they were all carrying rucksacks. (The ones we'd seen earlier that morning had appeared to be carrying supplies of some sort.)

I observed the various groups as they all continued down the trail. They were wearing various styles of PJs—some in khaki, some in green—and one even appeared to be wearing a sweater. The last group was moving in a loose single-file line. They walked slowly but casually, apparently unaware of our presence. Ten or twelve minutes later they reached the crook in the trail at the far end of the valley. At that point they turned away and disappeared into the trees.

After nearly two full days of watching that trail—and after watching a continuous stream of VC and NVA bringing in supplies—we got word from English that they wanted to bring in an air strike on the opposite side of the valley. We'd concluded that the hospital was situated just above the base of the mountain, where the trail entered the trees. The guys at command wanted to bring in an air strike to hit the entire area.

Pete and I decided to move the team back up the mountain a ways—not that we didn't trust the pilots, but we just wanted to make sure we were in the clear. There's not a whole lot of margin for error when it comes to an air strike—if you happen to get caught in the middle of it, you're pretty much toast.

We maneuvered back up the mountain a bit, about two hundred feet or so, toward the first trail we'd stumbled across that first day. As we were moving back up the slope, we came across an absolutely great place to view the air strike.

A rocky cliff jutted out and created a sort of natural set of bleachers to sit on. There was about a twenty-foot drop down to the ground below, and the wall was clean rock. I don't know how we'd missed it the first day, when we were looking for an observation post, but we'd found it this time—and it looked just about perfect.

The only problem with our new OP was that it was probably just a little bit close to the trail behind us—we were only about fifty yards or so below the trail—but that didn't really seem like too much of a problem, just something to be aware of.

We all got settled, and before long we could hear the roar of the jets emerging from off in the distance. And then, in just a matter of seconds, they appeared over the far end of the valley, coming in just above the horizon.

Our RTO—the rookie—quickly switched the radio over to their frequency and told them where we'd seen the VC entering the trees.

They came in low to get a fix on the location—first at tree level, then dipping along the valley floor.

The trail was well worn, about the width of two men, and it ran along the tree line on the opposite side of the valley. It meandered back and forth a ways, then crooked around and disappeared into the trees, just where the land started to slope.

From the altitude they were flying, it should've been fairly easy to spot, and just as they passed one of the pilots radioed back down and said, "We got it." They then headed off into the distance to circle back around for their first run. Of course, we knew they were coming back, but they flew so far out that it almost looked as if they were leaving.

With the jets off in the distance, the area got quiet. We all sat silently at the top of the cliff, just watching and waiting—we'd found a pretty good place to watch from and we sat eagerly along the edge, like fans at a football game. Pete had climbed up a tree for a better view, and as the jets circled out and around he looked back down at me and gave me a nod. The show was about to begin.

Then suddenly the sound of the engines grew louder, much louder, and the jets appeared in the sky, coming in hard from the right, one behind the other, on the same low pattern they'd taken before. This time, as they streaked across the valley floor, they flew just past the place we were sitting, and for a moment I could actually see the pilot, seated there in the cockpit, with his helmet and sunglasses on, coolly going about the business of being a jet pilot.

A moment later the bombs fell loose from the bottom of the plane and tumbled through the air like candy from a piñata. They disappeared in the wooded area at the bottom of the mountain, and then a ball of flame, orange and black, quietly appeared and engulfed the entire area. A full two seconds later—and it seemed like more—we finally heard the sounds of the bombs exploding. It sounded as if the earth had been ripped apart.

I looked up at Pete, and he raised an eyebrow.

The jets cleared the end of the valley, pulled up over the trees, and disappeared into the distance, just as they had before. A few seconds later, after they'd made the same loop they had the first time, they reappeared at the far right end of the valley and repeated the feat.

They continued like that for the next twenty minutes, making pass after pass, dropping their bombs and lighting up the side of the mountain like a Fourth of July parade.

When they'd finished their last bombing run, the two planes cleared the valley and started back toward the horizon, back toward wherever it was they'd come from. The valley was beginning to settle down when I heard one of the pilots speaking over the radio.

"Anything else we can do for you today?"

Just as calm and cool as could be. I looked over at Pfister, and he just shook his head. Those flyboys were cocky, but they did one heck of a job.

When they finally disappeared in the distance, our RTO switched the radio back to our normal frequency and contacted LZ English.

They were really excited about the air strike, and since we still had plenty of food left, they decided to leave us out there for one more day. They also told us they were planning to bring in a Special Forces unit to infiltrate the other side of the valley—to sweep the mountain in the wake of the air strike and try and locate the hospital or base camp that was over there.

Without the hospital to worry about—once the Special Forces arrived, they'd be able to secure that part of the valley—we turned our concentration to the trail to our rear. Since we were right there below that trail, it seemed like the thing to do was to go ahead and try to pull the ambush there, and then get extracted sometime early the next morning at the LZ on the other side of the mountain.

It was starting to get late, so there wasn't really much to do except wait and watch. We continued watching the valley for the next hour or so, until a couple of choppers arrived carrying the Special Forces unit. A lot of times they ran with a group of Montagnard tribesmen they'd recruited to help, and it looked as though they'd brought some of the Montagnards with them this time. They quickly departed the choppers and disappeared into the trees at the far side of the valley.

Once they'd infiltrated the trees, the choppers took off, leaving the Special Forces guys there to do their work. We sat and watched for a little while longer until the choppers disappeared in the distance; then we started preparing our perimeter for the night. We set out two claymores, facing in the direction of the trail behind us, then ate our Lurp rations and settled in for the rest of the evening.

It was just getting dark when I eased down on my back and pulled my half-blanket over my face. That was my usual way of doing things: I'd pull the little blanket out and drape it over my head to keep the mosquitoes out of my ears, then I'd lie very still for an hour or so, listening to the sounds of the bush, until I drifted off to sleep.

That evening things were pretty quiet—we hadn't seen any activity down in the valley since the air strike—and from what I could tell, it would probably remain that way for the rest of the night.

I lay quietly and continued to listen.

The sound of a transport plane, flying high overhead, emerged in the distance—softly at first, then growing louder, as it passed directly above us. I closed my eyes and listened to the distant roar of the plane's engines, wishing, in some ways, that I were up there on it.

A few seconds passed, and as the sound of the plane diminished, I thought I heard something else.

I eased the blanket away from my face and quietly sat up, rising slowly into a sitting position. I looked around at the others to see if anyone else had heard anything, but they all remained still, lying quietly on the ground.

I listened again. I was sure that I'd heard something.

The sound of the plane had since faded in the distance. Had it been the plane? My imagination? For a minute the plane had blocked out all other sound, blanketing the mountain with its dull, distant roar. But I was sure that I'd heard something. Something unusual.

I sat very still and listened intently. I didn't move a muscle, concentrating only on the sounds, concentrating on listening. I held my breath.

Seconds passed—a chorus of crickets and mosquitoes sang out in the twilight, nothing more—and then suddenly I heard it again. And this time it was very distinct: voices.

I reached over and put pressure on Pete's shoulder. He roused immediately but didn't say a word, just turned his head to me so I'd know he was awake.

I leaned into his ear and whispered quietly.

"I hear voices."

He sat up quickly, but without making a sound. We sat still, like the trees, listening intently to see what we could hear.

A few seconds passed before we heard anything, but this time it was much closer to our position: a Vietnamese voice, speaking clearly and calmly, floating across the brush.

We turned to each other, both now fully certain of what we were hearing. We quickly informed the others, not speaking but simply putting pressure on an arm or a leg—gently nudging everyone in the circle—and within seconds we were all up and on full alert.

As the others sat up it became clear that there were several Vietnamese—we were hearing multiple voices, talking back and forth—and some of them seemed to be female. After listening a bit longer, we also realized that they were nearing our position.

There was this idea that "Charlie" somehow ruled the night, that the VC were all out and about, creeping around out there in the dark—but in fact, in my experience, it was actually pretty unusual for a group of VC or NVA to be moving around like that after dusk. Whenever we gauged any serious enemy activity, it was usually during the day—most often early morning or early afternoon. But this time there was no doubt about it: there was a large group of NVA, and they were coming right toward our position.

As the voices grew louder it became obvious that they were coming up the trail we'd spotted that first day—the one that was now just fifty yards above us, to our rear. And even though they obviously didn't know we were there, they were still coming too close for comfort. As dark as it was, though, they wouldn't be able to see us down at the edge of the cliff where we were. So we all just lay there, as still and quiet as could be, and waited for them to pass.

Within minutes they reached the point in the trail directly above us, and at that point they did something none of us expected: they stopped.

For some reason—who knows why, just plain old bad luck, I guess—those guys decided to stop right there above us. We couldn't believe it. They'd gotten louder and louder as they approached our position, but then, rather than continuing on, they stopped right there and started setting up shop. We were dumbfounded.

I looked over at Pete, and he just shook his head in disbelief. Of all the places for those guys to stop, they had to pick here!

We continued sitting there for the next few minutes, just listening to the sounds of the NVA. The voices continued, but they were now joined by the moans and cries of the wounded. It was impossible to say if they'd been hurt during the bombing from earlier, but that seemed pretty likely. Whatever the case, some of them were clearly in pain.

And even more unusual, we now started smelling alcohol. Apparently they were trying to dress some of the wounds only a few meters up the slope from where we were sitting.

This was getting bad. The way we were situated, there was no good way to get away. The cliff behind us was a good twenty-foot drop, and the leaves all around us were about six inches deep. If we made any attempt to crawl away, they'd hear us for sure. And by that point it was becoming clear that they had no intention of moving. They were buckling down for the night.

I leaned over to Pete.

"This is okay for now, but in the morning these leaves ain't gonna cut it."

He nodded his head in agreement. The cover there was halfway decent—when it was dark, the lower limbs and underbrush gave us a fair amount of protection—but under the light of day it'd be a different story. The trees there were tall and thin, and the lower canopy was much thinner than we'd need to feel safe. Plus, with so many NVA up there, there just seemed like a pretty good chance that one of them would spot us.

At that moment one of the NVA shouted out in pain, probably as one of the nurses tried to apply the alcohol.

Things definitely weren't looking good. We continued sitting there for a few more minutes, just listening quietly as the NVA tended their wounded, until finally Pete broke the silence.

"I think I have an idea . . . ," he said.

No sweeter words could he have uttered.

". . . but it could get hairy."

Well, at that point any course of action seemed like it might be dangerous, so I was pretty much open for anything. I whispered back, "Well, what is it?"

Pete's plan was to have the guys at LZ English fire a single artillery piece at a location about a thousand meters from our position and then gradually work it in toward the NVA at fifty-meter increments. Of course, the obvious trouble with this plan was that they would also be working the artillery in toward us as well, since we were basically sitting in the exact same spot as the NVA. But the idea was that, by walking the artillery closer and closer to their position, we might eventually scare the NVA into moving.

When he finished telling me about it, he stopped to get my reaction: "Well, whatta you think?"

"It sounds risky," I said, "but I don't really see any other option."

I weighed the idea further in my mind, then nodded my head in approval.

"Let's give it a shot," I said. "What have we got to lose?"

We all had confidence in Pete when it came to reading a map. Not only could he pinpoint a location, read the terrain, and tell you just exactly where you were, even in high canopy, but he also understood the nuances of calling in artillery—that was a skill he even enjoyed in a way. Though, in this case, he'd be working with a much thinner margin than usual.

He got out his penlight to study the map, and I draped a couple of blankets over his shoulders to conceal the light. The first thing he had to do was determine the coordinates to give the guys at English so they'd know where to fire the first round.

Whenever we went out on a mission, we had these predesignated points that we'd give code names or designate as A, B, C, etc. Pete had already determined where we were, so all he had to do was figure out which of those coordinates would be the best spot to call in the first round.

Now normally they'd want to shoot the first round smoke, but in this case that didn't seem like the best thing. The smoke rounds were used to mark the coordinates—to make sure we were all on the same page. They could fire off a smoke round, and if we happened to have given the wrong coordinates or read the map wrong, then we wouldn't end up shooting ourselves.

But the problem with the smoke was that it would tip off the NVA that someone was watching—they understood what the smoke was used for just as well as we did, so if they saw it, they'd know that someone was in the area, looking out for the smoke, in order to adjust it. And the last thing we wanted to do was tip them off that we were there beside them—not to mention the fact that, as dark as it was, we might not be able to see it anyway.

Pete talked to the guys at command and explained the situation, but they still wanted to fire a smoke round for the first round. They just wanted to be safe, to make sure we didn't get caught up in a live round, but we thought the live round would be the best option. We all trusted Pete's judgment on that, and eventually, after several long exchanges over the radio, the guys at command did too. They finally agreed to fire the first round live.

In the meantime they sent up a spotter plane—an FAC, or forward air controller—to relay the artillery instructions. About thirty minutes later Pete heard from the pilot—he was in the area—and then, almost immediately after, we heard the first round coming in at the top of the mountain, about a thousand meters away. Right where Pete had figured.

He nodded his head, then got back on the radio to make the adjustment.

About thirty seconds later a second round arrived, this time about fifty meters closer. Again, perfect. He called in a second adjustment, again fifty meters, and again the round arrived, just that much closer. But unfortunately, the rounds weren't making much of an impact on the NVA—they didn't seem to have moved an inch.

So the next time, Pete told them to add a hundred meters, and this time when they fired there was no doubt that it was getting closer.

He continued calling it in like that for the next few minutes, just listening to the sound of the artillery and walking it down the ridge, until the rounds were about three hundred meters away. We were all hugging the ground, just keeping as low and as still as we could—but there was still no movement from the NVA.

And unfortunately, things were now beginning to get hairy. We could hear the shrapnel cutting through the trees. None of it had hit us, but it was getting awful close. If those guys didn't move soon, I didn't know what we would do—I mean, we couldn't very well call a strike in right on top of ourselves.

Pete decided to cut the adjustments back to fifty meters.

When the next one came, I noticed the Vietnamese voices getting a little bit louder. They might not have been planning to move, but if they were anything like us, they had to be getting concerned—I mean, I actually knew what was happening and I was getting concerned.

Pete called in another round. And then another. At that point the shrapnel starting coming down through the trees on top of us. It sounded like a bus flying overhead. I was hugging the ground as tight as I could, lying completely flat against the ground and just praying to God that we didn't get hit by one of those stray pieces of shrapnel.

It was cutting those trees to pieces, and it didn't take a whole lot of imagination to imagine it hitting one of us.

Pete called in one more strike—this time twenty-five meters closer, and as soon as it started cutting through the trees one of the pieces struck his wristwatch. Which was incredible—it was a miracle really that he didn't get hit any worse.

It shot through the trees, breaking up limbs and shredding the leaves, and when it hit the ground, it felt like the earth shook beneath me. But no sooner had it started to clear than the Vietnamese started moving out. We could hear their voices now as they moved back up the trail.

I clinched my hands together and thanked God. That was about as close as I ever wanted to come to getting caught in an artillery strike—but Pete's plan sure as heck worked.

The NVA were leaving, and we were all still intact. No casualties. Just one busted watch and a bunch of thankful Rangers.

We waited for a little while, just to make sure we were in the clear, and then, satisfied that the NVA weren't coming back, we all decided to settle in and try to get some sleep. We'd had a pretty exciting day, but we still had to get up and pull the ambush the next morning. I lay back down, adjusted my rucksack, and listened to the sounds of the night, now oddly quiet and still. And within the hour I was fast asleep.

That was one thing that came with experience: being able to shake off one close call to move on to the next, being able to recover, to refocus. With the exception of the new guy, we were all pretty experienced, so once the NVA had cleared we were actually able to get a pretty good night's rest. I think I slept for probably four or five hours, which was about as good as you could hope for anyway—we normally slept at night, but we never slept a whole lot. And it was usually just light sleep anyway.

When I woke up the next morning, I was thinking, of course, about all the NVA we'd heard, but I was more intent on getting ready for the ambush. We knew we'd had a close call, but you couldn't let your mind wander or you'd get into trouble. And the thing for us to do was to get ready for the ambush.

Pete suggested we sit tight for a couple of hours just to observe the area. Normally we liked to get up right at daylight and start moving early, but this time it seemed better to wait for a couple of hours to see how things would develop. After the air strike and those artillery rounds, we couldn't be sure exactly how the NVA would react, so it seemed best to just sit tight and observe.

We waited and watched for the next few hours. Just sitting and keeping quiet. We didn't see anything out of the ordinary, however, so after packing up our claymores and pulling on our rucks, we decided to move.

Naturally we headed straight up toward the trail where the NVA had been sitting. We wanted to see if they'd left anything behind—bandages, papers, anything of value. I was pulling rear security, so when I got up to the trail the others were already standing there looking.

I couldn't believe what I saw. Or more specifically, what I didn't see. Those guys hadn't left a single thing. There was no sign that they'd ever even been there. No bandages, no papers, not even any footprints. If I hadn't heard them myself, I wouldn't have believed they'd been there.

I looked over at Pete, and he just shook his head. Those Vietnamese made more use of less than any group of people I've ever been around. Weapons, bandages, everything—they just made do with whatever they had.

We studied the area for a few more minutes and then decided to move out. Pete pointed in the direction that the NVA had come from the night before, so we headed in that direction, moving cautiously up the trail. We were careful not to make any unnecessary noise—we didn't want to tip off any NVA that might be coming around the next turn—but we were also careful not to leave any unnecessary tracks or disturbances in the dirt. If a group of NVA came along and spotted a footprint or unusual marking, they'd figure out real quick that we were there—and probably try and turn the ambush around on us.

We normally didn't take to the trails like that, but in this case we felt pretty confident that there wouldn't be any booby traps there; with the NVA having just been there the night before, it didn't seem likely that they'd have stopped and laid out a bunch of booby traps. They normally wouldn't leave booby traps anyway, not in the areas where we ran, but in this case we felt *particularly* confident. Plus, it was pretty well packed, which meant that we probably wouldn't leave much of an impression with our boots. But I kept an eye out anyway. Just to be safe.

We were walking along like that—we'd covered maybe a hundred meters—when I started hearing voices coming up from behind us. Not loud, but very distinct: Vietnamese voices, exchanging casual banter.

I snapped my fingers and made a talking gesture with my hand to signal the rest of the team. We quickly disappeared into the bushes on the left side of the trail—the high side.

When I heard those voices, my adrenaline started pumping. Normally we had plenty of time to set up an ambush—time to contact headquarters, time to set out claymores, time to get ready—but these guys were walking right up our backs, so we just had to play it by ear. We all sat perfectly still and waited for them to appear.

They never did.

We waited for probably fifteen minutes, and those guys just never emerged. I'm not sure how many it had been, but it had sounded like two or three, maybe more. I guess they'd turned around and headed back in the other direction. Maybe they'd sensed something or just decided to go another way, I don't know, but in any event, they never came close enough for us to see them.

We stepped out of the bushes and continued on down the trail—going in the opposite direction from the voices—looking for a place to set up our ambush.

After another seventy-five meters or so, we found a place that looked pretty good. The cover was actually thin, but we decided that if we moved up into the brush a bit, we could position ourselves in a way that made the trail stretch out before us in perfect view—so whenever anyone made the turn, at the far end of the trail, they'd appear at the end of a straightaway and right in plain sight of our position.

Pete instructed two of the guys to set up to the back for rear security. Pfister and Peacock—Peacock was the guy running point that day—positioned themselves out to each side, while Pete and I took the center position.

We decided not to put out any claymores—we weren't sure how much time we had, and we felt like we were in good position to utilize our rifles. Pete and I were both situated behind a couple of trees, and Pete had set the barrel of his M-16 in the fork in a tree just beside me. It was just about at eye level, and he had his rifle just sitting there, steady as could be—wouldn't have been any better if he'd had it sitting on a tripod. We were about thirty yards from the edge of the trail.

Pete had instructed everyone to follow my lead on the ambush. That was something that would vary depending on the particular situation. In this situation he apparently wanted me to initiate the ambush. "Don't fire until after Shan," he'd said. "He'll be in the best position to see the trail."

So once all of that was clear, and once everyone was settled into their position, the only thing left to do was wait. We sat there for about forty-five minutes, rifles at the ready, but nothing happened. For all the activity we'd been seeing, you'd have thought they'd be walking by every five minutes. I crouched down on one knee and lowered my rifle to my lap.

Then all of a sudden, completely out of the blue, this chicken—and I'm talking about a real live, living, breathing rooster—just started going nuts about twenty-five feet down the trail from where we were sitting—*pock! pock! plock! plock! plock!*—like a dang fox in a chicken coop.

It was such a racket that I just about fell over when I heard it.

I looked up at Pete, and he was none too pleased: apparently the new guy—the rookie, *our RTO*—had seen the chicken and decided to throw a rock at it. To scare it off, I guess, but that thing just started making a racket like nothing else.

Pete couldn't believe it, and I couldn't either. With all the NVA around there, the last thing we wanted to do was draw attention to ourselves. Pete gave the guy a hand signal, telling him to cut it out, and soon enough the chicken started calming down.

But as it turned it, having that chicken around might've actually been a good thing. No sooner had it gotten settled down than all of a sudden a whole group of chickens just started going nuts a little bit farther up the path—and we knew that none of us had spooked them.

We quickly got ready. And sure enough, about fifteen seconds later a single NVA soldier came walking around the turn in the trail. I was pulling my rifle up to my shoulder to initiate the ambush when I heard the *tat-tat-tat* of an M-16 coming from over my right shoulder. At the same time I saw a stream of red tracers flying into that guy, like a laser.

I realized that Pete had just opened up on him, and as soon as he did the rest of the team, including me, followed suit. We all just started firing—there were red tracers bouncing all over the side of that mountain—and about thirty seconds later, when we realized there was nobody firing back, we stopped.

We let the dust clear and then quickly climbed out from behind the trees and proceeded over to the trail to check out the damage. We went through his pockets and belongings, finding a flashlight and a notebook with some writing inside, and then started back toward the LZ.

Our RTO contacted English, and by the time we got there and set up the perimeter, the choppers were already on the way. We waited for maybe twenty, twenty-five minutes before the chopper arrived and picked us up.

As we lifted off and flew back across the valley, I was none too sad to be leaving—that had been one very active mission, and I for one was looking forward to getting back to the base. But then, as we were just about to clear the crossing—and really, I wouldn't have expected anything less—we took incoming. Thankfully we weren't hit, though, and thirty minutes later we landed safely at the chopper pad at LZ English. I was never happier to see that place in my life.

The next day I saw Pete and Pfister sitting outside the radio shack with Bagpipes and some of the others. They were just sitting around taking it easy, catching up on things around the communications bunker. When Pete saw me walking up, he started smiling.

"Now everybody follow Shan's lead," I said playfully. "Shan's gonna be the one to start the ambush."

He had to laugh—he knew exactly what I was talking about.

"Hey, Shan, I'm sorry about that man, but that shot was just too perfect. I had my rifle right there in that tree, and that guy just walked right up the barrel."

"You can say that again," I said, turning to Bagpipes. "He just pulled the trigger back and let 'em fly—looked like a dern laser with all those red tracers barreling down through there."

Like I said before, they recommended using tracers every third or fourth round, but we used them every round. We realized we could make a much greater impact that way. Using tracers every round, it looked like there were probably thirty or forty guys out there instead of just the five or six that it actually was. They'd start flying around, bouncing off trees, marking up the woods, and it could be very intimidating to the NVA.

So when Pete opened up on that NVA, it was just a brilliant line of tracers hanging in the air, from the tip of his rifle to the chest of that soldier. He pulled the trigger back and kept it pinned until the magazine was empty—eighteen rounds later.

"I'm telling you, man, that guy just came walking right up there, right in my sights," Pete said. "I couldn't resist."

"Oh yeah, I see," I said, nodding. "Just couldn't resist, huh?"

I kidded Pete about that for a long time, for robbing me of that shot, but really it was only a joke. He was a good friend and a great Lurp, and he could open an ambush for me anytime. And in a situation like that, anyone else would've done the same thing; it was perfectly understandable.

I joined them there by the bunker, and we sat around for the next couple of hours, just relaxing. Eventually Pete decided to head over to the supply tent to see the supply sergeant.

"Hey, Shan, I need to go over and see the supply sergeant about next week. You want to walk over there with me?"

"Yeah, sure, no problem. I need to go by there anyway."

"I tell you what, I sure envy you guys," the supply sergeant said. "Getting to go out in the field like that all the time." He disappeared behind a wall of Lurp rations and then reappeared with a box under each arm. "It's got to beat sitting around this place all the time."

The supply sergeant liked to give us a hard time—he was always giving me a hard time about tracers and rations and stuff—but this took it to a whole new level. *Surely he wasn't serious?*

"I mean, a guy gets stir-crazy, you know? Sitting around a place like this all the time," he said. "You know what I mean?"

"Well, not really, but I sure wouldn't mind finding out. What about you, Pete? You think you could handle sitting around the base for a few weeks?"

"Oh, I don't know, Shan," he said, "I'd hate to get a case of stir-crazy."

"Yeah, yeah, well, you can joke, but I'm telling you, I wouldn't mind getting out there in the field for a while, out there where all the action is." He paused for a second to straighten a stack of boxes. "I'm telling you guys, running this deal here is enough to make a guy nuts."

"Apparently," Pete said.

"Ha-ha."

Well, this went on for a while, back and forth like that, until Pete finally got an idea. A lot of the TLs probably wouldn't have done this, but he knew the supply sergeant pretty well, and he figured it'd be okay.

"Well, look, Sarge, why don't you just come out with us?"

The supply sergeant stopped what he was doing and looked back over his shoulder. "Do what?"

"Hey, I'm serious, why don't you just plan on coming out with us this next time? I can talk to Top and get it all cleared with him. I'm sure he won't mind."

Pete definitely had his attention now. "Top" was our first sergeant, Jesse Ramil, and he was the one who could give the okay. Sarge quit fooling with those boxes and came over to where we were standing.

"Well, Pete, to be honest, I've got a ton of stuff to do around—"

"Aw, nonsense, I'll just talk to Top, and we can get somebody to help you out around here. And besides, it'd only be for a couple of days—surely you can take off two or three days to get out in the field for a while?"

He seemed a little reluctant at first, but after he listened to Pete talk about it for a while, I think he actually started building up his nerve a little bit.

"Well, you know what?" he said, nodding his head, gaining confidence with each moment. "That actually sounds okay. I think I might just do that. I mean, I've been wanting to get out of this place for a while now—"

"—Oh sure, I can see that—"

"—And really, there's no better time like the present, right?—"

"—None that I know of—"

"—Well, all right then! You talk to Top about it, and I'll just plan on taking a few days off?"

"Well, all right then!"

We finished up getting our stuff together, and as we were gathering up our things it was all I could do to keep from laughing. What in the world was Pete thinking? The supply sergeant had no idea what he was getting into. I loaded up my arms with chicken stew rations, and as we turned and starting walking away I noticed a grin forming across Pete's face.

I just shook my head. This was really gonna be interesting.

I looked back over at Pete. He just gave me a wink.

Two days later we met back at the supply tent to get the sergeant ready for the mission. The sergeant had been around a while, but he hadn't gone through all the training that some of the others had, so Pete wanted to help him get his equipment ready, get things packed up, that kind of thing.

When I came walking up, the sergeant was already standing there in his outfit, completely decked out in full Ranger regalia—camouflage, flop hat, the whole bit. And every bit of it was brand spanking new, with the creases still in the pants.

He had this big smile on his face, just like a kid in a candy store. I shook my head: "Looking good, Sarge. Looking good."

Pete was already there, taping up Sarge's rucksack, so I gave him a hand. We taped everything—the buckles on his rucksack, the sling on his rifle—to make sure he was securely fastened and that he wouldn't be making any unnecessary noise.

A few minutes later, convinced we had him all taped up, we headed down to the chopper pad to prepare for departure. Pfister and the others—Peacock, Chessmore, Arslanian, the regulars from Pete's team—were already there, waiting for us to show up.

When we arrived, Sarge walked over to the others to show off his new threads. They were all duly impressed—"Hey, check him out, man, he looks like he's fresh out of basic training with them new duds!" "Oh yeah, Sarge, you're looking sharp, man, real sharp!"— that kind of thing.

They were all giving him a hard time, and he was just grinning from ear to ear, enjoying the attention, but even so—and this was before we'd ever even gotten on the chopper—I thought I noticed him getting a little bit anxious.

A few minutes later Pete gathered us around for a final word about the mission, and I noticed Sarge shifting back and forth from one foot to the other. I just sort of shook my head and thought, *Uh-oh, here we go.*

About ten minutes later the pilots cranked up the choppers, and we all piled aboard. Half an hour later, and we'd be back out in the bush.

To Sarge, it had seemed like something he wanted to do, but once you got out there, well, if you hadn't been specifically trained for it or prepared for it, it could really be overwhelming. I mean, in truth, there was a lot of security in those small teams. Being mobile for us meant security. And being able to keep hidden and keep quiet, it was really a far better situation than being, say, in a line company. But if you'd never done it before, or if you'd been doing something else like Sarge had, and were going straight out there into a mission like that . . . well, I can definitely see how it might be a little over-whelming.

Of course, Pete wouldn't have brought Sarge along if he thought he might get hurt or be in any unnecessary danger, or that he might hinder the mission in any way. This was one of those missions that was supposed to be fairly quiet: we weren't scheduled to pull an ambush, just to watch and observe. Of course, you really couldn't predict what might happen out on a mission—there were no guarantees, obviously—but still, I think Pete felt pretty comfortable with it.

Unfortunately, almost as soon as we got out there Sarge started getting uneasy. We were supposed to watch a trail that ran along the valley floor—the intel report had indicated enemy movement throughout the valley, apparently with the intention of cutting off Highway 1—so as soon as we got there, we moved across the top of the mountain and set up an observation post just below the ridge.

Well, we sat there for the next couple of hours, watching the valley, but we didn't see anything—I mean nothing, not even a farmer or a straggling VC or anything—so eventually, after sitting there for a while, we decided to start getting ready to go to sleep. It was getting too dark to see anyway, and with such little activity going on, I think we all felt pretty comfortable about calling it a night.

But Sarge wasn't quite so relaxed. I was getting my blanket out when I noticed that Sarge was still sitting up, not like on alert or anything, but still, just sitting up, not really moving. Pete must've noticed too, because he leaned over to him and whispered, "Hey,

Sarge, I think we're gonna call it a night. There's nobody around here."

A few minutes later, when I was lying there listening, just lying there on the ground with my blanket over my face, listening for noises like I normally did, I noticed that Sarge was still awake. He was lying pretty still, but then I noticed that every few minutes he'd start fidgeting around a little bit, just sort of readjusting, like he was getting comfortable or something. I didn't really think much of it, and a few minutes later I dozed off to sleep.

The next morning we woke up early and started moving along the side of the mountain, moving parallel to the valley in a southeasterly direction. We had found a decent observation post the night before, but we usually liked to keep moving, just to cover more territory and keep from feeling like a bunch of sitting ducks.

We continued along the mountain, moving just below the ridge, for about three hours or so, until we found a spot that offered a clear view of the valley down below. We stopped and watched for about an hour, but still didn't see anything.

We started moving again at about half past twelve, moving just below the ridge of the mountain, again in a southeasterly direction. We normally didn't move along the ridge of the hill because we didn't want people to see our profiles. So we'd usually just move slightly below it. This time, as we were walking along the edge of a cliff, we spotted an old, abandoned base camp, about thirty meters below us, down at the foot of the cliff.

It was situated along a small trail that wound down along the mountainside and opened up into a slight clearing. Unlike some of the other bases we'd seen that were overgrown with grass, this one was still fairly clean. But it was definitely abandoned—didn't look like it had been used for over a month or so. There were some foxholes and a raggedy-looking shelter and even a couple of bamboo bed frames scattered around. At one time this had been a good-sized NVA base camp. And at the near side, along the foot of the cliff, there seemed to be an entrance to a tunnel complex.

Tunnels were something we saw fairly frequently, and normally there weren't any signs of inhabitants—or rather, current inhabitants. Usually the ones we came across were all abandoned. Every now and then we might find a good-sized cave system, but that was a little more unusual. In any case, we didn't like to go sniffing around them—there were some guys who would explore those things, but we certainly weren't among them.

The whole complex—the camp and those tunnels—looked like it'd been uninhabited for several weeks, so we felt pretty comfortable stopping and hanging around. Pete suggested that we go ahead and set up camp there at the top of the cliff, so we broke down and set up another OP, this time overlooking the old abandoned camp and the trail down below. From where we were sitting we could also see a good stretch of the trail, out in the valley, nearly four hundred meters across.

That night it started getting dark about seven o'clock. By nine I'd drifted off to sleep, to the sounds of the supply sergeant once again wrestling around in the dark.

The next day we had another uneventful outing. We did see a couple of groups of VC, but in general, their numbers were small. The first group appeared in the valley at about six-thirty that night, and then the second group—in khakis and black helmets and armed with AK-47s—appeared shortly thereafter. But in general, things remained quiet.

By the time we bedded down to go to sleep again, it became obvious that the supply sergeant hadn't been getting any sleep. He had bags under his eyes, and his manner was just completely on edge. He was jerky and fidgety, wide-eyed and nervous, and he looked like somebody who'd drunk too much coffee—or, for that matter, hadn't slept in three days.

I was lying there with my eyes closed, just about to fall asleep, when Pete squeezed my arm. I pulled my blanket off my face and turned to see what was up. That was about ten o'clock.

"Hey, Shan," he said, "Sarge is hearing things."

I slowly sat up to see what was going on. And there was Sarge, on the other side of Pete, just sitting up with his rifle at the ready, staring intently at the trail down below.

I quickly tapped the others awake to make sure everyone was alert.

"Hey, Sarge," I whispered, "what's going on?"

He looked back over his shoulder at me, then quickly looked back to the trail. "I just saw a VC," he said, "coming down the trail."

I looked back at Pete, and in the dim light of the night I could see him shaking his head, slightly from side to side. I relaxed a little, but still wasn't sure exactly what was happening.

We sat there for another five or ten minutes, just sitting there listening, to see if we could hear anything. Then suddenly the Sarge raised two fingers prominently in the air. "Two more," he said.

Now, I knew there wasn't anybody out there. We were bedded down in an area that was completely covered over with leaves, and the trail down there looked like it had about two feet of leaves on it—and these were dry leaves, not wet and sticky, but big piles of dry leaves like right after you rake up your front yard. So if anybody had been moving around down there, we all would have heard it instantly.

I looked back at Pete and noticed a slight grin across his face, and that's when it finally hit me what was happening. The sergeant had gone so long without sleep, and he'd gotten so shook up being out there in the field for so long, that he'd started to hallucinate.

I tapped Pete. "Is he okay?"

"Yeah, he's all right," he said, "but I think he's hearing things."

Suddenly the Sarge spit out under his breath, "I think we're *surrounded!*"

Well, at that point Pete and I looked at each other, and we just started cracking up. This guy was so out of sorts that he'd just started seeing things.

"There's another one," Sarge announced. "He's coming up the trail."

I started laughing so hard I had to cover my mouth with my blanket to muffle the noise.

By that point we all realized we weren't surrounded. After the initial fear, we'd figured out what was happening, and we got a pretty good kick out of it. Of course, we still couldn't make any noise, but we definitely got a laugh out of what was going on.

Eventually Pete got Sarge calmed back down, and we all settled in to go back to sleep. I lay back on the ground, with my blanket over my face, and drifted back to sleep.

About an hour or so later I heard him again.

"*Did ya'll hear that?*"

A moment of silence, followed by Pete's voice.

"What is it, Sarge?"

"I think I just heard an elephant."

I took my blanket and pressed it tightly against my mouth. I had to do something to suppress the laughter.

When we got back to LZ English the next day, I think the sergeant went straight to bed and didn't wake up for two days. I actually went by to see him a little bit later, and the guy who was helping out over there told me he was still asleep—there was a little space in the back of supply where he kept his bunk, and he was just sacked out there, sleeping it off.

Of course, in a situation like that, it was understandable that the sergeant got a little spooked—I mean, some people just didn't take to combat, and he was one of them. But his job was about as important as any other; everyone played a part, some small, some big, but everyone played a part that contributed to the whole overall effort. And keeping the supplies flowing and regulated—I can guarantee you, that was an important job.

But nonetheless, we definitely got a kick out of it. Pete and I laughed about that mission for a long time. As it turned out, it also meant an easier time at the supply tent. I never had any trouble getting my chicken stew again—or anything else for that matter. From then on out, the supply sergeant was like an angel.

The next day I got word from Pete that the first sergeant wanted to see me. Ramil was the one we usually talked to about things not directly related to running missions—promotions or R&R or things like that. I wasn't exactly sure what he wanted to talk to me about, but I had a pretty good idea: I'd been there for nearly a year, which meant I was coming up on the end of my one-year tour.

Within the next few weeks I'd have to make a decision about what I wanted to do—whether I wanted to go ahead and head home or sign up for another round. Re-upping is what they called it, and believe it or not, it was actually pretty common, especially among the guys on the Hill—a lot of those guys were there on their second and third tours.

So I figured that that's what he wanted to see me about. I stopped by the hooch for a couple of minutes, then headed across the Hill to see him.

"Hey, Top, you wanted to see me?"

The first sergeant was sitting behind a small desk just within the front door of his tent, going over some paperwork. When I popped my head in, he looked up from his work and waved me in.

"Oh, sure, Shan, come on in."

His tent was a lot like the others, located there on the Hill at the end of the row of hooches, and it was a convenient meeting place for whenever we needed to see him—just a short walk away from pretty much any point on the Hill.

"You doing all right?" he asked.

"Oh, yeah. Doing fine." I walked on in and took a seat in one of the metal chairs out in front of his desk.

"Things okay with the new team?"

"Oh, yeah, things are good."

"How's Arslanian? Is he back yet?"

Arslanian had gotten sick and had to miss a couple of missions. He'd just gotten back when I went to see Top.

"Oh, yeah, he's a lot better. We just got back from a mission."

"Oh, okay, well, good, good, glad to hear that."

He set down the papers he was holding and walked around to the front of his desk and leaned back against the edge of the desk.

"Well, Shan, I guess you know what I wanted to see you about?"

"Well, yeah, I think I've got a pretty good idea."

He smiled, and nodded.

"All right, then, I guess I'll just tell you straight out, I'd like for you to come back." He paused a second to let it sink in. "We need all the veterans we can get around here, and with the company growing the way it is, it looks like it's just gonna get worse."

I knew I'd finally get around to having this conversation at some point. All of the guys were offered a chance to re-up, and it was usually the first sergeant who made the offer.

He laid out some options and ideas about coming back, making his case as to why a person might want to come back for a second or even third tour. We talked for a while, discussing the various issues at stake, and of course, he made the best case he could. But in the end it was my decision to make, so he left it up to me.

"Take your time, talk to some of the others about it, see what they have to say, I'm sure they'd be glad to fill you in on some of the details."

I stood up to leave, and he stood along with me. We shook hands, and I pushed open the door.

"But don't worry about it too much," he said. "I'm sure you'll do the right thing either way."

I pulled my hat back over my head, then started out the door. As I was walking away, I heard him call out from over my shoulder, "See ya round."

And with that I walked slowly back to my bunk—to sit down and make my decision.

PART THREE
------------------------------------------------------------------

# THE EXTENDED TOUR

# LZ English and the
# Company N Rangers

So why in the world would anyone want to come
back? Why would someone go home to the United States, back to
their families, back to their lives, back to their friends and their
schools and their jobs and their houses, and then turn around and
come back? Actually *choose* to come back? *To Vietnam.*

It's a good question. And to be honest, when I first got there, I
never thought I'd end up coming back. Even after I'd been there for
a while, I still didn't think I'd end up coming back—*especially* after
I'd been there for a while. After that first week with the line company, I don't think you could've paid me enough to come back. But
after I joined the Lurps and found a system that actually seemed to
work and to make sense, well, things began to change. The envi-
ronment changed, the people changed, even I changed.

When I first got there, I wasn't worried about company loyalty or
patriotism or anything like that—I mean, maybe, during those first

few days, when everyone's still all fired up and green—but after linking up with the line company and covering the Vietnamese countryside for two or three weeks, I realized pretty quickly that staying alive was the number-one priority.

And for a lot of the guys that's all it ever was. You've probably heard about these guys marking off their calendars until it was time to DEROS (Date of Eligibility Return from OverSeas). Well, that was pretty much true. Being in the rifle company, that's exactly what you wanted to do—just survive those 365 days and get the heck out. I know when I first got there, that's how I was.

But when I joined the Lurps, it wasn't like that anymore. I didn't feel like I was about to get shot at every fifteen minutes. I felt comfortable and in control. And I also started to realize the importance of another quality: loyalty. Though my top priority would always remain my own safety, I eventually came to realize the debt I owed to some of those others, the ones who helped me make it, both physically and emotionally, from day to day.

And there was even a sort of responsibility I felt toward the ones I didn't know—the new guys who would be coming through, the ones who would carry on the tradition after we were gone. The company was growing, and a group of new recruits would arrive soon. Coming back would give me the opportunity to help out those guys, and help out the company in general, by helping to nurture and develop the next generation of Company N Rangers. Coming back would give me an opportunity, once again, to make a difference—to contribute.

But if it sounds a little crazy, well, there was one other thing that helped to sway my decision:

"Now, of course, we realize that not everybody sees this as that great an option, so we try to make it worth your while."

The first sergeant had spoken candidly, but at that point I still wasn't convinced. Coming back for another tour was a big commitment. And not something to take lightly.

"You may already know some of this from talking with some of the others—Tad and those guys—but basically, if you come back, you can get the early-out."

He raised his brow and held my gaze for a couple of seconds, as if waiting for me to respond; then he crossed his legs and continued talking: "Obviously, we don't expect something for nothing."

I'd already talked to Pete about it a little bit. We both knew we'd be having to make the decision at some point or another—it was a decision that everyone had to make eventually, even if it just came down to saying, Hell no, I'm not coming back.

But all of the guys I'd run with—Dave Brueggemann, Patrick Tadina, Cameron McAllister—all those guys were vets, back for their extra tours.

"And also, if you come back for another tour, I'll make sure you don't have to run any more missions."

See? So maybe it wasn't so crazy after all.

I mean, I wanted to help out the outfit, but I didn't have some kind of a death wish either. The way Top described it, I'd be able to make the perfect compromise—to come back to LZ English and help out the company, without having to put myself in the line of fire. I could *contribute,* but without taking the unnecessary risk of running more missions.

The way it worked for most of the guys was that they'd give you some sort of incentive to make you want to come back or to at least make it worth your while—in other words, they'd cut you a deal. For a lot of us that deal was getting the early-out—a reduction in our overall military commitment in exchange for an extra tour of service in Vietnam. And then, in addition to that, they might promise you a new job that wasn't so dangerous or as taxing as the one you had before—which in our case, as Rangers, was a pretty good deal, because we had one of the toughest jobs you could have.

In my case, the first sergeant offered to get me a job helping out around the base—working with the new recruits, helping out at the canteen, that kind of thing. Instead of being out in the field all the time, chasing VC, I'd be back at the base, helping out with things at the rear. He also promised me my sergeant stripes, but that was more or less just an added bonus—to me the main thing was getting to do what I wanted, which meant *not* having to be out in the field all the time.

And really, that was a good compromise. I don't think I could have come back and run another year of missions like we had. From the time I'd gotten to LZ English to the end of those twelve months, we'd run missions practically nonstop, and that's a tough life to lead, even if you are taking breaks every few days. But coming back and helping out around the base, now that seemed like a reasonable compromise. And after I'd gone back to my bunk and thought about it for a while, that's exactly what I decided to tell Top.

As it turns out, a lot of the other guys made the same decision: a surprisingly high number of Lurps decided to re-up, and a bunch of them even decided to keep running missions. Of course, there were also those who told Top where he could shove it. And it was probably different for the guys in the line company—I can't imagine a whole lot of those guys deciding to re-up—but there in the Lurps we had a pretty good number who opted to come back.

Of course, it may have been a matter of personality—the Lurps were, after all, volunteers, so maybe we just had a more aggressive mindset than some of the others. Or maybe it was the fact that we were all so close-knit; after running missions together in such small teams for so long, the guys usually became very close. I know in the teams that I ran with, we often developed such close relationships that we could communicate without even having to speak—just by giving a certain look or gesture.

I went back and talked to Top, and he explained the various details I'd need to know—how the early-out worked, the one-month leave, when I'd be scheduled to leave, that type of thing—and then that was pretty much it. I ended up running a few more missions after that—the Tet campaign lasted another month, so we stayed extremely busy for the next few weeks—but then, after that, I got to go home for my one-month leave.

The one-month leave was pretty standard for those of us who decided to come back, and we definitely looked forward to having the chance to go home and regroup before coming back for the second round. I went back home to Alabama and spent the majority of the time just hanging around the house. I saw some old friends and caught up with my family, but mostly I just tried to catch up on my sleep. I relished the time off—the rest and the comforts of home—but by the end of the four weeks I was actually sort of ready to get back. I still had a lot of friends over there, and I was anxious to see how they were doing.

As it turned out, Pete had gotten basically the same deal that I got, so he decided to come back for another round too. He wanted to get his early-out so he could start back to college when he got back to the States. He'd left school at the end of his junior year and wanted to return to college in the summer of 1970.

The other part of his deal was that he would get to help out with operations, back on base—that meant joining up with Bagpipes and those guys at the radio shack and helping to coordinate team insertions and extractions. That was actually something that Pete was pretty well suited for—he'd always been good at reading maps, and he had a knack for coordinating. Plus, everyone liked Bagpipes, so that was a pretty good job to get.

When I got back to LZ English later that spring, it was just like Top had promised. They gave me a job back at the base, helping out around the canteen and at the post office, sorting mail. I also helped out with the new recruits whenever they came through—overseeing the training program, that type of thing. And with only one or two early exceptions, I never had to run a Lurp mission again.

Even though I got the job as promised and was pleased to be back with the company, not everything would turn out so well. When I got back to the base, I found out that Pfister had gotten hit and had to go back home. Pete had been helping out with the choppers that day, so he filled me in on what had happened.

It was part of a two-team mission into the mountains to the north of LZ English, and they'd actually already finished their assignment when it happened. The teams had hit a pretty good-sized base camp and were waiting to be extracted when the first choppers arrived and started taking incoming.

The teams had established a perimeter in an old, dried-up rice paddy, and they were loaded down with supplies: bicycles, hardware, rice, food, all kinds of things they'd found at the base camp. As they moved across the clearing and were about to board the first chopper, the VC opened up on them from a line of trees at the edge of the clearing, from just outside the perimeter. Pfister quickly climbed on board, but before the chopper could lift off, an AK-47 round caught him in the hand and took off two of his fingers.

Pete had flown out with Bagpipes and those guys to pick them up—he was riding in the first chopper that had settled down in the field—and from what he said, the rifle fire was so fierce that he just about got hit himself. As soon as he realized they were taking incoming, he instinctively jumped out the chopper door to get down on the ground—he ended up doing a swan dive about twenty feet down with his headset still attached to his head—but as it turned out it was a good thing he did. When he got back in the chopper, there were a couple of rounds lying there at his feet, right where he'd been sitting.

Pfister was only a couple of weeks short when that happened. In fact, he probably shouldn't even have been out there, but it was one of those situations where they needed two full teams and he happened to get the call. It was actually a pretty big mission from what I was told, a hunter-killer type, and even Captain James had gone out in the field with them. But still, getting hit like that when you only had a couple of weeks left—that was a tough way to finish out your tour.

And the weird thing was that they didn't even get hit while they were out in the middle of the mission—it was while they were being picked up. Apparently the rest of the mission had gone really well—they'd hit a base camp and found a large cache of supplies—but just at the end they'd started receiving gunfire. It was just one of those things. A quirk of fate.

In a way, though, Pfister was actually lucky. Being so short like that, it's a good thing he didn't get hurt any worse, or even killed—that round could've just as easily hit him somewhere else. Of course, that's little consolation for somebody who just got shot in the hand, but for some it would've been an improvement. As the war went on and the company continued running missions, there were others who didn't have it so lucky.

When I quit running missions with Dave Brueggemann, Harry Bell, who'd been at LZ English for several months, took over my spot and started running as Dave's ATL. He and Dave had run a number of missions together, but beyond that, they'd hit it off as friends in a way that few others had. They shared the same sense of humor and a similar laid-back philosophy, and they were both just always real pleasant to be around.

Though I'd probably gotten to know Dave better over the course of the year, I'd certainly gotten to know Harry as well, and like everyone else who knew him, I considered him a very competent Lurp and a great guy to have around. He was from the South like me—he was from Mississippi—so we sort of had a similar perspective on things. And he was always laughing about something or cutting up with Dave and the others.

I'd only been back for a couple of weeks when it happened. I was back at the club, helping out at the bar, when one of the guys came by and told me the news: Bergy's team had been hit, he said. Bergy's been shot, and Bell's been killed. I couldn't believe it. I took a jeep down to B-Med to see if I could help, but the choppers were still in the air, so there was nothing anybody could do. I rode back up to the radio shack to find out what had happened. Apparently they'd had their ambush reversed—they were trying to pull an ambush, and the NVA had somehow reversed it, taking the offensive and managing to hit both Bergy and Bell.

Having an ambush reversed was actually one of the most dangerous things that could happen—when you opened up on somebody in an ambush, there was always a chance that he might be the forward point, or the scout, for a whole line of other guys following somewhere along behind him. And a lot of times, with the foliage as thick as it was, you just couldn't tell. Like the time I'd seen all those NVA when I was running with Tad—we easily could've opened up on those first couple of guys, not even knowing that there was a whole battalion of NVA coming right up the trail behind them.

When the choppers finally arrived, we found out that the information we'd heard was correct. Bell had been killed, and Dave had been shot. As it turned out, though, Dave, thank God, had only been shot in the arm—an extremely serious injury, but not nearly as bad as it could have been. It wasn't life-threatening, and for those of us who knew him, that was definitely something to be thankful for. When I finally got a chance to talk to him after they'd seen him at B-Med, I asked him what had happened, and he told me the story.

They were set up to pull an ambush along the edge of a trail—just like we'd heard—and a single NVA soldier had come walking right down the middle of their kill zone. When he reached the center of their ambush, they all just opened up on him—Bell, Bergy, the whole team—but somehow, and this is the strange part, he managed to make it through unscathed. They hadn't set out any claymores, but still, this guy managed to slip right through a fifteen-foot kill zone and a barrage of M-16 fire without getting hit.

Well, when that happened, Dave and Bell went after him—that was just too much, to watch this guy disappear into the brush like that, having slipped right through the ambush. So they gave chase.

They followed his trail for as long as they could until it disappeared into some thick, kudzu-like grass. At that point they decided to split up. Dave went off to the right, and Bell went off to the left.

A few minutes later Dave heard a single shot, coming from the direction that Bell had gone. He started over in that direction, but as soon as he got close there came a second round—and this time he felt it himself, right below his right elbow, on the underside of his forearm.

They'd opened up on him and hit him in the arm—which knocked his rifle out of his hands. Instinctively, he started to reach for his pistol, but when he did, he realized he couldn't move his arm—at which point he fell back and rejoined the team.

As it turned out, there was a platoon of NVA there, about twenty or thirty strong, and they'd managed to turn the ambush around. Dave and those guys eventually managed to break contact and get out of there—but not before Bell had been killed and Dave had been seriously wounded.

Dave's arm was in such bad condition that he couldn't run any more missions after that, so he went home to recover and rehab his arm. I think he partly blamed himself for what happened to Bell, but that was just one of those things that happened—if you ran enough missions, it was almost impossible not to have a bad run at some point. Heck, that's the main reason I got out—if you put yourself out there enough, the odds were that something bad would happen eventually.

And as it turned out, that was true for others as well. The company kept running missions at the same ragged pace, and unfortunately, the bad luck didn't end with Bell.

Cameron McAllister was one of those guys that just loved running missions. He was a natural soldier in a way that few others were: many tolerated the war, but Mac actually seemed to thrive on it, and that was no more evident than when he was out there in the field running missions.

He went back to the States for his one-month leave shortly after Dave had left, and apparently Mac went by and saw Dave while he was there—they even drove down to New Orleans together—but then, as soon as he got back, he was right back out there again, running missions.

I was up on the Hill when I heard he'd been killed. He'd only been back for a couple of months and was running a mission near a village in the An Do Valley. It was just after midnight, and the ATL had come over the radio, saying that Tango had been hit, which meant that Mac had been shot—Tango was code for "team leader," so we all knew immediately that it was Mac.

They scrambled the choppers to go pick them up, and I went down to the chopper pad to wait for them to get back. About an hour or so later the choppers all returned, carrying Mac and the rest of the team. When I got a chance to look at him, it was unbelievable how clean he was—he didn't look like he had a scratch on him, except for a single gunshot wound to the eye.

I wasn't sure, but it looked to me like he'd only been hit the one time—though I guess in a case like that, if you get hit in the wrong place, that's all it takes. They unloaded him off of the helicopter and transported him down to B-Med.

The next day I saw one of the guys from Mac's team, and he told me what had happened. Apparently they'd opened up on a group of VC that was about twice the size of what they were expecting. Which made sense considering it was a nighttime ambush.

Normally we didn't pull ambushes at night like that, but in this case it was the only option—the VC were using the trail to access one of the villages, and unfortunately they were only doing it at night. They'd come in there during the middle of the night to get food and resupply, and then by the time morning rolled around they'd be gone, leaving scarcely any sign that they'd even been there. Then that trail would be just as quiet as could be throughout the rest of the day, until they'd come back again later the next night.

We'd sent in a team to check it out a couple of days before—Mac's team—and they'd seen a group of VC that they figured to be about twenty or thirty strong, moving down the trail and entering the village. But when they went back in the second time to pull the ambush, they would encounter probably twice that number—and with it being as dark as it was, it was really hard to distinguish.

Of course, they got a bunch of VC in the process, that was for sure. They'd carried about four claymores apiece, and after they blew them, they estimated nearly twenty enemy KIA, which was a ton. But since there were more like fifty or sixty VC instead of the twenty or thirty they were expecting, when they went in to check out the damage (they'd triggered the ambush from a pretty good distance away), there were still several VC lingering around in the dark. As soon as Mac and those guys got in there close, one of them just opened up on the team and ended up hitting Mac.

In a way, though, it didn't surprise me that Mac got killed that way—he was one of those guys who was always right in the middle of the action. He wasn't content just to sit back and watch; he wanted to be at the front, where the action was. Before he left for that last mission, I had told him to be careful—they were scheduled for the nighttime ambush, and I knew there'd be a whole lot of VC coming down through that trail—but he just shrugged and said, "Ah, well, you know me, Shan."

And that was Mac—he loved what he did and was gonna be himself regardless.

Mac had no fear—he was brave and tough and as hard-core as they came. Most people would've been too afraid to pull a nighttime ambush—for all anyone knew, it could've been a hundred VC coming down through there—but not Mac, he wasn't afraid of anything.

It also seems like a fitting ending for Mac that, although he ended up getting shot and killed that night, the group of VC that they ambushed, despite outnumbering the Ranger team five to one, turned and retreated. Of course, it doesn't make up for getting shot, but I think Mac would've liked hearing that.

As the months went by and I continued working back at the rear, the number of teams that got hit just continued to grow. One team got ambushed and had one guy killed—Pete Campbell and Captain Frank Norton (our XO, or executive officer, at the time) had to go in there and help pull those guys out after it happened. Another team tripped a booby trap down in the Tiger Mountains, and everyone in the whole team got hit. The only one who got by without any serious injury was the RTO, but even he had his eardrums blown out when the artillery shell exploded.

I think a lot of the casualties were due to the fact that the company was trying to expand. With the success of the early Lurp teams, people had finally started to realize that using smaller teams, like the Lurps and the Rangers, was a whole lot better way to go about doing things than using those larger, more cumbersome infantry companies. The old search-and-destroy tactic had all but run its course, and the higher-ups were looking to try something new.

The thinking was that if four teams could do this, then think what twenty-four could do—and in theory that seemed fine. But in actuality it didn't really work like that. When they started expanding the company, they created such a great need for men to come in and fill the slots that they ended up fielding a whole squad of guys who hadn't really been there before, guys who didn't have enough experience to run a Ranger team. This wasn't necessarily the reason for all the casualties, but it had to have had an impact.

To put it into perspective, by November 1969 we had 128 members there in the Ranger company at LZ English. That was nearly 100 more than we'd had in the outfit when I first got there in the summer of 1968—in other words, there were over three times as many as there were in the beginning. Even with the most experienced teams, if you had that many guys out there running missions, there was just a much greater chance that somebody was going to run into trouble. And apparently that's what was happening.

That second year, because I was back at the rear, I could watch the company in a way I hadn't been able to the year before. As the war dragged on, from month to month, I could actually see the toll that running so many missions took on a lot of the guys—guys getting hit, guys getting killed, and just the physical and mental exhaustion of it. Despite the problems, however, despite whatever troubles we had—the injuries, the KIA, all the bad things that happened that year—the Rangers persevered. Despite whatever was going wrong everywhere else—politically or even militarily—the Rangers always answered the call of duty.

I think a lot of that was probably due to the training—even later on when we started expanding and bringing in so many new guys, they were still really well trained. We'd put them through the works there at LZ English, and then we'd send them off to Recondo School for their advanced reconnaissance training. Recondo School was down at Nha Trang where the Special Forces trained all the recon units from around the country, including the South Vietnamese, the Australians, and the Koreans. I'd been there myself for a couple of weeks, and it was absolutely top-notch, very professional.

But the heart and soul of the operation was still the leadership, from the top down: guys like John Buczacki, Dick James, John Lawton (our newest CO)—they were all different, but they all led from the front and motivated us to do our best and to push the boundaries. Officers like Rick Jones and Matt Dezee—our XOs—took a personal interest in the personnel, and they inspired us to give that extra bit of effort. And of course, the team leaders—guys like Patrick Tadina and Dave Brueggemann and Pete Campbell and Cameron McAllister, and even guys I didn't run with like Santos Matos and Don Sexton—those were the guys who gave the company its heart and kept it going when times got bad.

And really, the bad times were far and away the exception—we did have a number of guys get hit there in 1969, but in general, our guys almost always ended up getting the better end of the stick. Most of the TLs were incredibly competent, and they did a remarkable job of keeping everybody safe. In fact, that's why it was so unusual for someone to get hurt.

Under Captain James we ran something like 450 missions, and we only lost six guys. That was one number that we were especially proud of; it was tough when somebody got hit, but thankfully it was also uncommon.

Regardless of how bad things got, the one thing you could always count on was that the teams would keep working hard, keep persevering. Our guys on the ground always fought hard, no matter what. And more times than not they ended up getting the better of their guys.

That was sort of a trademark of the teams there at LZ English— our guys had heart. And our team leaders were known for their courage. Over the course of my time there at English, I saw guys giving themselves to the company over and over, taking risks to protect each other, putting their lives on the line to serve the team.

When Pete and Captain Norton went out in the field to pick up that team after they'd been ambushed, that was a great example— going into a hot LZ, armed with only their side arms, they ended up hiking across a long stretch of open field to get to those guys, and they could've gotten hit themselves. But they did it, and they didn't hesitate to do it.

One of the early Lurps, a guy by the name of Laszlo Rabel, committed what was really the ultimate sacrifice—he smothered a live grenade with his body to protect his team. He was out on a mission with Mac and Bell, and when a VC soldier managed to hit their perimeter with a hand grenade, he did the only thing he could've done to save the rest of the team—he sacrificed himself.

I don't know what it was about the company, or the situation, that gave rise to such great acts of courage, but I saw guys doing things, over and over, that could only be described as heroic.

Patrick Tadina was another guy who always went beyond the call of duty. There's a level of professionalism—just doing the job, just getting by—and then there's another point somewhere beyond that, and that's where Tadina operated. Going literally beyond the call of duty.

I'd seen him do a lot of things, in a lot of different situations, but the most amazing thing I ever saw him do was to try and infiltrate an NVA hospital. It was while I was working back at the rear, in the fall of 1969, and for a long time after that it was the talk of the base. It all started when Santos Matos showed up with an NVA prisoner.

A few days prior to the mission, Santos Matos's team captured an NVA officer, and when they brought him back in for questioning, he just started singing: he told the interrogators about an NVA hospital, and he said he thought there might be Americans there, which naturally sparked the interest of the guys at S-2.

Our new CO, Captain John Lawton, decided immediately that he wanted to go in and check it out. If there were Americans there, there was no question that we wanted to go in and get them, but there was the question of just how to go about it. It was a mission that seemed ill suited to an infantry company. There were no good landing zones anywhere around, and even if they did get close to the hospital, they'd probably scare everyone away before they managed to get to it. It seemed like a mission that might be tricky for a

Ranger team as well: finding the place would be easy enough, but getting inside without being detected would be difficult, and camouflage or no camouflage, six American soldiers were gonna look pretty conspicuous at an NVA hospital. Even if they could get inside, there remained the problem of force: a six-man Ranger team would be severely outmanned at an NVA compound.

It became apparent that the mission would require some creative thinking. To address the problem of force, they decided to combine two Ranger teams, which actually wasn't that unusual—teams were often linked together for communication purposes, and for missions in areas considered particularly hostile, like this one, they were sometimes added together for fire support. But it was the problem of actually getting inside that required some innovative thinking.

They decided that at the front of the first team they would place a Ranger wearing complete NVA attire—black pajamas, flop hat, and Ho Chi Minh sandals. He would be accompanied by the actual NVA soldier they'd just captured, and together the two of them would try and penetrate the enemy perimeter. The other Rangers would be close behind, of course, but the gist of the mission—penetrating the perimeter—would rest heavily on the shoulders of the point-man. Now, the idea was to fool the NVA just long enough for the Ranger to get inside, but as the old saying goes, that would be easier said than done—and for whoever was running the point—well, I could guarantee you it was gonna get pretty darn hairy.

I remember that when I first heard about the mission, I couldn't believe it. Going in there, practically single-handed—I thought it sounded just about crazy. The NVA would be swarming around like bees, and the NVA prisoner would be little help if things went badly. But then I found out who it was they'd gotten to run point, and the whole thing started to make a little more sense. When I found out that right there at the front of the team, fully clothed in NVA garb and equipped with his own AK-47, would be Patrick Tadina, I began to wonder if maybe it wasn't the NVA that were in for the rough time.

Now, Tad was known around the base, and even throughout the 173rd, for wearing the traditional NVA garb now and then. Sometimes he'd go out wearing the black pajamas, Ho Chi Minh sandals, and wrinkled-up flop hat that the NVA wore—and he already carried an AK-47 anyway.

Unlike anyone else in the outfit, Tad's physical appearance vaguely resembled that of the Vietnamese—slight build, Hawaiian features, and a dark complexion that could pass for Vietnamese, especially out in the thick, low visibility of the jungle.

He did it to get an edge for his team. If they were out in the bush and the enemy spotted him coming through the brush, there might be a split-second of confusion before they figured out what was going on—and who he was—and that split-second of confusion might just mean the difference between staying alive and not.

But this time, not only would he need to get an edge, but he'd have to get his guys past the NVA and right on into the camp.

The day they left I went down to the chopper pad a few hours before they were scheduled to leave. There were already a couple dozen people hanging around there—some, like the pilots, were there to get the choppers ready, and a few others, like me, were just there to see them off.

There was a sense of electricity in the air—people were starting to get excited about the mission, even more so than usual. Tad was there at the end of the pad, standing off by himself, keeping quiet. A few of the guys from his team started showing up, and they gathered down by the pilots at the end of the pad.

Tad was decked out in black PJs, just like they'd planned—checkered cravat around his neck, flop hat on his head, and Ho Chi Minh sandals on his feet.

They'd retrained the prisoner Santos Matos and those guys had captured, and apparently he'd ended up being a pretty willing participant—he was actually gonna go along with them and point out the way to the camp.

It wasn't that unusual for one of the VC or the NVA to come over to the Americans—to swap sides—but this one was truly a model capture. He was an NVA lieutenant, and he seemed willing to guide these guys right on into the NVA hospital. They had him decked out in his normal NVA attire, even to the point of giving him a rifle to carry to make him look more authentic—with the firing pin removed—and from what I could tell, he was ready to go.

A few minutes later Matos showed up, followed by several of the guys from his team, and then Captain Lawton and a Vietnamese interpreter—to make sure Tad and the prisoner could communicate—appeared.

The plan was to use a two-team combination—Tad's team and Matos's team—with the company commander and the NVA prisoner coming along as well. The way they configured the teams, it would end up being about twelve people in all, so it was shaping up to be a mission of pretty significant size.

As the time for takeoff grew closer, I could sense the anticipation growing. People were standing around talking. The teams they'd arranged to be on standby had arrived, and they were milling around at the edge of the pad. I just sort of stood off to the edge watching everybody get ready and praying that things would go well.

The sky to the west was beginning to cloud up, but the conditions there at LZ English looked adequate. Normally the choppers wouldn't fly if there was too much cloud cover, but right then the weather looked like it might actually cooperate—at least long enough to start up the mission anyway.

Captain Lawton gave the word, and about forty-five minutes later they cranked up the choppers, loaded everybody on board, and headed out to the hills. I stood at the edge of the pad and watched as the choppers flew up over the base, then disappeared in the distance, right above the peaks of the mountains.

After the choppers had cleared out, I caught a jeep back over to the communications bunker; I knew the teams would be keeping in contact with the guys at the bunker, so I wanted to get over there so I could stay informed. Of course, I'd have to wait until they got back to LZ English to get the *real* details, but I'd at least be able to keep up with what was going on. By the time I got over there they were already nearing the LZ.

After they landed and the choppers dropped them off at the LZ, the mission started developing as planned. Tad's team went in first—they were supposed to be the lead team—and Matos's team followed in behind them.

Before the mission the NVA prisoner had showed them on the map exactly where the hospital was located, and as soon as they got on the ground he started leading them down through some trees, right toward the area where it was. As usual, Tad was running point, but the prisoner was right along beside him, showing them the way the whole way in.

Things seemed to be going well. At one point they moved down by a riverbank and Tad spotted a group of VC over across the way, on the other side of the river. It was a pretty good ways away, but the VC spotted him too and apparently mistook him for an NVA—they waved at him at first and then signaled for him to come on over, across the river. Tad just waved back, and then led the team back away from the river and farther down the trail.

They continued like that for a couple of hours, with Tad leading the way and the prisoner continuing to point out the direction, getting deeper and deeper into the heart of enemy territory. And before long they started seeing signs of a base camp.

One of the things about Tad was that he'd been doing this stuff for so long that he could just about figure out where the NVA were better than the NVA themselves. He knew the tricks, the secrets, the signals—and around those base camps there were plenty. They would leave subtle signs for each other, trail markers that communicated different things to their own people—like where to look out for punji stakes, that kind of thing. Of course, most people wouldn't know what the signs were, but Tad had a knack for these things. He'd run so many missions, he had so much experience, that he'd learned to read their signs, and once you figured them out, you could just about tell what was coming up ahead—just like reading a map.

That was one thing that was unique about Tad: things that might be difficult for another person, that might look strange or even dangerous, were often just second nature for him. It almost seemed like he'd developed a sort of sixth sense that nobody else had—so when he told you in earnest that there were VC nearby, you'd better believe that they were somewhere there in the area.

That never ceased to amaze me—how he could sense the presence of the enemy. Like the time he realized we were being followed by that Montagnard tribesman—I have no idea how he knew that guy was back there, but he sure did. I was pulling rear security, but I hadn't heard anything myself or picked up on any sign that someone might have been following us. Sure enough, though, just like Tad had said, that guy was right there, following along behind us.

One thing they couldn't hide, though, was the smell. In Vietnam there was a really popular sauce that the Vietnamese ate with their meals; it was a salty, strong-smelling fish sauce called *nuoc mam*—kind of like soy sauce, but with a much stronger smell that you could pick up a mile away. You didn't have to be Tad to smell that stuff—it was potent. So if you were out in the field and started smelling that nuoc mam, you definitely knew you were getting close to a camp.

Well, they were moving down a ridge line, just below the edge, and as they were easing down the slope of this mountain, they started seeing some of these signs—the grass lying down, the smell of the camp, that sauce, even the alcohol from the hospital. Tad knew they were getting close, and he could tell they'd be getting to the camp within a half an hour.

But just before they had a chance to close in on the base, they started hearing voices—and right about that same time they spotted a group of three NVA coming up the trail.

They were all decked out in their standard garb—black PJs, cravats, rifles slung over their shoulders—and they were apparently unaware that Tad and those guys were sitting there in the brush.

They came walking down the trail, casually talking among themselves, and they unfortunately headed straight toward the area where Tad's team was situated. There wasn't enough room for Tad and those guys to slip around them, so the team had no choice but to confront the NVA head-on. As the NVA drew near, they knew they would have to do something very soon.

Tad was still intent on pushing his way on into the hospital, so whatever they did, he knew they didn't need to make a whole lot of noise. He turned quickly back to his team and signaled for them not to shoot—he wanted to try and jump the three soldiers and somehow secure them, without firing off their weapons. If they could knock out the three guys or take them prisoner, they would still be able to slip on into the camp and continue with the mission.

When Tad gave them the signal, the rest of the team eased back in the bush, to conceal themselves from the now rapidly approaching NVA soldiers. The NVA still hadn't spotted them, but they were now within thirty meters of the first team's position.

Tad hunched down in his spot, waiting for the three to draw close. He was coiled like a spring, ready to fly out of those bushes and knock those guys out.

They waited. Seconds passed.

And then suddenly, somebody just opened up on those NVA— M-16 fire spattering everywhere, coming from back behind, just kicking up dust and sending those guys running like Olympic sprinters.

For a split-second Tad couldn't believe it—but then he realized what had happened and started firing them up himself.

Apparently the guys in the second team hadn't gotten word, and the guy running point had just opened up on them as soon as he'd seen them coming down the trail. That, of course, alerted everyone else within a ten-mile radius that they were there.

And what was worse, when the point-guy opened up on those guys, he'd missed them, just flat out missed them. Of course, that happened from time to time—I'd done it plenty myself—but it sure didn't make things any easier for the guys up front.

When Tad realized what had happened, he reacted quickly—he just pulled up his rifle and finished them off. No point in wasting any time at that point, because that valley was about to be running over with NVA. And there was no reason to think they'd be able to finish the mission anyway. All hope of making it into the hospital was pretty much shot—their cover was blown, and within a matter of minutes the NVA would be out there looking for them—so Captain Lawton told them to pull back. They started back toward the LZ where they'd been dropped off earlier, and that's when the action started.

Just as they'd expected, the rifle fire had woken up the NVA—as soon as they'd finished off that first group, they started hearing movement from down past the ravine. They couldn't tell how many there were, but based on the commotion they were hearing, it sounded like a bunch.

They continued quickly toward the LZ but soon realized that the NVA were right behind them. They started firing back, and before long they found themselves in the midst of a running battle. They were firing down through the trees, and the NVA were doing the same, just back and forth, back and forth—and every time they'd try and pull back, the NVA would just come up that much closer, inching bit by bit across the hillside.

And then, to make the situation worse, the weather started getting bad—the wind kicked up and the rain started coming down in waves, just saturating the ground. They were still intent on getting out, but the ground was turning muddy and wet, and the side of that hill grew so slippery that getting back to the LZ became next to impossible.

At that point they decided to have the helicopters come in and try to lift them out by rope. A rope extraction wasn't exactly a favorite option at any time, but with the NVA right there, and the rain coming down, it was definitely a tough plan.

I talked to Tad about it later, and he said he almost decided to just E&E (escape and evade), which basically meant getting the hell out of there as fast as you could in hopes of somehow just outrunning the contact. But after they talked about it, they decided to call in the choppers; it might not have been ideal, but it was still the best option they had.

Usually on a rope extraction you'd have six ropes. They'd drop them down through the trees, and you'd hook yourself up to the end, using a modified Swiss seat. Then, once everyone got hooked up, they'd pull you all straight up through the canopy and hopefully out of danger.

Unfortunately, the helicopters that arrived about forty-five minutes later didn't have enough lift power to do that. Some of the choppers at the base were more powerful than others—it depended primarily on the year and model—and unfortunately, these were some of the less powerful models. The first chopper could only pick up four guys at a time. Sometimes if you had two teams out like that, the teams might even get pulled out two at a time—piggyback style we called it—but in this case, there was no chance of that at all.

Normally when the choppers couldn't get everyone, the TL and the RTO would stay behind and the rest of the team would be extracted—and in this case, since the company commander was there, he'd stay too. Then the choppers would come back and get the team leader and the RTO later.

That was one responsibility that Tad took very seriously: putting his team first. He may have been something of a maverick in his methods, but his top priority was always protecting his team. If the higher-ups wanted them to do something that he didn't agree with or that he thought seemed overly risky or unnecessary, he'd stand up for his team—and I can guarantee you that to all the guys who ran with him, that meant a lot.

Before long the choppers left, carrying the first group of Rangers and leaving Tad, Captain Lawton, and the RTO on the ground. Tad had actually had a similar experience the week before—getting chased out from a mission and having to get extracted by ropes. On that mission the first chopper wasn't powerful enough to get the whole team up over the trees, so they'd had to cut the ropes on them—while the team was hanging in the air, about forty feet above the ground.

They'd gotten banged up pretty bad naturally, but they hadn't really had a choice—Tad said later that he could hear the chopper's RPMs revving up so high that they thought the chopper was going to crash right down through the tops of the trees. So when it came to getting pulled out that next week, he was in no hurry to overburden one of those old choppers again.

The three of them continued across the hill as the NVA maintained their pressure, following closely behind and spraying the hill with intermittent rifle fire. Finally Tad said, "Hey, you guys just go ahead without me, I'll stay down here and E&E. I can E&E right through those guys." But of course, Lawton didn't go for that at all. "Hey, look, we got to get out of here," he said, "and there's no way we're leaving you down here on the ground."

They continued moving, but as the minutes ticked by they realized they were about to be faced with yet another problem: the darkness. They'd been out there so long that the sun had set, and it was about to start getting dark. Which meant a whole other set of problems in using those ropes. Getting pulled out at night is a whole different ballgame from getting pulled out in the daylight.

Well, right about that time, the NVA started closing in on them—they sent a round of AK-47 fire up through the trees above them, shooting up the side of the hill right above where they were sitting—and after that Tad didn't take any more convincing. When the choppers came back, the three of them quickly hooked up their ropes and got the heck out of there.

A few days later they went back in to try and complete the mission, and this time they were successful in getting all the way into the camp—but by the time they got in there the NVA had all left, and whatever Americans might have been there before certainly weren't there now.

What they did—going into the camp like that, trying to penetrate an actual, active hospital complex—was a brave thing to do, especially for Tad, who was running the point, wearing an NVA uniform, and packing his AK-47. If the mission hadn't gotten off track when it had, things would've really gotten interesting once they closed in on the camp. They might even have pulled it off—Tad was the kind of guy who, once he'd set his mind to something, you could bet he was going to do it.

He received a real high award for trying to make it into the hospital like that. But medals usually don't reflect how dangerous something like that can be, or even how much courage it takes to get out there and risk your life. Not that people didn't appreciate getting medals—they were great—but they never truly captured the strength and heroism of those guys.

Tad himself would never admit to being a "hero" or being brave or courageous or any of that stuff. To him it was all just a part of the job; he was very modest that way. When I talked to him later about that mission, he wouldn't take any credit for being brave; he was just upset that they hadn't made it all the way into the hospital. "If we hadn't made contact," he said, "it would've been a real good one. We could've slid right on into that camp."

But what he'd done, that was a real act of courage. When they were at that ravine at the point where the NVA came walking up the trail, they were probably within a few hundred yards of the hospital, headed right into the heart of the dragon's lair. And he was the only one who could've worn an NVA uniform like that—nobody else could've done it because he was the only one who resembled the Vietnamese.

He was one of those guys who just never seemed to be afraid, no matter how dangerous the mission or how difficult the task. He'd go out there and do whatever needed to be done—if he had any fear or hesitation at all, I never saw it.

To me, and to a lot of the others, he was someone who almost appeared fearless. I mean, if you stop and think about it, what would've happened if they'd actually made it into that camp? They might not have ever gotten out of there, but Tad wasn't one to think about that; he just concentrated on doing the job—getting in there and doing what he had to do.

Of course, he wasn't crazy—he knew when to be smart and when to avoid certain things. He could tell when something wasn't right or safe—like when they were overloading those choppers and had to cut the ropes—but he didn't seem to worry about that kind of stuff either. He just never let it get to him.

What looked to a lot of us like fearlessness was largely just a reflection of his own self-confidence—confidence in his men, confidence in his training, and ultimately an unwavering confidence in himself. More than anyone else, he knew what he was capable of, and whenever the sounds of duty called, he believed honestly (and not incorrectly) that he was the best man for the job.

That was characteristic of many of the team leaders there at LZ English. Everyone had so much confidence in each other that they were often willing to put themselves on the line—to put their own self-interest aside to support and help one another.

It was incredible to watch. Over the course of the year so many guys—like Tad and Bergy and Mac and Pete and Rabel—those guys were always willing to help, no matter how difficult or dangerous a situation might be. Whenever something needed doing, they were always willing to do it, right there at the front of the line.

Tad, though, was probably a special case. I saw him risk his life over and over, far beyond the call of duty, but in a lot of ways his heart and his character were the company's heart and the company's character. He embodied the Ranger ideal: committed to the company and loyal to his men. He was truly committed to being the best Ranger he could be, and when he pushed himself, he brought the rest of us along with him.

Over the course of my time at LZ English, that is something I saw over and over—guys giving themselves to the company in selfless acts, helping each other, supporting one another.

I saw Rangers compromising their own self-preservation—overriding their instinct to survive—to act for the greater good and for the benefit of the others, to protect, to save, to contribute.

When we looked out at our enemy—at the soldiers from the North or the rebels from the South—we saw men with a cause, people with a political motivation for doing what they were doing. They answered to a bigger issue, and that's what gave them their motivation and made them fight as hard as they did.

In the Rangers we didn't have that, or at least we didn't have that from a political standpoint. We wanted to serve our government, to answer the call of duty, but we didn't have that one common belief that linked us together. In fact, most of the guys didn't even understand the politics of the war—I'm not sure that anybody did. But what we did have was each other.

Running with the Rangers and being at LZ English—with Tad and Bergy and Pete and Pfister—I realized that I wasn't just out there for myself, trying to survive and make it through my tour. I was there for a greater good, a bigger purpose, something greater than one man's own individual need to survive. And that greater good was the very thing that made the Rangers special, that made us rise above, persevere, and come back and contribute.

Ultimately, I guess, we all had our own individual motivations, our own personal reasons for being there and doing what we were doing, but in the end we were all linked together, by fate and by choice. It didn't matter whether or not we all believed in the same cause or supported the same ideology. We believed in each other. And when it was all said and done, when the last rifle had been fired and the last chopper was flown, that's really what the whole thing was about.

# Going Home

I left Vietnam in April 1970, two full years after I first arrived. For some of the guys, especially the ones in the line company, those last few days were like walking on eggshells—nobody wanted to get hit right before he was scheduled to DEROS, so people had even more caution in their step than usual. They moved a little slower, talked a little lower, and held their eyes just that much wider. For some guys those last days were like waiting to get out of jail.

Coming to the end of my second year, I was actually a little bit more relaxed than that; in fact, I was pretty comfortable with where I was. For the rest of that second year I'd continued helping out at the rear and trying my best to stay out of trouble. We'd had a bunch of new guys coming through, so I spent a lot of my time helping out with those guys, putting them through training and trying to keep them organized. I also spent a lot of time doing things for the other guys, like helping out with the mail and at the bar.

When I'd first gotten to LZ English, we didn't have anything in the way of a bar—some place to spend our downtime when we weren't running missions, to get a drink or just sit around with the fellows. So during that second year I'd helped to put a canteen together, and I spent a lot of time running that.

Sometimes I had to drive down to Phu Cat with a bunch of ration cards to pick up supplies for the canteen—Phu Cat was the big air force base down below Bong Son. One time I took Top down there, and on the way back an MP stopped us for speeding and gave us a ticket. That was kind of funny because, whenever you got a ticket with two people in the vehicle, the ticket always went to the higher-ranking person, so in this case, of course, it went to the first sergeant. But he was pretty good about it. As soon as those MPs cleared out, he just said to step on it—better to make it back in one piece, with a ticket, than to not make it back at all. So I floored it and kept right on going.

I may have been pretty comfortable with where I was, but I could also tell when enough was enough. By the time the end of that second year came rolling around in April 1970—well, that was enough.

During the two years I spent in Vietnam I saw a lot of action—a lot of highs and a lot of lows—but the one thing I saw that just never seemed to change was the enemy. I went from the line company to the Lurps, made the transition to the Rangers, and spent months and months humpin' some of the most hostile territory in the land. And the one constant, throughout it all, was the enemy. They were elusive, they were a mystery—but above all, they were just always there.

The Vietnamese had been fighting over that land for hundreds of years—previously with the French and before them the Japanese and the Chinese—and through that entire time they'd never been defeated. They had a mindset that was just doggedly determined, the sort of commitment that could only come from someone with a passionate belief in what he was doing—in their case, fighting for control of their homeland.

Our guys had the best technology, there was no doubt about that. We had the choppers, rifles, grenades, mines, artillery, planes, ships, tanks—anything you could think of, we had it—but those guys had the commitment. They had the willingness and the drive to see the war through to its end, no matter how long it took. They'd lost no telling how many men, and yet they still continued to fight—and as far as I could tell, were in no hurry to quit.

From a military perspective, we had a lot of success in Vietnam. When I was running with the Rangers, we were able to penetrate some of the most remote parts of the country, where the VC and NVA considered themselves safe. And from the relative security of those teams, hidden there among the trees, I was able see those successes firsthand: the ambushes, the air strikes, the artillery.

We saw NVA and VC on a nearly daily basis—usually in groups of five or six—and we saw ten, maybe fifteen, groups a day. By the end of each mission we almost always initiated contact, whether an ambush or an artillery strike or even a strike from a battleship like the time we coordinated with the USS *New Jersey*.

Despite the successes—those small, individual victories that seemed to accumulate over time—the NVA just never gave up. It was incredible how resilient they were. We'd clear out a valley, we'd sweep up a hill, we'd pressure the countryside with our screens and our campaigns—but every time, regardless of what we did, they just kept coming back.

I think they felt that they could outlast us. We were Americans after all, not Vietnamese, and eventually we'd have to make the decision to leave. As it turned out, they were right.

If the NVA were one constant during my time in Vietnam, then Patrick Tadina was definitely the other. From the time I got to LZ English to the time I left, he was there running missions. Leading his team and doing his best to defend that countryside in and around Bong Son. In a lot of ways that war was a lost cause, but I guarantee you, if we'd had a few more like Tad, we would've come out on top.

He had the opportunity to go home several different times, but he always opted to stay. Every time his tour would come up, he'd re-up, and always with the understanding that he'd get to stay with the Rangers. Even after he got hurt—he got shot three different times during his service in Vietnam—he'd always opt to come back. And not just come back, but actually get out there in the field again and run missions.

When I was there that second year, he ran a mission into the An Do Valley that ended up being one of the bad ones—he got shot and had to be extracted—but just as soon as he was able to, he was right back out there again. It was a perfect example of the way he was and the sort of devotion he had to his job and his team.

The mission was a classic example of a reversed ambush. After Tad and his team had pulled an ambush on a small group of NVA, the surviving NVA sprung an L-shaped ambush on them farther up the trail. Tad actually spotted the NVA, off to the side of the trail, before they had a chance to initiate contact, but he ended up getting shot anyway—he was shot in the back of both legs—after firing them up himself. When the dust settled and his team had broken contact, he was evacuated on a Loach helicopter and taken back to LZ English.

He stayed there for over five years—which made him the longest continuously serving Ranger of the war. During that time he ran hundreds of long-range patrols and was awarded numerous medals and honors. In fact, a 1985 article in *Stars and Stripes* called him "the most decorated enlisted man of the Vietnam War."

But the most impressive thing to me was the fact that, during all that time, running all of those missions, not a single one of his team members was shot or killed. Not one. And it's even more remarkable considering that he ran his own point and got shot himself three different times. He put himself out there, in front of his team, and by doing so, he ensured the safety of no telling how many men. Today he's a very deserving member of the Ranger Hall of Fame.

When I left Vietnam that April for the last time, I left alive and in one piece—so in that sense, my decision to join the Lurps had been a great success.

I'd survived two years of Vietnam during some of the most difficult times of the war and operating throughout some of the most hostile parts of the country. I'd joined the Lurps not knowing entirely what I was getting into, but it worked out about as well as I could've hoped. I'd gone from the noise and chaos of the rifle company to the relative order and discipline of the Lurp company, and in doing so, I'd managed the one thing that I'd wanted all along—to survive.

Of course, I'd also done something else—I'd become a part of a team, a part of a family. And I was sad to leave that family behind. I understood what a hard life it was, and when I left, there were a lot of guys still there running missions.

I was proud of being a Ranger, of being associated with those men, and I'd learned a lot from them. But like I said, I also knew when it was time to get out, and by that point a lot of the other guys had already left anyway. Pfister was gone, and so was Pipkin and Moose—Dave Brueggemann had been gone for nearly six months. Pete was still there, but he'd be leaving shortly too, just behind me. Tad was still there, but he, of course, would be there until they *made* him leave.

I talked later to Pete about his departure. He'd left a little bit later that same April—though apparently he just about missed his flight. He went down to Cam Ranh Bay to catch the plane and fell asleep while he was waiting there on the staging area. When he woke up, he had to flag down a jeep to take him out to the plane, and he got there right as they were pulling up the ramp.

As for Tadina, they really did have to force him to quit running missions; the NVA had a bounty on him, and the Pacific commander didn't want him getting killed. They actually had to call him out of the field one day, right in the middle of a mission.

The company itself was inactivated in August 1971, and like most other areas of the country, observance of our AO was turned over to the South Vietnamese army—in this case, the 22nd ARVN Division.

As for me, my last few days were uneventful. Thankfully.

Leaving Vietnam turned out to be a whole lot like arriving: it all happened through Cam Ranh Bay. They flew me down to Cam Ranh Bay, where I met up with a bunch of other guys arriving from around the country, doing the same thing I was doing—getting ready to fly back to the United States. Then they loaded us all up on one of those big passenger planes and off we went, back to the homeland.

Before I left, I made a point to go down to Bong Son one last time to walk around. After that, I went back around the base, to say good-bye to all the guys who were still there—Pete, Tad, Chief, Top, everybody. I even went by the supply tent to see the supply sergeant.

After the mission he'd run with us, he was an absolute angel and started giving us anything we wanted—which was kind of funny because he'd always given me a hard time before about getting certain rations and things. Normally we'd only get one case of rations, but he'd give us three cases of rations and let us pick out whatever we wanted—which for me was great, because I always liked to get in there and get that chicken stew.

When I went by the tent, he was standing there fooling around with a stack of those Lurp rations, just like always. He just about knocked them over when he heard me walk up.

"Oh, hey, Shan, you scared me." He looked back over his shoulder at me, then quickly finished up with those boxes and turned to greet me. "I hear you got one more mission to run. This is the big one, huh?"

"Yeah, that's right—you ought to come with me," I said. "Won't be any VC on this one."

We'd kidded the Sarge about that mission for a good bit after that. Pete would always go by and say, "Hey, Sarge, we got another mission coming up, we need an extra man, how 'bout you come back out with us?" And of course, the Sarge would say something like, "Oh, I don't think so, not this time. You know, they need me around here"—that kind of thing.

"Well, Shan, I tell you what, you ought to take a box of these rations back with you," he said. "I know how much you love that chicken stew."

Well, I think he was halfway joking, but the funny thing was that I really did like that stuff—so I decided to take him up on his offer.

"Well, Sarge," I said, "as a matter of fact, I think I will. I wouldn't mind having a case of that stuff at all."

Early the next morning I caught a flight down to Cam Ranh Bay, and then later that afternoon I boarded a plane and headed back to the States.

The funny thing was, for a long time after I got back, I still ate those Lurp rations. After doing it for so long, I guess you just kind of get used to it.

# APPENDIX
# THE LURPS AND RANGERS OF THE
# 173RD AIRBORNE BRIGADE

The following is a partial listing of those who served with the 173rd's long-range reconnaissance companies during the Vietnam War. It includes members from the 173rd LRRPs, the 74th Infantry LRPs, and the Rangers of Company N, 75th Infantry.

Billy M. Acox

Jimmy Akuna

Richard Aldridge

James Andrews

Frank Aragon

——— Arslanian

Keith Augerbright

Dan Austin

Thomas Baird

Jim F. Balch

Carl Baldwin

Henry D. Banks

Jesse Barber

Michael S. Barber

Robert K. Barnes

David G. Barnette

Curtis S. Bartrug

Herbert Baugh

Bruce L. Baughn

Paul C. Beckwith

Arthur F. Bell

Richard L. Benet

Alton G. Bird

Donald F. Bizadi

John W. Blake

Roy Boatman

John Boehnu

Frank B. Bonvillian

Juan S. Borja
Michael Bowers
Joseph F. Brand
Bob Brooks
Rick Brooks
J. J. Brown
Joe E. Brown
Roger Brown
David J. Brueggemann
John Buczacki
Roger Bumgardner
Dennis P. Burgess
Douglas P. Bush
Gary Bushinger
Donald L. Caldwell
Peter J. Campbell
Bruce C. Candrl
Robert L. Cantu
Charles Capach
Steven Carazo
David Carmon
Henry Caro
James E. Carroll
Robert Carroll
John Carson
——— Carter
Walter Casebolt
Paul Catozzi
David D. Chaisson
Thomas H. Chann Jr.
Kirk Cheney
——— Chessmore
Chris L. Christenson
Arthur E. Clark

Robert Clark
Charles Clayton
Roger Cleary
William E. Collins
Donald G. Costello
Michael E. Creamer
Patrick B. Crebbs
David Cummings
Reed Cundiff
Gary L. Cupit
Jerry Curtain
Lyle V. Daniels
Brian P. Danker
David R. Dankert
Anthony Dapell
Ron Davenport
Dick Davis
James A. Davis
John Davis
Victor Del Greco Jr.
Charles G. Denham
Gregory De Perio
Weymouth Derby
Wendell J. Derr
Paul L. Desmond
James E. Dewey
Matthew R. Dezee
David C. Dolby
Richard R. Dudley
John B. Dukes
Tommy L. Duncan
Leroy Dymond Jr.
Gary A. Ebel
Tom Eckhkous

Thomas R. Eckhoff
Nicholas M. Ergas
Rivers Evans
Dolph K. Farrand
James E. Fatheree
Leslie D. Flegel
Larry A. Fletcher
Kenneth C. Floyd
Robert E. Foti
James Fowler
Rick Frame
Gain F. Francis
Stephen Fryer
Vernon M. Furniss
Mike Gaddy
Arthur W. Galbreath
D. Bruce Gardner
Kenneth Gaudet
—— Gayler
Michael A. Gerome
Roy Gilmore
James P. Glenn
—— Gooseff
David J. Gowen
Larry Gregersen
Frederick Hanbury
Rob Handley
James A. Hardin
Fred D. Hardman
Wayne Harland
Joseph D. Hayes
Don Heath
Robert Henricksen
Sven Henricksen

John E. Henry
Roy K. Henry
Hal Herman
Raymond Hill
Charles M. Hines
John W. Hodgkin
Ronald S. Holeman
Charles J. Holland
Thomas F. Honan Jr.
Gregory E. Hooks
Minor Hopkins
William L. Horne
Kenneth House
Rocky Houser
Johnnie M. Howard
R. J. Huckaby
Raymond H. Hudson
Robert Hughes
Charles Hunt
Hubbie Imhoff
Sydney K. Ingram
James J. Israel
Alan T. Jackson
Vladimir Jakovenko
Richard D. James
Bill Jang
John Jasinski
John Jersey
Abraham Johnson
Robert L. Johnson
Stephen A. Joley
Rick Jones
Harold Kaiama
Charles E. Kankel

John W. Kelly
John Kelner
Joe Keshlear
John J. Kirk
John R. Knaus
Phillip S. Kossa
David Kuamoo
Dave Lang
John P. Lawton
Clifford Leathers
——— Leblanc
James G. Leik
George Leininger
Joseph Lerhinon
David Liebersbach
John E. Lilholt
——— Lindsey
James B. Long
Chip Loring Jr.
Andrew Love
Dennis Lovick
Peter F. Lynch
Charles T. Lyons
Stephen H. Macomber
Albert K. Marcus
Joe Mariani
Ernest Martinez
Santos Matos
Cameron T. McAllister
Chester McDonald
Michael McDonald
Michael D. McDonald
Patrick McKeough
Craig R. Mclarin
Sylester Mcnair Jr.

Ed McNeil
James McSorley
Albert Mendez
Frank T. Mendez Jr.
Theodore Mendez Sr.
Jeffrey S. Meriwether
Daniel P. Miller
George L. Miller
Carl E. Millinder Jr.
David A. Moloney
Frank Moore
Irvin W. Moran
Jack Morrison
Peter G. Mossman
——— Mowrey
Manuel Moya
Kenneth W. Murray
Gerard B. Nery Jr.
Allen D. Nickles
Wayne G. Nisby
William P. Nissen
Frank Norton
Scotty Norwood
Tony Novella
Douglas Nunnally III
James E. Nutter
Patrick O'Brien
Shane O'Neal
Albert Ortiz
Larry A. Osborn
Andrew J. Pack Jr.
Roger D. Palmateer
Ward R. Palmer
Wilbur L. Palmer III
William T. Palmer

Roberto L. Patino
Phil Peacock
Lawrence R. Peel
Kim Pennington
Kenneth T. Perry
Lawrence Pezza Jr.
William A. Pfister
Charles A. Phelps
Allan B. Phillips
Darrel R. Phillips
Larry Phillips
Roger Phillips
Velmon D. Phillips
Clifton S. Pierce Jr.
Leroy Pipkin
Greg Poorman
Doc Potter
Richard R. Pou
Henry Prozorowski
Laszlo Rabel
Jesse A. Ramil
Michael J. Ramirez
Paul L. Ramos Jr.
Jack Ramsland
Charles W. Ransom
Ralph A. Raperto
Merle H. Redcay
Raymond S. Reeves Jr.
John R. Reitzell
——— Reyes
William Ricca
——— Rice
Junius L. Riddick
Chase E. Riley
John F. Robertson

Barry Rottman
Tommy L. Roubideaux
Fletcher Ruckman
Norman Ryman
Fred D. Salazar
James R. Samples
Raul Santiago
Charles Sayles
John V. Scalf
Samuel S. Schiro
Steven T. Schooler
Anthony E. Schoonover
Lamont C. Scott
Santiago Serna
——— Severinson
Don Sexton
Billy W. Shanahan
John R. Shelton
William Shippey
Dale W. Short
Chris Simmons
Joe Simons
Richard Skinner
James E. Slade
Scott S. Smith
Sid Smith
Thomas E. Smith
Jimmy E. Smithee
Walter Solgalow
John Sotilo
Guy Sparks
Jerry R. Speelberg
Ray D. Spencer
Steve Spradlin
Michael Staffin

Bart Stamper
Gary Stephens
Bill Stimpson
Delono Stones
Lamont C. Stott
Robert M. Stouch
Robert Stowell
Harold Strassener
Joseph E. Sweeney
Michael Swisley
Patrick Tadina
David D. Taitono
Richard M. Tanaka
G. Michael Tardif
Udo Taring
Rudolof A. Teodosio
Ronald G. Thomas
Charles R. Timmons
Robert C. Tingdale
Joseph J. Tompkins
—— Torres
Alain J. Tremblay
Murray D. Tucker
Gerald A. Turner
James C. Turner
Ronald E. Tussey
Victor D. Valeriano
Donald E. Vallencourt

Frank W. Vanservers
William L. Varble
Carl Vencill
Stephen Vogt
Ron Wafer
James Wagner
Donald G. Waide
Martin K. Waldhe
David P. Walker
Dennis I. Warwick
—— Webb
Joseph R. Welke
Richard S. Wells
Edward Welsh
Earl S. Wemple
Russel J. Weyl
C. E. Whitlock
Freddy J. Williams
Clyde Willis
Peter A. Wolf
Ronald K. Wooley
Lawrence T. Yegge
Mick Young
Ed Zapata
Thomas T. Zaruba
Michael A. Zemon
Edward M. Zezlina
Terry Ziegenbein

# POST-TRAUMATIC STRESS DISORDER

For all their courage and dedication, many former Lurps and Rangers suffer today from post-traumatic stress disorder. PTSD is an anxiety disorder that occurs in response to a traumatic event and can affect a person for years in the wake of significant trauma. Statistics suggest that over 30 percent of the combat veterans who returned from Vietnam have suffered from PTSD at some point.

For information on PTSD, call the National Center for PTSD at 802-296-6300. The center maintains an information line and will send you a free information packet containing fact sheets and current contact information. If you're interested in seeking treatment, the most immediate way is to contact your local VA medical center. To find the facility nearest you, call 877-222-8387, or consult the blue pages of your local telephone directory. If you're online, you can consult the Veterans Health Administration at www.va.gov/health_benefits.

# INDEX